The Origins of Hospitality and Tourism

Kevin D O'Gorman

The Origins of Hospitality and Tourism

Kevin D O'Gorman

Editing Consultant: John Cousins

Never let the future disturb you.
For you will meet it, if you wish to,
with the same weapons of reason
which today, arm you against the present

Aurelius, *Meditations*, VII:viii
Marcus Aurelius Antoninus (AD 121–180), Emperor of Rome from AD161

(G) **Goodfellow Publishers Ltd**

(G) Published by Goodfellow Publishers Limited,
Woodeaton, Oxford, OX3 9TJ
http://www.goodfellowpublishers.com

British Library Cataloguing in Publication Data: a catalogue record for this title is available from the British Library.

Library of Congress Catalog Card Number: on file.

ISBN: 978-1-906884-08-6

Design and typesetting by P.K. McBride

Printed by Lightning Source, www.lightningsource.com

Contents

Background to the book

During the initial reading and before undertaking the research which underpins this book, it became clear that in current hospitality and tourism literature, the history and philosophy of hospitality was an overlooked area for investigation. In particular, the portrayal of the historical evolution of the phenomenon of hospitality was prone to a great deal of rhetoric and little research; and in certain cases some of the assertions were manifestly wrong.

The research underpinning the content of this book is essentially hermeneutical; that is investigating ways of engaging with and interpreting textual data. It has to depend upon on textual data, as there are very few other practical ways of accessing Classical Antiquity. The research was also carried out within the interpretivist paradigm as it is seeking to observe the general trends and perceptions of a social phenomenon. Some of the problems of using literature and translation (compounded by the fact that this research is using texts that have been written in at least seven ancient or modern languages) and the surrounding controversies arise from four principal difficulties: differences in ancient manuscripts; obscure text and vocabulary; denominational bias; and translation philosophy.

What proved to be important, along with research skills, was familiarity with the texts and period of time under investigation albeit for previous and different purposes. Without the necessary language and translation skills, this project would not have been possible. The interdisciplinary combination of classics, theology and philosophy in tandem with the atmosphere of a business school brought together a unique set of interests, skills and abilities to underpin the research.

Preliminary findings underpinning the content of the book have been presented in a variety of publications and conference papers at various stages prior to the book being finalised. This process has been valuable not only to test the methodological processes but also to develop the findings. Opening up both the research process and the preliminary findings, in essence requiring the need to explain and justify the research and outcomes, certainly contributed to enhancing the process.

The key focus of the book is on exploring the textural evidence from and about Classical Antiquity in order to identify aspects of the origins of hospitality and tourism. In nearly all cases the prime purpose of the texts was not to do with recording the history of hospitality. The content of this book focuses on the analysis of the incidences of hospitality that were identified. Consequently this is not a history book, although references are made and detail provided to help the reader to locate the incidences within the historic framework.

Now, finally, standing back from the work there are key aspects of hospitality that apparently are constant: it is only when the contents of the book are examined, that the true rewarding richness of the outcomes become evident. The principal outcome is that the hospitality phenomenon in its broadest sense has been recorded since the beginning of human history and it embraces a wide range of activities beyond the commercial provision of food, drink and accommodation. In particular, the essence of the hospitality phenomenon, within Classical Antiquity, is characterised by a reciprocally beneficial two-way process that takes place within three distinct, and separate, contexts: domestic, civil and commercial, which can also be summarised and represented by dynamic visual models.

Exploring the origins of hospitality can aid the practitioner within the hospitality industry today; awareness of the past can always help to guide the future. The current increasing debate on, and research into, the origins of hospitality can enhance the future of the industry. Professionalism and greater expertise can surely come from a deeper understanding of the dimensions of hospitality, that have been evolving since antiquity, and on which the industry now relies.

Aims of the book

The key aims of this book are to:

◊ Consider the social, economic and geographical influences on the development of hospitality principles and practices within Classical Antiquity;

◊ Provide a structured approach and supporting information for those wanting to develop their knowledge and understanding of the phenomenon of hospitality;

◊ Provide a contribution to the literature as a book about the true origins of hospitality and identify how an understanding the past can help in developing modern approaches to hospitality and tourism management, and

◊ Meet the needs of students and practitioners of the hospitality, tourism and leisure industries and provide a sound foundation on which to build future studies.

Structure of the book

The text of the book can be approached as a whole or individual chapters can be considered signally. The book is presented in ten chapters:

Chapter 1 Historical Perspectives presents the focus, content and coverage of the book. The hospitality lexicon is traced including the identification of the origins of host and guest and other associated words and the chapter ends with exploring the links between oral tradition and texts.

Chapter 2 Philosophical Perspectives on Hospitality presents a critical analysis of the relationship between philosophy and hospitality through the analysis of key writers and discusses moral philosophy and the host, nation states, refugees and hospitality and language. The chapter end with a note on potential for bias and provides a summary of the key philosophical issue identified.

Chapter 3 Judaeo-Christian Origins identifies, through a review of Judaeo-Christian theological and scriptural thought, many of the presuppositions that underpin hospitality conventions and practices. The Chapter also includes a section on the potential problems of the Teleological Fallacy and provides a summary of the key issues identified from the biblical and theological literature.

Chapter 4 Classical Greece explores hospitality in early Classical Antiquity focusing on domestic hospitality: the nomad and the homestead; civic hospitality: communities and the emergent city; and commercial hospitality: the geneses of an industry.

Chapter 5 Classical Rome presents hospitality at the height of Classical Antiquity, focusing on: domestic hospitality: consolidation of power; civic hospitality: growth of an empire; and commercial hospitality: diversified industry.

Chapter 6 The Five Dimensions of Hospitality concludes the main exploration of Classical Antiquity through to the fall of the Roman Empire and summarises the identified aspects of hospitality into five dimensions of hospitality. To complete the foundation of the underpinning knowledge for the thematic chapters that follow, the emerging influences through to the dawn of the Renaissance are explored.

Chapter 7 Charitable Hospitality explores caritable perspectives of hospitality as a cross-sectional theme. A brief historical summary of hospitality, based on the Abrahamic model, is presented and the development of charitable hospitality is explored. It concludes by reflecting on the constantly evolving religious practice of providing hospitality to those in most need.

Chapter 8 Monastic hospitality explores the Western European monastery traditions of the Middle Ages, starting with the Rule of Benedict and identifies how, during the 1000 years of mediaeval times up to the beginning of the Renaissance, the monastic traditions were affected at the time and subsequently and emphasises their significance in laying the foundations for the later formalising of modern civic and commercial hospitality. The chapter concludes with an identification of the principles of hospitality that had been established by the traditions of western monasticism.

Chapter 9 Along the Silk Routes examines examples of hospitality practices along the Silk Road and in particular focuses on the religious/commercial caravanserais and the home (gers and yurts) in Iran and Mongolia.

Chapter 10 The Dynamic Model of Hospitality With the phenomenon of hospitality becoming recognised as a field of study, to which this book is intended to contribute, this chapter considers the implications of the publication of *Hospitality: A Social Lens* and brings into the thematic framework the aspects of hospitality identified throughout the writings of Classical Antiquity. The chapter then presents a dynamic model for hospitality and ends with an overall reflection of the origins of hospitality and tourism within Classical Antiquity.

Four appendices are provided to support the chapters:

A **Glossary of names and terms** – provides quick reference guide to names and terms used within the book.

B **Frequently used Latin and Greek terms** – provides a quick reference guide to terms used within the book.

C **Methodological issues** – presents a summary of the key methodological approaches that were used in the research unpinning much of the content of this book.

D **Augmented bibliography** – contains all references (both classical and modern) within the text and more and also provides a standalone useful resource for academics, researchers, practitioners and students.

Further work

The content of this book raises issues that should require further consideration either because they will extend the existing work or because further investigation could refine it.

This work was restricted primarily to the Greco-Roman civilisations of Classical Antiquity, therefore other projects that explore different but contemporaneous civilisations should be possible. Further research could be developed horizontally. For example, an exploration of ancient hospitality practices outside Europe could be particularly enlightening, as it would provide a useful comparison to the hospitality practices of early Europe. This comparative study could help to answer the question posed earlier and further explore the view that hospitality is inherently a basic human trait and not born out of a particular faith and system of belief.

Another option would be to develop the research vertically into other periods of time within the same geographical region. For example, if the research were progressed into the modern age of European history it would be fascinating to see how hospitality continued to develop and evolve over a longer period of time. This could also be true if the research was to be developed horizontally in this time period.

One final question for further research: Is there really anything different in the modern notions of hospitality that is not contained within the origins identified within this book?

Kevin O'Gorman, March 2010

Acknowledgments

The preparation of this book has drawn upon a variety of experiences and information but could not have been undertaken without the assistance of a variety of people. In particular I would like to thank John Cousins, Director of The Food and Beverage Training Company, London, for acting as editing consultant.

I would also like to express my thanks to my colleagues in the Business School of the University of Strathclyde, and particular thanks to my supervisors and examiners of the original thesis for their advice and support: Cailein Gillespie Charles Harvey, Conrad Lashley, Paul Lynch, Alison Morrison and Richard Prentice.

Additionally I would like to thank: the journal editors and conference organisers who published works coming from the process, in particular the organisers of the many conferences and anonymous referees; David Brooks for his help in drawing the dynamic hospitality models; Iain MacLaren of Wylie Shanks Architects, and most importantly, Gladys Chapman (my mother) for reading endless articles and proofs.

KDO

About the author

Dr Kevin O'Gorman is director of under-graduate hospitality and tourism programmes in the Department of Management, Strathclyde Business School.

His doctorate is in the history and philosophy of hospitality in the Greco-Roman world of classical antiquity. He has published extensively on topics relating to the history, practice and philosophy of hospitality management. He is also to be the guest editor of a special issue of the International Journal of Contemporary Hospitality Management that is investigating the History of the Commercial Hospitality Industry from Classical Antiquity to the 19th Century.

1 Historical Perspectives

In contemporary hospitality literature the history and philosophy of hospitality seem to have been largely overlooked areas for investigation. In particular, the portrayal of the historical evolution of the phenomenon of hospitality has often been based on random conjecture rather than historical fact. Through exploring classical history and philosophy, and contemporary hospitality literature, it is clear that modern hospitality has its foundation in the culture of Classical Antiquity. In addition, the analysis of texts requires an understanding of evolution of language and how the modern words associated with hospitality have evolved.

1.1 The phenomenon of hospitality

Investigating the genesis and the evolution of the phenomenon of hospitality has suffered from relative neglect. However the importance of the historical perspective is supported by O'Connor (2005, p. 267) who states that: 'only once an understanding of hospitality's origins and its place in human nature is achieved can one expect to discover what hospitality means today, and more importantly what it will mean to those entering the industry in the future'. This recognises hospitality as a broad concept alongside hospitality as a profession, with historical literature contributing to informing industry practices of today and tomorrow: awareness of the past can always help to guide the future.

Going back in time to primitive and archaic societies, hospitality in its broad sense was seen as essentially organic, as a vital and integral part of such societies revealing much about their cultural values and beliefs. Muhlmann (1932, p. 113) notes that the principles which governed the peoples' attitudes towards hospitality in these societies were: religious practices and beliefs; the advancement of trade and commerce; transactional expectations; social status and the household; a system of communication, and the fear of strangers.

From an initial review of the history and evolution of commercial hospitality, two basic approaches are to be found within the current literature. The first is declarative and the second is judgemental.

The declarative statement approach is designed to illustrate common roots or starting points, for example, Rutes and Penner (1985) claimed to trace the development of contemporary commercial hospitality to four basic roots:

1. Commercial hotels can be traced to facilities provided to expedite trade or mail delivery, or to accommodate government and religious travellers.

2. Resorts and entertainment-based facilities are related to Greek and Roman spas.

3. Rental housing and rooming houses eventually led to condos, time-shares and bed and breakfast facilities.

4. Royal courts led to super-luxury hotels, castles and condominiums.

Similarly, King (1995) argues that commercial hospitality has developed from only two roots: the luxury accommodation of aristocrats, and particularly minimum level accommodation provided for commoners. Other examples include: Lattin (1989) who states that a history of lodging dates back 12,000 years, without offering any evidence as to why; Medlik and Ingram (2000) claim that the hotel industry has 200 years of history, and Bardi (2007) declares that the founders of the hotel industry are Statler, Hilton, and Marriott, etc.

The judgemental approach is aimed at implying that commercial hospitality is somehow ignoble compared to other forms of hospitality. This type of questionable rhetoric can be traced to Muhlmann (1932) (succinctly summarised by Wood (1994)) where the commercial context of hospitality is described as a:

formal and rational system of (usually monetary) exchange whereby hospitality is provided in particular institutional forms (hotels, restaurants) that are essentially impersonal… for the most part, hospitality is no longer about the personal giving of the host's own food and accommodation but a matter of impersonal financial exchange.

This reflection on the hospitality industry within a narrowly and poorly defined commercial context has permeated through hospitality literature. When discussing commercial hospitality, Wood (1999, p. 738) considers:

in essence, the organic and spiritual qualities of hospitality have disappeared, replaced in the public sphere by a formally rational system of (usually monetary) exchange whereby hospitality is provided in particular institutional forms (hotels, restaurants) that are essentially impersonal and

> *for the most part, hospitality is no longer about the personal giving of the host's own food and accommodation but a matter of impersonal financial exchange.*

These ideas were also developed, for example, by Morrison (2001, p. 784) amongst others, when she argued that commercial hospitality provision 'arose from a general process of modernisation, the gradual breakdown of the importance of kinship and social obligation based on status ascription, and the process of urbanisation'.

These two approaches are further characterised by sweeping statements not backed up with any apparent empirical research evidence. Analysing examples of the history of commercial hospitality, looking for examples of similar practices in contemporary cultures in the world today, whilst being illuminating can have its difficulties. All writing is the product of a particular time and culture, the views expressed in it and the language in which they are expressed reflect a particular cultural conditioning; often making them quite different from contemporary ideas and concerns. Both the declarative and judgemental approaches illustrate the potential error of considering any hospitality event out of its proper time, location or context (domestic, civic and commercial) and then subsequently comparing it to any other hospitality event from another time or context. This atemporal and cross-contextualisation is referred to by Finley (1983) as the Teleological Fallacy (as detailed in Chapter 3, section 3.5).

The declarative and judgemental statements made may be given some credibility because they sound convincing and echo characteristics within other hospitality literature; that humanity's organic and spiritual quali-ties have disappeared and everything is being replaced with commerce. Fortunately, this is at worst simply not true, or at best a myopic and one-sided view of society.

1.2 Hospitality is as old as recorded human history

The provision of hospitality is as old as recorded human history. The span of written history is roughly 5000 years, with Sumerian cuneiform being the oldest form of writing discovered so far. This writing tends to be used as the beginning of history by the definition used by all historians; the period before writing is known as prehistory. The oldest collection of texts that refer to hospitality would be from a literary genre known as 'Ancient Near East texts'. These texts belong to a large family of Eastern Mediterranean traditions from Mesopotamia, Asia Minor, Syria-Palestine, and Egypt. Normally these texts are seen in parallel with the Old Testament; certain works date back to around 3500 BC, and are as old as the history of writing itself.

A brief overview of the history of hospitality in Egypt and Mesopotamia, demonstrates the illuminative capacity of historical exploration. The texts and key events that these examples have been drawn from are summarised in Figure 1.1; they form an illustrative beginning for the story of hospitality as they offer a glimpse of what hospitality was like when writing began; but unfortunately this is all the literature that has been identified from that very early time period. Between the contemporary era and the time when these texts were first written, there is a gap of up to 5000 years and a very limited literature base from which to draw conclusions.

5000 BC	4000 BC	3000 BC	2000 BC	1000 BC	0	AD 1000	AD 2000

3500 BC	Beginnings of writing
	'Ancient Near East' hospitality text
2700 BC	Great pyramids in Egypt
2100 BC	Laws of Hammurabi
	Teachings of Khety
	Hotels in Mesopotamia
1500 BC	'Tourist' graffiti written on the inside of the Great Pyramid
	Hostels in Crete

Figure 1.1: Timeline of 'Ancient Near East texts'

The teachings of Khety are a satire that celebrate the work of scribes and makes fun of every other trade in Egypt; they were written around 2100 BC. In the text, there is a clear directive on how to treat strangers, and the rewards, both in the temporal sphere through benefits to the household and the spiritual sphere, by pleasing the gods.

Give the stranger olive oil from your jar,
And double the income of your household.
The divine assembly desires respect for the poor
More than honour for the powerful.
(Khety XXVIII in Matthews, 1991b, p. 282)

Clearly domestic hospitality is not a new phenomenon. Neither is commercial hospitality. Hostels and inns in Mesopotamia date back to at least 2000 BC; they were in the business of supplying drinks, women, and accommodation for strangers. As yet no archaeological remains of the hostels (as referred to in Pritchard 1955) have been discovered; however, in Crete there is evidence of a hostel erected at around 1500 BC. According to Evans (1921) it was a small elegant structure placed alongside the highway at the approach to the palace at Knossos. Details are given of kitchens, dining rooms, and bathing facilities, all designed to allow travellers, after the long ride across the island, to rest and refresh themselves before entering the palace. Oppenheim (1967) observes that at least some of the roadside government hostels in Mesopotamia welcomed casual non-official travellers, whilst Jacobsen (1970) notes that in towns, travellers would be accommodated in the local inn.

In Egypt some characteristics of tourism, travel for curiosity or pleasure, can be found from about 1500 BC. Firth and Quibell (1936) note that in 1500 BC, the Sphinx and the three great pyramids were over a thousand years old, and on the wall of one of the chapels connected to the pyramids there is 3500-year-old graffiti. What facilities for food and lodging were available for ordinary holidaying Egyptians is unclear. Yoyotte (1960) hypothesises that more than likely they slept in the open and fed themselves as best they could, leaving the locals to clean up after them. However priests or those on government assignment had everything provided for them. As they travelled they would be cared for at temples and government depots along the way; this was standard procedure in Egypt for all who were travelling on official business.

There is also a large diorite stela in the Louvre Museum containing inscriptions commonly known as the Code of Hammurabi. Although the original purpose of the stela is somewhat enigmatic, within the inscription there are laws governing commercial hospitality from at least 1800 BC. Hostels and inns in Mesopotamia were in the business of supplying drinks, women, and accommodation for strangers. Drinks included datepalm wine and barley beer, and there were strict regulations against diluting them. Driver and Miles (1952), in the translation of the stela, identify that the punishment for watering-down beer was death by drowning, there was also a requirement

The Code of Hammurabi - the upper part of the stela (left) and the inscriptions on the reverse (right)

that tavernkeepers, on pain of death, report all customers who were felons. Other hospitality-related laws include one that states that a woman who had retired from the priestly office caught entering an inn was to be burned alive. According to Richardson (2000) the assumption was that she was going there for sex. The general level of the clientele and surroundings are illustrated by the saying: 'If a man urinates in the tavern in the presence of his wife, he will not prosper... He should sprinkle his urine to the right and the left of the door jambs of the tavern and he will prosper' (Gelb, 1956: s.v. *astammu*). The commercial hostels were even discussed in religious hymnody as in the following:

> *I enlarged the footpaths, straightened the highways of the land,*
> *I made secure travel, built there 'big houses' [hostels of some sort],*
> *Planted gardens alongside of them, established resting-places,*
> *Settled there friendly folk,*
> *(So that) who comes from below, who come from above,*
> *Might refresh themselves in its cool,*
> *The wayfarer who travels the highway at night,*
> *Might find refuge there like in a well-built city.*
>
> (Pritchard, 1955, p. 585)

The official referred to in the hymn founded fortified settlements to maintain sizeable government hostels along the major roads to service the needs of the travellers, regardless of whether they were official visitors or traders. Jones and Snyder (1961) give a detailed account of large-scale hospitality in operation at Lagash in Babylonia (modern-day Iraq). It ensured efficient movement of administrators, couriers, and army personnel between the capital and the subject cities; distances which varied from 100 to 400 miles away. The travel orders included an issue of one day's food rations. At the end of this they stayed for the night at a government hostel and then received rations for the next day. The amount and quality of the food differed according to rank, with administrators eating better than dispatch riders.

Within these illustrations of hospitality from 3500 BC to 1500 BC certain characteristics of hospitable behaviour are clearly recognisable: a disposition towards hospitality is prevalent; generous hospitality can bring certain rewards whereas a lack of hospitality can lead to retribution; hospitality is a personal duty and should not be delegated to others. It is also clear that hostels and inns in Mesopotamia date back to at least 2000 BC and they were controlled by the laws of the time.

1.3 Focusing on Classical Antiquity

This book concentrates on the historical period directly following that of the Ancient and Near East texts: known as Classical Antiquity. This is a broad term for the period of cultural history centred on the Mediterranean Sea, which begins with the earliest-recorded Greek poetry of Homer (*c*.770 BC), and coincides with the traditional date of the founding of Rome in 753 BC. Classical Antiquity continues through the death of Alexander the Great and decline of Greece, the advent of the Roman Empire, the rise of Christianity and the fall of the Western Roman Empire (fifth century AD), ending in the dissolution of classical culture with the close of Late Antiquity. The time period and these events are summarised in Figure 1.2.

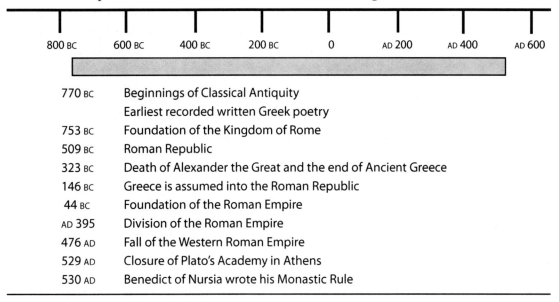

770 BC	Beginnings of Classical Antiquity
	Earliest recorded written Greek poetry
753 BC	Foundation of the Kingdom of Rome
509 BC	Roman Republic
323 BC	Death of Alexander the Great and the end of Ancient Greece
146 BC	Greece is assumed into the Roman Republic
44 BC	Foundation of the Roman Empire
AD 395	Division of the Roman Empire
476 AD	Fall of the Western Roman Empire
529 AD	Closure of Plato's Academy in Athens
530 AD	Benedict of Nursia wrote his Monastic Rule

Figure 1.2: Key events in Classical Antiquity

Although the ending date of Classical Antiquity is disputed, Liebeschuetz (2001) notes that currently most Western scholars use the abdication of Romulus Augustus, last Western Roman Emperor in AD 476 as the end of ancient European history. However, as Ward-Perkins (2005) observes, the date used as the end of the Classical Antiquity is entirely arbitrary and is a matter of some dispute amongst historians; alternative dates that are often used for the end this period are: 293 – Persecution of the Christian by Roman Emperor Diocletian; 395 – Division of Roman Empire into the Western Roman Empire and Eastern Roman Empire; and 529 – Closure of Plato's Academy in Athens by Byzantine Emperor Justinian I.

The period of time known as Classical Antiquity offers a suitable volume of literature for the focus of this book. At the beginning of the 20th century, the Cambridge scholar F.M. Cornford reflected on the enduring allure of Classical Antiquity, saying:

> *The ancient classics resemble the universe. They are always there, and they are very much the same as ever. But as the philosophy of every new age puts a fresh construction on the universe, so in the classics scholarship finds a perennial object for ever fresh and original interpretation.*

(Cornford, 1903, p. 19)

As identified in section 1.2, when the example of hospitality in Ancient and Near Eastern Texts was given, it became clear that no matter how tempting it might be to go as far back in time as possible, there is not the textual foundation to make that possible. The next period allows for a large collection of texts and sufficient temporal focus; and indeed as Cornford (1903) observed 'classics scholarship finds a perennial object for ever fresh and original interpretation' and in this book the object for interpretation is hospitality.

Classical Antiquity begins with the writings of Homer, as the first textual source of Classical Antiquity, and concludes with the Rule of St Benedict (c.AD 530), arguably the last text of the period or the first of the Middle Ages. The Rule is the foundation for the spread of monastic life across Western Europe, and Chapter 53 was recognised by Borias (1974) as the key focus for subsequent hospitality. During the Middle Ages the monasteries (as well as being the custodians of civilisation, knowledge and learning) had also provided the blueprints for detailed and formalised rules for religious hospitality, the care of the sick and the poor, and responsibilities for refugees, which were all to be adopted later within the nation states and by secular organisations. In addition the scriptoria (writing rooms) of the mediaeval monasteries had been the centres for the production of copies of the works of Classical Antiquity.

As Benedict was writing his Rule, Classical Antiquity was at an end and the next period of time is known as either the Dark Ages or the Early Middle Ages began. In historiography the phrase 'the Dark Ages' is most commonly known in relation to the European Early Middle Ages (from about AD 476 to about AD 1000). According to Mommsen (1942) it is generally accepted that the term 'Dark Ages' was first used by Petrarchae (c.1330) when writing of those who had come before him. He said that 'amidst the errors there shone forth men of genius, no less keen were their eyes, although they were surrounded by darkness and dense gloom' (Petrarchae, 1554, p. 1194). Petrarchae was reversing the traditional Christian metaphors of 'light versus darkness' to describe 'good versus evil'. Classical Antiquity, so long considered the 'Dark Age' for its lack of Christianity, was now seen by Petrarch as the age of 'light' because of its cultural achievements, while Petrarch's time, lacking such cultural achievements, was now seen as the age of darkness. Later historians expanded the term to include not only the lack of Latin literature, but a lack of contemporary written history and material cultural achievements in general: an age more silent than dark. Most modern historians dismiss the notion that the era was a 'Dark Age' by highlighting that this idea was based on ignorance of the period combined with popular stereotypes: see for example Smith (2005) who illustrates the pluralism and cultural diversity of Europe in a time period that is more appositely described as the early Middle Ages.

To set the context of the authors and writings, and indeed the interrelationship between the various historical events considered for this book, Table 1.1 identifies the texts and demonstrates, on a timeline, the historical location of each of the authors. The left-hand column gives the dates of major historical events that may have had an influence on the various authors cited. The right-hand column gives a list of the major authors or works investigated; here the texts are grouped according to age. This also demonstrates the importance of the oral tradition to the ancient cultures. It is interesting to note that the events surrounding the life of Abraham for example, have been dated to around 1850 BC, whilst it is generally accepted that Genesis did not begin to take written form until 1000 BC. A more recent example of the importance of oral tradition would be the observation that Jesus died around AD 30, and the Gospels did not begin to take written form for at least 40 years after; therefore, dates of particular happenings have been included along with the date of the redaction of the actual work. The 'Age' column has been divided up according to standard form of the archaeological periods.

For the preparation of this book, texts have been considered from all the authors in the right-hand column, however, the main periods of investigation run from approximately 540 BC to the writing of the Monastic Rule of St Benedict as that consolidates much of what had been written before that.

Table 1.1: Context of authors and writings

Historical events	Age	Authors and writings investigated
The Judges 1200–1025 King David 1010–963 Capture of Jerusalem by Israelites 1000 Building of The Temple 966 Sack of Thebes 633 Fall of Jerusalem 587	Iron Age 1200–539 BC	Book of Genesis starts to take a written form 1000–800 Homer 850 Prophet Elisha 850 Codification of Deuteronomy 800 Prophet Isaiah 722 Solon 638–560 Editing of Books of Kings 622
Building of Second Temple in Jerusalem 515 Revolt of Cyrus 401	Persian 539–332 BC	Simonides 556–468 Book of Job 500 Euripides 485–406 Socrates 470–399 Compilation of Psalms 450 Xenophon 431–360 Plato 428–347 Aristotle 384–322
Conquests of Alexander the Great 332 John Hyrcanus 134	Hellenistic 332–64 BC	Titus Maccius Plautus 254–184 M T Cicero 106–43 Redaction of 1 Maccabees 124 Writing of 1 Maccabees 100
Augustus Emperor 29 BC Birth of Jesus 7–6 BC Pontius Pilate Prefectship AD 26–36 Death of Jesus AD 30 Paul's martyrdom under Emperor Nero in Rome AD 67 Destruction of the Jerusalem Temple in AD 70 Clement of Rome, Pope 88–97	Rise of Roman Empire 64 BC	Livy 59 BC– AD 17 Ovid 43 BC– AD 17 Plutarch AD 50–120 Writings of St Paul AD 50–67 Synoptics, Acts and the Didache around AD 70 or 80 Letter of Clement to the Corinthians AD 94 Gospel and Apocalypse of John about AD 95
Death of Tacitus in 120 Emperor Hadrian 117–138 Emperor Marcus Aurelius 161–180 Emperor Decius 249–251 Emperor Diocletian 284–305 Emperor Constantine I 306–337 Battle of Milvian Bridge 312 Conversion of Constantine II 313 Edict of Milan 313 Julian persecutions 362 Council of Carthage 419	Patristic Period AD 60 – 460	Shepherd of Hermas 100 Letters of Ignatius 117 Martyrdom of Polycarp in Smyrna 166 Gospel of Thomas 200 Clement of Alexandria, Stromata 210 Tertullian 212 Cyprian of Carthage 258 Origen 253 Lucius Caecilius Lactantius 240–320
Emperor Justinian granted legal status to poor 530 St Benedict 480–543 Pope Gregory 590–604 Augustine of Canterbury 595–604	The Mediaeval Period AD 460 – 1500	Monastic Rule of Benedict 530 St Isidore, Bishop of Seville 610

1.4 The hospitality lexicon

Investigating the history and philosophy of the phenomenon of hospitality has to depend on original written sources and then their translation into English. In addition, the analysis of texts requires an understanding of the evolution of the language used in the texts and should provide both a template and also the linguistic background against which the investigation is conducted. Equally important is how these words are now used and translated into contemporary English. The first part of this section considers the evolution of English and the second part provides an in-depth review of the etymological evolution of the words readily associated with hospitality.

Proto Indo-European beginning

Indo-European is the name given for geographic reasons to the large and well-defined linguistic family that includes most of the languages of Europe, past and present, as well as those found in a vast area extending across Iran and Afghanistan to the northern half of the Indian subcontinent. It is held by Mallory and Adams (2006) that sometime around the middle of the fifth millennium BC, people expanded from the steppe zone north of the Black Sea and beyond the Volga into the Balkans and adjacent areas. These were the Kurgan peoples, who bore a new mobile and aggressive culture into Neolithic Europe, and they became the Indo-Europeans. However, with this movement of people into Europe in about 4500 BC also began the Proto Indo-European language. By the middle of the second millennium BC, this single language was to develop into forms as divergent as Mycenaean Greek and Hittite. As Renfrew (1990) observes, English words can be derived from Indo-European languages back to their fundamental components in Proto Indo-European, the parent language of all ancient and modern Indo-European languages. The dialects or branches of Indo-European, still represented today by one or more languages, are Indic and Iranian, Greek, Armenian, Slavic, Baltic, Albanian, Celtic, Italic, and Germanic. In modern times, this family of languages has spread by colonisation throughout the Western Hemisphere.

English is the most prevalent member of the Indo-European family, the native language of nearly 350 million people. As Mallory and Adams (2006) record, there are four main sources for English words that have evolved from an Indo-European root: direct descent from Indo-European to Germanic to Old English to English; borrowed from Old Norse during the Norman conquest; borrowed from French as a result of Norman French domination;

and borrowed from Latin at various times. These four sources and their development towards English words are supported by a timeline and shown in Figure 1.3.

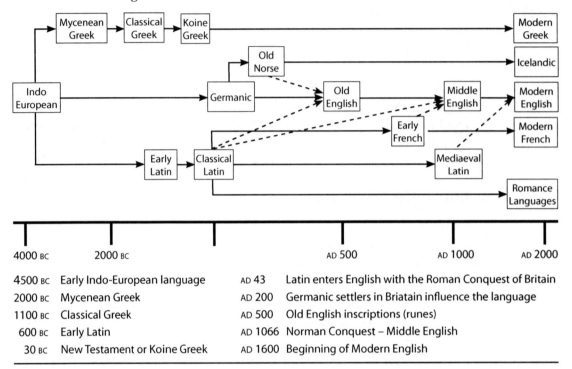

4500 BC	Early Indo-European language	AD 43	Latin enters English with the Roman Conquest of Britain
2000 BC	Mycenean Greek	AD 200	Germanic settlers in Briatain influence the language
1100 BC	Classical Greek	AD 500	Old English inscriptions (runes)
600 BC	Early Latin	AD 1066	Norman Conquest – Middle English
30 BC	New Testament or Koine Greek	AD 1600	Beginning of Modern English

Figure 1.3: The evolution of English

This identifies the key stages in the evolution of Modern English and summarises that evolution: the black lines show the direct descent of words, whereas the broken lines illustrate the borrowing of words from other language families.

Origins of 'guest' and 'host'

All the words that are readily associated with hospitality are evolved from the same hypothetical root *ghos-ti*; conventionally, whenever an * is used it shows that the word is hypothetical; it has been constructed by linguistic scholars; there is no written evidence for its existence. According to Watkins (2000) the 'guest' in Indo-European times (*c.*4000 BC), was also the 'stranger', and the 'stranger' in an uncertain and warring tribal society may well be hostile: the Latin cognate hostis also means 'enemy'. Figure 1.4 has been developed as means of summarising the evolution of the words 'host' and 'guest' and associated Modern English words from their Indo-European roots. The language families are shown within rectangular dotted lines, the dotted lines show borrowings from other language, whereas solid lines show a direct descent from the Indo-European root. For example, 'guest' can be directly traced from the Indo-European root *ghos-ti* through the Germanic *gastiz*, then entering Middle English as gest, but only after having been influenced/ borrowed from the Old Norse *gestr*; it eventually became 'guest' in current English.

'Stranger', 'guest', 'host': properly 'someone with whom one has reciprocal duties of hospitality' (Watkins, 2000, p. 89). As Ringe (2006) notes, the modern English word 'guest' has evolved from Old Norse *gestr*, 'guest'; from Old High German *gast*, 'guest'. Both come from Germanic *gastiz*. The compound forms the Proto Indo-European *ghos-pot-*, *ghos-po(d)-*, have given 'guest-master', one who symbolises the relationship of reciprocal obligation. From the same root the classical Greek ξένοςxenos meaning 'guest', 'host', and/or 'stranger' has evolved. The classical Greek word for hospitality was φῐλόξενος/philoxenos, literally the 'love of strangers'. For the Greeks φῐλόξενος/ philoxenos was the law or custom of offering protection and hospitality to strangers. English today still uses the word xenophobia (from the Greek 'fear of strangers') but has lost the word philoxenos.

In current usage, according to the Oxford English Dictionary, the word 'host' assumes three basic definitions, summarised as:

◊   a great company, a multitude;

◊   a large number; a man who lodges and entertains another in his house: the correlative of guest;

◊   the bread consecrated in the Eucharist, regarded as the body of Christ sacrificially offered; a consecrated wafer.

Watkins (2000) notes that 'host' as with 'guest', also originated with the Indo-European root, *ghos-ti-*. Kurzová (1981) argues that this root evolved into two Latin terms: *hostia*, meaning 'sacrifice', and *hostis*, 'army', 'enemy', and 'stranger'. Compound forms *ghos-pot-* subsequently evolved into the Latin *hospitem* or *hospes*, meaning 'proprietor', 'guest', 'stranger', 'foreigner; and subsequently hospice, hospitable, hospital, hospitality, host. 'Host' as 'multitude' appeared in Old French as *ost*, carrying with it a military connotation deriving from the Latin *hostis*. At almost the same time, a word pronounced identically yet trailing an 'e' – *oste* – turned up with the suggestion of 'host' as a person of hospitality. Around the year 1290, both words came into usage in Middle English as *ost*. Over time, the 'h', lost from the Latin, alternately appeared in and vanished from variant spellings (*hoste, host, oste, oost, oyste, hoaste*, etc.) until, 'host' as 'multitude' had shed its dominantly

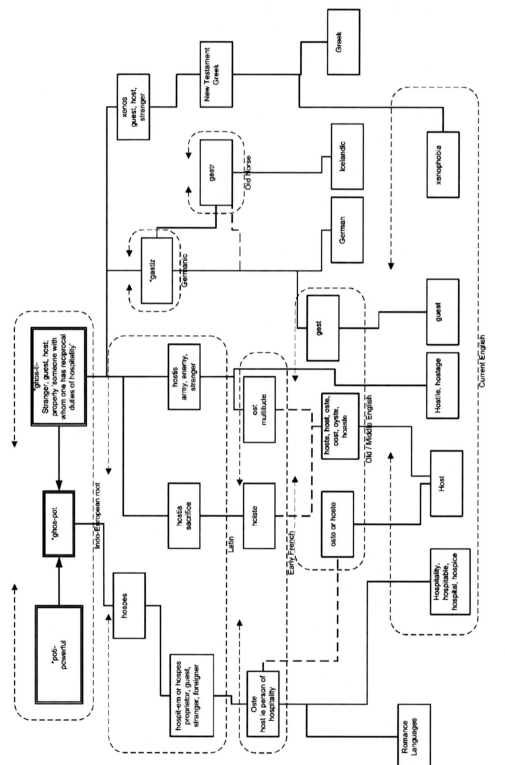

Figure 1.4: Evolution of 'host' and 'guest'

military evocation and, though still often used in reference to armies, could stand for multitudes of any kind.

Bickford (2002) observes the antagonistic flavour of the word was increasingly subsumed into a Biblical vernacular, as 'host' came to describe a 'host of angels' or a 'heavenly host' (though often passive, gathered around God, this 'heavenly host' could also be warlike and menacing). For a while – between 1390 and 1560 – 'host' as 'proprietor' was used interchangeably with 'guest', semantically returning it to its Latin roots. Meanwhile, the Eucharistic 'host' had an incarnation as hoiste in Middle French, before appearing in the early 14th century as the Middle English oste or hoste. Until very recently, 'guest' and 'host' were understood to be two different roles. Some popular television programmes even have the 'guest host' where a different person, 'guest', presents, 'hosts' the show each week.

1.5 Links between oral tradition and texts

The works of Homer provide the first textual source of Classical Antiquity; however when exactly these works were redacted is unclear. Graziosi (2005) states that papyrus copies of the Homeric writings could be found throughout the Greek World in the 4th and 5th centuries BC. There must also have been texts in circulation in the 6th century, because certain classical authors refer to official recitations in Athens, and there are echoes of Homer in the writings of 6th century poets. Fagles (1990, p. 6) notes that other poets of the 7th century BC, whose work survives only in fragments, have phrases and even half-lines that are also common to Homer, and argues that 'these echoes betray acquaintance with the work we know as Homer's'. Fagles (1990) also records that there is also a vase, dated to about 750 BC, that has an inscription that refers to the cup of Nestor described in the *Iliad* (11:745–53).

The Homeric writings concern the Trojan War and surrounding events. Thomas and Conant (2005) observe that Ancient Greek authors date this war to about 1200 BC and that Homer was believed to live around 900 BC. Bakker (1997) records that history and traditions attribute the first written composition of the Homeric writings to 770 BC and thus this date is generally accepted as the beginning of Classical Antiquity. Lord (1960) and Parry (1936) addressed the issue of who Homer was and what the Homeric writings are. Their contributions reconsidered the foundational assumptions that framed the ideas about where written texts had originated. Until this point it had been assumed that it was Homer himself who wrote down his works; there was no concept of a pre-existent oral tradition.

In a separate development, Ong (1987), whose research interests are in cultural history, psychology and rhetoric, included investigating ways in which the media used to communicate the story also shape the nature of the content conveyed. Ong (1987) articulated the contrasts between oral and literate cultures, and made possible an integrated theory of oral tradition. This allows for certain assumptions or hypotheses to be made about a text; these include when the text was first redacted in written form and how long it has existed in oral form. This is generally known as the theory of traditionality and textuality. This theory, which was also adopted and used in Biblical studies, highlights levels of formulaic compositions within the texts that include the type-scene: A basic pattern of narrative details, some of which could show how the original oral story was remembered and told (traditionality) and then in what form it was originally written down (textuality). As noted by Zumthor (1983), an oral poet needs devices to facilitate the production of the poem at a more detailed level, and this is the reason for the use of formulae and specific type-scenes. Type-scenes such as 'arrival', 'messages', 'dreams', etc., are a fundamental element of oral poetry: they allow the poet to compose by selecting from a more-or-less pre-determined range of detailed narrative units. In the case of the Homeric writings, a summary of all the type-scenes can be found in Edwards (1992).

Drawing on the work of previous authors including that of Lord (1960) and Parry (1936), Reece (1993, p. 190) undertakes a study of one category of Homeric type-scene, that of hospitality, 'the most pervasive type-scene in the *Odyssey*'. The study is about how oral poetry works, however the subject taken for investigation is the hospitality in the Homeric writings, which according to Reece (1993, p. 191) is 'everything that occurs from the moment a visitor approaches someone's house until the moment he departs'. Reece (1993, p. 189) attempts to present the *Odyssey* as a series of variations on the theme of hospitality; stating that he has:

> *often wondered how an oral poet, when performing a large-scale epic of the size of an Iliad or an Odyssey, would, on a very practical level, go about arranging and structuring the larger units of his epic, the major scenes and large-scale narrative patterns, and, having devised a satisfactory arrangement, how he would remember that arrangement accurately in subsequent performances.*

The hospitality scenes, as defined by Reece, are much larger narrative units; some are second only in size to the poems in their totality comprising many smaller type-scenes. Reese (1993, p.5) identifies 18 hospitality scenes within the writings:

twelve in the Odyssey *(Athena-Mentes in Ithaca; Telemachus in Pylos; Telemachus in Sparta; Hermes and Calypso; Odysseus and the Phaeacians; Odysseus and Polyphemus; Odysseus and Aeolus; Odysseus and the Laestrygonians; Odysseus and Circe; Odysseus and Eumaeus; Telemachus and Eumaeus; and Odysseus' homecoming); four in the* Iliad *(the embassy to Achilles; Nestor and Odysseus in Phthia; Thetis and Hephaestus; and Priam and Achilles); and two in the* Hymns *(Demeter in the home of Celeos; and Aphrodite and Anchises).*

The first four hospitality scenes in the *Odyssey* are seen to establish the paradigm of proper hospitality, with which all the other hospitality scenes are to be compared or contrasted. These scenes follow a structure, consisting up of 38 conventional elements that, to a greater or lesser degree, are common, though no scene presents every element and some of them are hardly represented at all; some of these elements are type-scenes in their own right. These elements are shown in Table 1.2.

Reece (1993, p. 7) whilst conducting a discussion of the extensive hospitality type-scenes in the Homeric writings, accepts that the structure, presented in Table 1.2 is a 'highly artificial abstraction, a mechanical device' from which there are a number of hospitality deviations. In particular the contrast made between the pious Nestor and King Menelaus, in whose palace no sacrifices are offered. By contrasting between humble and extravagant hospitality in their respective residences, the hospitality of the former is less grand but warmer and more personal than that of the latter. There is also humour contained in the hospitality scenes, particularly when Menelaus forgets his own remarks about the duty of the good host and detains Nestor against his will:

> *I would condemn any host who, receiving guests, acted excessively hospitable or excessively hostile; all things are better in due measure. It is as blameworthy to urge a guest to leave who does not want to as it is to detain a guest who is eager to leave. One must grant hospitality to a guest who is present and grant conveyance to a guest who wants to leave.*
>
> *(Homer,* Odyssey *15:69–74)*

Table 1.2: Structure of Homeric hospitality type-scenes

	Sub scene	Other elements
I	Maiden at the well /youth on the road	
II	Arrival at the destination	
III	Description of the surroundings	a. Of the residence b. Of (the activities of) the person c. Of (the activities of) the others
IV	Dog at the door	
V	Waiting at the threshold	
VI	Supplication	
VII	Reception	a. Host catches sight of the visitor b. Host hesitates to offer hospitality c. Host rises from his seat d. Host approaches the visitor e. Host attends to the visitor's horses f. Host takes the visitor by the hand g. Host bids the visitor welcome h. Host takes the visitor's spear i. Host leads the visitor in
VIII	Seat	
IX	Feast	a. Preparation b. Consumption c. Conclusion
X	After-dinner drink	
XI	Identification	a. Host questions the visitor b. Visitor reveals his identity
XII	Exchange of information	
XIII	Entertainment	
XIV	Visitor pronounces a blessing on the host	
XV	Visitor shares in a libation or sacrifice	
XVI	Visitor asks to be allowed to sleep	
XVII	Bed	
XVIII	Bath	
XIX	Host detains the visitor	
XX	Guest-gifts	
XXI	Departure meal	
XXII	Departure libation	
XXIII	Farewell blessing	
XXIV	Departure omen and interpretation	
XXV	Escort to visitor's next destination	

Source: Reece (1993, p. 6f)

More general issues of hospitality, in particular the Phaeacians' ambivalent attitude towards strangers, are discussed by Reece (1993, p. 104) and also how the dynamics of delay show that there may be 'a hint of potential hostility' contained in hospitality.

Reece's general methodology of hermeneutical textual analysis, and in particular his observations regarding the form and centrality of hospitality within the Homeric writings, promote a significantly richer understanding of the structure of the Homeric epic. Linking stories of hospitality together was used both by Homer and successive oral poets to construct the epic poem, and Reece (1993) demonstrates how 3000 years later the concept of hospitality was used to analyse how the poem had been constructed and redacted.

2 Philosophical Perspectives on Hospitality

Although no specific studies into hospitality and classical philosophy have been identified, certain contemporary philosophers have written on the philosophy of hospitality. Examining the work of these philosophers allows for exploring the complexity of the phenomenon of hospitality, through critically evaluating the studies and thoughts of contemporary philosophers who have considered the phenomenon of hospitality. In reviewing the relationship between philosophy and hospitality, three separate issues are evident in the writings:

◊ moral philosophy of hospitality from the perspective of the guest/host relationship;

◊ hospitality between peoples and nation states; and,

◊ the use of language in hospitality provision and consumption.

2.1 Individual moral philosophy: host

Derrida (2000b) defined hospitality as inviting and welcoming the 'stranger'. This takes place on different levels: the personal level where the 'stranger' is welcomed into the home; and the level of individual countries. Derrida was credited as the inventor of 'deconstruction', the practice of dismantling texts by revealing their assumptions and contradictions. Normally life is lived at the level where things are presumed; people are accustomed to think in narrow ways. Deconstruction attempts to highlight just how much is taken for granted in contemporary conceptual thought and language.

Derrida's interest in hospitality was heightened by the etymology of Benveniste (1969) who analysed 'hospitality', which is from a Latin root, but derived from two proto Indo-European words that have the meanings of 'stranger', 'guest' and 'power'. Thus in the 'deconstruction' of the word, there can be seen:

an essential 'self limitation' built right into the idea of hospitality, which preserves the distance between one's own and the 'stranger', between owning one's own property and inviting the 'other' into one's home.

(Caputo, 2002, p. 110)

Derrida (2000a, p. 13) observes that there is always a little hostility in all hosting and hospitality, constituting what he called a certain 'hostipitality': 'If I say 'Welcome', I am not renouncing my mastery, something that becomes transparent in people whose hospitality is a way of showing off how much they own or who make their guests uncomfortable and afraid to touch a thing.' To Derrida then, the notion of having and retaining the mastery of the house underlies hospitality.

'Make yourself at home', this is a self-limiting invitation ... it means: please feel at home, act as if you were at home, but, remember, that is not true, this is not your home but mine, and you are expected to respect my property.

(Caputo, 2002, p. 111)

Telfer (2000) also explores this when discussing the motivation behind hospitality. There is a limitation to the amount of hospitality that 'hosts' can and wish to offer, just as important are the intentions that lie behind any hospitable act: there surely is a distinction to be made between hospitality for pleasure and hospitality that is born out of a sense of duty. She considers hospitality to be a moral virtue, and articulates hospitable motives to be:

Those in which concern for the guests' pleasure and welfare, for its own sake, is predominant. These can include entertaining for pleasure where that pleasure largely depends on knowing that one is pleasing the guests, and sense of duty where there is also concern for the guests themselves. And hospitable people, those who possess the trait of hospitableness, are those who often entertain from one or more of these motives, or from mixed motives in which one of these motives is predominant.

(Telfer, 1996, p. 82)

The distinction made between hospitality offered for pleasure and hospitality that is born out of a sense of duty is developed by Telfer to include the type of guest to whom a host would offer hospitality. This classification is summarised as:

1. *Those in a relationship to the host. This includes guests within a social circle, that the host is obliged to offer hospitality to, for example, colleagues, neighbours, fellow parishioners, parents whose children are friends and relatives.*

2. *Those in need. This Telfer (1996, p. 91f) terms 'good-Samaritan hospitality', this encapsulates all who are in need of hospitality. It may be a need for food and drink; however, it also includes 'a psychological need of a kind which can be met particularly well by hospitality, such as loneliness or the need to feel valued as an individual'.*

3. *Friends of the host. Hospitality is shown to friends because 'liking and affection are inherent in friendship; the liking produces a wish for the friends' company (as distinct from company in general), the affection a desire to please them'.*

(Telfer, 1996, p. 93)

On several occasions arguments are based on simple assertions rather than an elaboration of philosophical underpinnings, or on the use of descriptive categories as universals of human conduct. For example, Telfer (1996, p. 107) notes gluttony may come in several forms but always involves 'caring too much for the pleasures of eating and drinking'; this is a rather sweeping statement to cover all of human society.

Telfer (1996, p. 93) argues that there is a special link between friendship and hospitality, because it involves the home of the host: 'hospitality (provided it is not too formal) is an invitation to intimacy, an offer of a share in the host's private life'. This can cause a paradox when the friends start visiting without invitation and therefore they stop being guests and start to become like part of the family. Telfer (1996, p. 93) then asks 'Is turning friends into family the essence of this kind of hospitality, or does it go beyond hospitality?' Hospitality in this situation is double edged: the host can either make a special fuss over them or the special fuss can be deliberately avoided to allow them to feel at home. Telfer (1996, p. 101) concludes that the reason why hosts choose to pursue the virtue of hospitableness is that they are attracted by an ideal of hospitality. 'The ideal of hospitality, like all ideals, presents itself as joyful rather than onerous, and provides the inspiration for the pursuit of the virtue or virtues of hospitableness.'

In stark contrast to the individualistic perspective offered by Telfer on hospitality in a domestic context, Derrida (2000b) offers a more encompassing philosophy of hospitality. In an attempt to clarify terminology, this section adopts Derrida's differentiation between the 'law of hospitality' and 'laws of hospitality':

The law of unlimited hospitality (to give the new arrival all of one's home and oneself, to give him or her one's own, our own, without asking a name, or compensation, or the fulfilment of even the smallest condition), and on the other hand, the laws (in the plural), those rights and duties that are always conditioned and conditional, as they are defined by the Greco-Roman tradition and even the Judaeo-Christian one, by all of law and all philosophy of law up to Kant and Hegel in particular, across the family, civil society, and the State.

(Derrida, 2000b, p. 77)

This distinction is useful because it clarifies that there is a universal truth of hospitality; however, the way that hospitality is offered is normally governed by a set of rules dependent on the context: domestic, civic or commercial.

In his discussions, Derrida (2000b) makes a distinction between unconditional hospitality, which he considers impossible, and hospitality that is always conditional. A distinctive aspect of Derrida's approach to the phenomenon of hospitality is his reflection on how achieving an absolute hospitality is impossible. In trying to imagine the extremes of a hospitality to which no conditions are set, there is a realisation that unconditional hospitality could never be accomplished. It is not so much an ideal: it is an impossible ideal. The phenomenon of hospitality necessarily contains the concept of the other or foreigner within it, since hospitality requires, a priori, a concept of the outsider or guest. From the perspective of the host, Derrida distinguishes between a guest and a parasite:

In principle, the difference is straightforward, but for that you need a law; hospitality, reception, the welcome offered have to be submitted to a basic and limiting jurisdiction. Not all new arrivals are received as guests if they don't have the benefit of the right to hospitality or the right of asylum, etc. Without this right, a new arrival can only be introduced 'in my home,' in the host's 'at home,' as a parasite, a guest who is wrong, illegitimate, clandestine, and liable to expulsion or arrest

(Derrida, 2000b, p. 59f)

Derrida (2000a) argues that hospitality is therefore conditional in the sense that the outsider or foreigner has to meet the criteria of the a priori 'other'. He is implying that hospitality is not given to a guest who is absolutely unknown or anonymous, because the host has no idea of how they will respond.

Absolute hospitality requires that I open up my home and that I give not only to the foreigner (provided with a family name, with the social status of being a foreigner, etc.), but to the absolute, unknown, anonymous other, and that I give place to them, that I let them come, that I let them arrive, and take place in the place I offer them, without asking of them either reciprocity (entering into a pact) or even their names. The law of absolute hospitality commands a break with hospitality by right, with law or justice as rights.

(Derrida, 2000b, p. 25)

Derrida (1999b, 1999c) argues that absolute hospitality requires the host to allow the guest to behave as they wish; there must be no pressure or obligation to behave in any particular manner. Absolute hospitality does not make a demand of the guest that would force them to reciprocate by way of imposing an obligation. The language used by Derrida could be held to imply that make a guest conform to any rules or norms is a bad thing.

2.2 Hospitality and the nation states

The hospitality relationship also exists on a wider scale: between peoples and states. This can be illustrated by using the example of the French Revolution and the declaration of national hospitality as providing a case example of hospitality offered by the states. This is echoed in the writings of Derrida and two other post-colonial theorists Rosello and Ben Jelloun, recognised philosophers who have devoted a considerable amount of thought to hospitality.

Kant ([1780] 1998) argues that individuals have a universal right to shelter in any country, but for a limited time period and not if they would jeopardise the security of the country in question. This philosophy was codified in French national hospitality during the revolution when Saint-Just in the 'Essai de Constitution' stated:

Refugees at Kibati camp in the Congo, 2008.
Photo by Julien Harneis, from Wikimedia Commons

> *The French people declares itself to be the friend of all peoples; it will religiously respect treaties and flags; it offers asylum in its harbours to ships from all over the world; it offers asylum to great men and virtuous unfortunates of all countries; its ships at sea will protect foreign ships against storms. Foreigners and their customs will be respected in its bosom.*
>
> *(Saint-Just 1793 cited by Duval, 1984, p. 441)*

This quote illustrates the original rhetorical gestures used to present the French Republic as generous and hospitable: the promise a generous and welcoming attitude to all strangers.

When reviewing French revolutionary hospitality, Wahnich (1997b, p. 346) identifies that its *raison d'être* was in offering sanctuary and security to all: 'first and foremost, citizens are men, and the purpose of national law is not to identify the frontier but to guarantee universal law, without limits.' However, as soon as this principle of hospitality was established it was betrayed. Wahnich (1997b, p. 346) asserts that 'the enigma of a hospitality subverted by suspicion, of friendship experienced in terms of treason, and of a fraternity that invents the most radical forms of exclusion.' Wahnich (1997a) also highlights a modern hospitality enigma: the situation where nation states want their emigrants treated as sacred guests but pay scant attention to their own laws of hospitality regarding immigrants. In contemporary times, nations admit a certain number of immigrants – conditionally. This is echoed in the writings of Schérer (1993, p. 7) registering his concern that hospitality has become an impossible luxury:

> *Isn't hospitality the madness of our contemporary world? To praise hospitality just when, in France and almost everywhere else in the world, the main concern is to restrict it, from the right to asylum to the code of nationality! Disturbing, excessive, like madness, it resists all forms of reason, including raison d'être.'*

Studying hospitality and the nation states, Derrida (1999b) notes that to the best of his knowledge there is no country in the world that allows unconditional immigration. Individuals may consider themselves to be practically hospitable; however, they will not leave their doors open to all who might come, to take or do anything, without condition or limit. Derrida argues the same can be said about nation states; conditional hospitality takes place only in the shadow of the impossibility of the ideal version. Derrida (1998a, p. 70) reflects on the conceptual possibility of unconditional hospitality in order 'to understand and to inform what is going on today in our world'. This is reflected in the following quote:

Unconditional hospitality implies that you don't ask the other, the new-comer, the guest to give anything back, or even to identify himself or herself. Even if the other deprives you of your mastery or your home, you have to accept this. It is terrible to accept this, but that is the condition of unconditional hospitality: that you give up the mastery of your space, your home, your nation. It is unbearable. If, however, there is pure hospitality, it should be pushed to this extreme.

(Derrida, 1998a, p. 71)

Derrida (1998a, p. 70) also questions the restricted nature of national hospitality to legal and illegal immigrants:

We know that there are numerous what we call 'displaced persons' who are applying for the right to asylum without being citizens, without being identified as citizens. It is not for speculative or ethical reasons that I am interested in unconditional hospitality, but in order to understand and to transform what is going on today in our world.

In Derrida's later works, he is interested in many unconditionals: such as an unconditional gift, an unconditional pardon and an unconditional mourning. As each of these is deemed impossible, impossibility takes on an increasingly strong resonance in his late work. Derrida's views on hospitality illuminate a transition in his philosophical project from earlier writings (Derrida, 1981, 1997a). Whilst considering hospitality, there is a progression of thought in relation to 'ideals' and depiction of the 'other'; the preceding Derridean writings concerning depictions of maternity, gender, nature, community and family values in popular culture an 'ideal' version is considered impossible. With hospitality, Derrida stresses impossibility in a different way and makes an alternative use of the idea that ideals are impossible. This impossibility amounts to an 'otherness' with which there is an everyday relation. Derrida (1999b) quotes former French minister of immigration Michel Rocard who in 1993 stated, with respect to immigration quotas, that France could not offer a home to everybody in the world who suffered. Derrida (1999b) asserts that Rocard's immigration quota is set through mediation with a threshold of impossibility. For Derrida impossibility opens up possibilities of transformation; the case of Rocard highlighted the fragility of brutal authority. Some of the French 'hosts' might respond with quick agreement about the strict limitations on 'guests'; however, others might be provoked into asking why more and better hospitality should not be offered, and what does set the limit.

In considering hospitality more generally Derrida (1981, p. 163) identifies 'otherness' in reference to 'the other, the newcomer, the guest'; interrogating humanities ethical relationship with itself, receptiveness and in relationship with others: strangers; foreigners; immigrants; and friends – guests.

For pure hospitality or a pure gift to occur, however, there must be an absolute surprise. The other, like the Messiah, must arrive whenever he or she wants. She [sic] may even not arrive. I would oppose, therefore, the traditional and religious concept of 'visitation' to 'invitation': visitation implies the arrival of someone who is not expected, who can show up at any time. If I am unconditionally hospitable I should welcome the visitation, not the invited guest, but the visitor. I must be unprepared, or prepared to be unprepared, for the unexpected arrival of any other. Is this possible? I don't know. If, however, there is pure hospitality, or a pure gift, it should consist in this opening without horizon, without horizon of expectation, an opening to the newcomer whoever that may be. It may be terrible because the newcomer may be a good person, or may be the devil.

(Derrida, 1998a, p. 70)

This quote demonstrates an important distinction between messianicity and messianism (messianic structure or messianicity is the expectation of future coming of the messiah and bringing of justice whereas messianism is the identification in time and history of the messianic structure; messianisms say that the Messiah has already appeared in time, tradition, and history), another way of reading his 'impossibility' and related notion of otherness. A messianism is considered by Derrida as a kind of dogmatism, subjecting the divine other to 'metaphysico-religious determination' (Derrida, 1994, p. 89); forcing the ultimate guest, the Messiah, to conform or at least converge to the host's preconceptions of them. When imagining the coming of the Messiah, the host attributes a new kind of origin and centrism to a divine other and assumes the latter suits their imaginative picture.

Faith for Derrida (1997b, p. 120) is undeconstructible, while religion, like law, is deconstructible. Faith is 'something that is presupposed by the most radical deconstructive gesture. You cannot address the other, speak to the other, without an act of faith, without testimony.' To speak to another is to ask them to trust you.

As soon as you address the other, as soon as you are open to the future, as soon as you have a temporal experience of waiting for the future, of waiting for someone to come; that is the opening of experience. Someone is to come, is now to come.

(Derrida, 1997b, p. 123)

The faith in the other to come, according to Derrida, is absolutely universal, thus the universal structure of faith is an undeconstructible. In contrast, Derrida (2002, p. 67f) suggests invoking messianicity: as 'the unexpected surprise. ... If I could anticipate, if I had a horizon of anticipation, if I could see what is coming or who is coming, there would be no coming.' Derrida's view of messianicity is not limited to a religious context, but extends to his depiction of otherness more generally. His comments about the other apply to a friend, someone culturally different, a parent, a child; where the issue arises of whether the host is capable of recognising them, of respecting their difference, and of how the host may be surprised by them. Thus Derrida allows for a pure form of hospitality. However, in the case of surprise the unsuspected guest is received on the terms of the host; unconditional hospitality is still impossible. Similarly when a country's borders are open to guests or immigrants, conditional hospitality places the country in relation to the impossible; the impossible greater generosity inhabits the act of conditional hospitality.

Engaging with the writings of Derrida's writings on hospitality, Rosello (2001) adopts a postcolonial philosophical stance, combines a brief historical enquiry into the nature of French hospitality as a metaphor for public acceptance of the other, and close textual analysis of several recent French and francophone novels and films; addressing what issues might be at stake if the immigrant (legal or otherwise, and usually non-European) were considered a guest. Examining France's traditional role as the *terre d'asile* (land of sanctuary) for political refugees, Rosello (2001) shows how this image of a welcoming France is now contrasted with France as part of the 'Fortress Europe' (a land that seeks to close its borders to unwelcome immigrants). Rosello's (2001) analysis also discusses the entire decade of the 1990s in France, when media reports of demonstrations and sit-ins by hundreds of *sanspapiers* (immigrants without papers) demanding amnesty and regularisation of their status, filled newspapers almost every week.

Rosello develops her stratification of private concepts to public or state hospitality by examining the novel *Un Aller Simple* (*One-Way Ticket*). This novel, written by van Cauwelaert (1994), is a humorous story about a young man (born in France, raised by gypsies) deported to a non-existent Moroccan village because his fake passport names this fictional place as that of his birth. Rosello links this story to French and European Union immigration laws and treaties of the same decade (1990s). The absurdity of immigration laws that seek to reduce individuals to their official documentary identity, without regard to the fluctuating and ethereal nature of national identities are highlighted within the novel by van Cauwelaert. Rosello's textual analysis reveals different hospitality scenarios between groups and between individuals, especially the notion of hosts and guests and their respective responsibilities. Emphasising this, Rosello (2002, p. 176) notes:

The very precondition of hospitality may require that, in some ways, both the host and the guest accept, in different ways, the uncomfortable and sometimes painful possibility of being changed by the other.

Within 'Fortress Europe' there does not seem to be the political will to allow increased immigration and the thought of European hosts being changed is an anathema. Rosello expresses grave concerns regarding the future of immigrants in Western Europe. It is unlikely that they be perceived of as honoured guests deserving of consideration, whereas it is more probable that they be likened to guests who have fallen into the category of parasite; they have overstayed their welcome and must be brutally ushered out.

Rosello's philosophical concerns are also reflected in the writings of another postcolonial theorist Tahar Ben Jalloun; a Moroccan who emigrated to France in 1971. Drawing upon his personal encounters with racism he uses the metaphor of hospitality to elucidate the racial divisions that plague contemporary France. Ben Jelloun (1999) states that laws of hospitality are a fundamental mark of civilisation, observing that he comes from a poor and relatively unsophisticated country, where the stranger's right to protection and shelter has been practised since time immemorial. On moving to France, Ben Jelloun discovered that hospitality was not reciprocal, despite the benefits that France had clearly gained from its former colonies. Although France had enjoyed one side of the reciprocal arrangement, hospitality was not reciprocated to those who wished to come as guests to France; the former hosts were not welcomed as guests. Hospitality was conditional; a right to visit was not a right to stay. Ben Jelloun (1999, p. 39) wishes to 'open windows in the house of silence, indifference and fear'; French society seems to remain inhospitable, even frightened by immigrants. Ben Jelloun (1999, p. 116) suggests that former colonials feel abandoned by the authorities of their own countries and in France, live in fear of being returned to them: 'in France he dreams of the country he left behind. In his own country, he dreams of France... he thumps back and forth a bag full of small possessions and of grand illusion'. Despite having lived for about 30 years in France the author states that:

yet sometimes I feel I am a stranger here. That happens whenever racism occurs, whether it is virulent or latent, and whenever someone lays down limits that mustn't be transgressed.

(Ben Jelloun, 1999, p. 133)

Ben Jelloun (1999) concludes with a plea aimed at policymakers; instead of laws that restrict hospitality, i.e. entry and residence, he advocates a policy that establishes links between morals and everyone's right to acceptance and equity.

For current postcolonial philosophical theory, hospitality is a multifaceted concept. What are commonly referred to as 'laws of hospitality' are largely unwritten and thereby subject to flux and interpretation. For Rosello (2001), what makes the phenomenon of hospitality relevant for philosophical investigation is the potential for redefinition in the traditional roles and duties of the guest and the host. Alternating between notions of duty and voluntary charity, hospitality between individuals and states of different racial, ethnic, or religious, backgrounds entails its own ramifications. Ben Jelloun (1999) argues that racism is caused by the existence of hospitality thresholds and boundaries.

2.3   Hospitality and language

The underlying principle established by considering moral philosophy of the host/guest relationship both at the individual level and at the national level is that during any hospitality relationship the host and guest inhabit the same moral universe and are subject to transcendent laws of hospitality. However, the hospitality relationship is further complicated by the use of language and culture. Ben Jelloun (1999, p. 8) highlights the problem of language and cultural difference within different laws of hospitality:

> In an unpublished novella called 'The Invitation' I tell the true story of a television crew who went to Algeria to produce a program about an immigrant who had gone home. The shooting lasted a week, and throughout the whole time the villagers entertained the crew. The immigrant's father went into debt to provide presents and sumptuous meals all around. The director, touched by such warmth and generosity, gave the old man his business card. 'If ever you're in Paris,' he said in typical Parisian style, 'be sure to come and see me!' But when one evening six months later the old man rang at his doorbell, it took the director some time to realize who he was. Very embarrassing for all concerned.

Ben Jelloun (1999, p. 3) notes that this illustration shows 'hospitality does not always imply reciprocity'; however, what this story also highlights is the embarrassment of the difference between expectations and behaviour.

Both the guest and the host speak the same language, but are from different cultural backgrounds and their language and cultural differences led to confusion between how to extend and accept invitations.

Derrida (2000a) proposes that issues of language cannot be dissociated from the most basic level of hospitality; guests can be discomforted and fundamentally disadvantaged by the host's language.

> *The question of hospitality starts here: must we require the strange to understand us, to speak our language in all the meanings of the words, in all its possible extensions, before being able to, in order to be able to, welcome him or her.*
>
> (Derrida, 2000a, p. 21)

Derrida (2000a) argues that this imposition and use of language is the first barrier to hospitality that is imposed by the host on the guest. Using Ancient Athens, Derrida (2000a, p. 16) notes 'the foreigner had some rights', the threshold of the host's domain establishes a social relation by delimiting the difference between those who are and are not of Athens. In the case of language, the social relations and understanding distinguish between sameness and difference; hospitality is extended on the host's terms and not those of the guest.

> *Because intentionality is hospitality, it resists thematization. Act without activity, reason as receptivity, a sensible and rational experience of receiving, a gesture of welcoming, a welcome offered to the other as stranger, hospitality opens up as intentionality, but it cannot become an object, thing, or theme. Thematization, on the contrary, already presupposes hospitality, welcoming, intentionality, the face. The closing of the door, inhospitality, war, and allergy already imply, as their possibility, a hospitality offered or received: an original or, more precisely, pre-originary declaration of peace.*
>
> (Derrida, 1999a, p. 48)

The example of France is used: when the Prime Minster Michel Rocard closed the door on unconditional hospitality, Derrida (1999a) argues that he opened up a conceptual paradox; similarly with this pre-originary hospitable declaration of peace there is another paradox at work. For the declaration to be understood, it has to be, a priori, inherently and universally understandable to everyone. This means, in turn, that a monolingual communication is required. In this situation Derrida (1998b) considers hospitality from the punitive side of what he refers to as a politics of language, within which monolinguism is imposed as a precondition for hospitality.

According to Derrida (1998b, p. 10) monolinguism refers to a paradox that formed what he calls the rule of language:

We only ever speak one language…

(yes, but)

We never speak only one language.

Derrida was noticing in Ancient Athens where the foreigner was welcomed according to the duties and obligations that appropriated the foreigner within Athenian law. This is a sovereign law that belongs to Athens, certainly, but that as in the case of all monolinguisms seem to originate from somewhere else, since even the native Athenians are always striving to appropriate it to themselves in the name of becoming the perfect and most native of citizens.

> *First and foremost, the monolingualism of the other would be that sovereignty, that law originating from elsewhere, certainly, but also primarily the very language of the Law. Its experience would be ostensibly autonomous, because I have to speak this law and appropriate it in order to understand it as if I was giving it to myself, but it remains necessarily heteronomous, for such is, at bottom, the essence of any law. The madness of the law places its possibility lastingly inside the dwelling of this auto-heteronomy.*
>
> *(Derrida, 1998b, p. 39)*

Belonging to the monolinguism of a native tongue is difficult for the simple reason that this language is not entirely perfectible; therefore, there is always the slight sense of being a stranger or foreigner to it. This self-perception of being alien or foreign despite your native tongue or status is what Derrida calls auto-heteronomy. For Derrida the identification with the native tongue is important because being a native speaker is a sign of political identity and the consequential legal rights. Speaking a language, therefore, is a means of dwelling or remaining within a political identity even when you are a foreigner abroad.

The politics of language can protect, since it is politics that prepare the way for hospitality in the Athenian sense, in which citizens and foreigners are both known quantities with formal contractual relations of hosting and being a guest. However, Derrida notes that the law under which people gather themselves to that language, gives them their political identity and security, is not as hospitable as one might like to imagine, precisely because it is political.

> *[Language is] one of the numerous difficulties before us, as with settling the extension of the concept of hospitality… In the broad sense, the language*

in which the foreigner is addressed or in which he is heard, if he is, is the ensemble of culture, it is the values, the norms, the meanings that inhabit the language.

(Derrida, 2000b, p. 132)

In terms of language and hospitality this would mean that if language shelters the guest, it does not incorporate or assimilate the guest into itself. Derrida (1998b) notes that at the same time 'we speak only one language...' because there is always the possibility of speaking otherwise, a speaking differently that is the condition of the essence of speaking one language properly.

Earlier in Chapter 1, when studying the evolution of English, Figure 1.3 showed the language's linguistic pedigree. It was clearly shown that English is made up of different languages that, over time, have not only become incorporated into the native language but have been so incorporated as to become indistinguishable. This illustrates Derrida's observation that in speaking a single language it is impossible to speak one language alone. Derrida emphasises the difficulty of establishing a hard and fast difference between the native and the foreign.

2.4 Potential for discontentment and bias

Discontentment and personal bias are issues that arise when reviewing the philosophical literature. This comes across clearly in the writings of Ben Jalloun, in his homesickness and general discontentment with his host country. Derrida too was an immigrant to France; his background could have had a strong influence on his thinking and writing. He was a Jewish adolescent in Algeria in the 1940s, during and after the anti-Semitic French colonial regime under German occupation. He had been excluded in his youth from his school after it reduced the quotas for Jews to 7 per cent. Confronted with violent racism, he avoided school during the period when he was obliged to attend a school for Jewish students and teachers. He eventually managed to gain entry to study philosophy in Paris. His subsequent experiences as a young student in Paris were isolated and unhappy, consisting of intermittent depression, nervous anxiety and a seesaw between sleeping tablets and amphetamines resulted in exam failures in the early 1950s. It may well be that neither Ben Jalloun or Derrida had any political bias or underlying propagandist tendency but the fact that neither of them seem to explicitly discuss their potential bias does leave room for doubt.

In addition, in investigating the hospitality of the classical Greco-Roman world Derrida was then drawing conclusions and writing for the modern age. When undertaking this type of work, care must be taken to avoid what is characterized as the Teleological Fallacy; the tendency to use ancient documents as 'a springboard for a modern polemic' (Finley, 1983, p. 110). Telfer, through her treatment of domestic hospitality, and Derrida, Rosello and Ben Jelloun with their investigation of the state and the relationship to the individual, all to a greater or lesser extent seem to expect that the hospitality relationship should be the same. There is limited consideration given to the motivations of either the guest or the host, and even less recognition given to the fact that the hospitality relationship exists in dissimilar contexts: domestic, civic or commercial, each with their own different sets of laws. This lack of contextual consideration potentially creates the foundations a hospitality fallacy. (The Teleological Fallacy is discussed in Chapter 3, Section 3.5.)

For Derrida the hospitality given to the 'other' is an ethical marker, both for an individual and a country. Everyday engagement with the 'other' is fraught with difficulties; sometimes the 'other' is devalued or in extreme cases rejected. In the case of hospitality, the 'other' is often forced to take on the perceptions of the 'host'. The 'guests' are unable to be themselves; they must transform their 'otherness'. For Derrida, being open and accepting the 'other' on their terms opens the host to new experiences, what Pope John Paul II (1994, p. 1) prophetically described as the possibility of 'crossing thresholds of hope'. The true gift of hospitality is an act of generosity experienced by the 'guest', which turns a stranger into a friend for a limited period of time. Even when they have the best of intentions people may fail in their attempts to behave hospitably and this adds to the complexity of the hospitality relationship:

We do not know what hospitality is.
Not yet.
Not yet, but will we ever know?

(Derrida, 2000b, p. 6)

From Derrida's writings it seems that true hospitality is somewhat of an enigma. This is not due to any philosophical conundrum, but perhaps because hospitality is not a matter of objective knowledge. Hospitality exists within lived experience; it is a gift given by the 'host' to the 'guest', and then shared between them. Hospitality cannot be resolved on the pages of academic writing; the true gift of hospitality is an act of generosity experienced by the 'guest', which turns a stranger into a friend for a limited period of time.

Within the various biographies and obituaries, it is clear that Derrida was undoubtedly a controversial character; his early dramatic failures were contrasted by the outstanding successes in later life. His work advanced the deconstruction of nothing less than concepts of knowledge and truth themselves, and provoked strong feelings within his readers who, just like the Senate of Cambridge University (that only awarded him an honorary doctorate in 1992 after a vote), were often divided over his writings; considering them to be either on the one hand absurd, vapid and pernicious or on the other hand logical, momentous and lively.

2.5   Summary philosophical issues identified

In reviewing the current thinking of philosophers about hospitality, three issues have been explored: moral philosophy of hospitality from the perspective of the guest/host relationship; hospitality between peoples and nation states; and the use of language in hospitality provision and consumption. This separation, although artificial (because the distinctions are not entirely delimited), serves as a useful way to gain an overview of the interrelated ideas.

Based on the discussion, review and analysis of the contemporary philosophical literature within the chapter, one of the key words or concepts that appears is welcome, however hospitality clearly transcends the initial welcoming act. Hospitality is recognised as a fundamental mark of civilisation and the study of the phenomenon of hospitality leads to a basis for the comprehension of the complexity of the world around us. Hospitality is identified as a moral virtue and motivations behind offering hospitality can emanate from people being attracted to the ideal of it. However with the philosophical literature, the concepts of a typology of guests is readily apparent.

There is a special link between the home and hospitality where guests are offered an invitation to intimacy. Although there may be a universal right to shelter this is for a limited time only and it also requires the guest to do no harm. Hospitality also requires a priori the concept of a guest not becoming a parasite.

Language gives hospitality to the other people, ideas or culture but there is a need to speak the same language for the offer of hospitality to be understood or received. True hospitality requires some element of surprise –

however this does not make it unconditional, as the guest is still received on the terms of the host. All hospitality is seen as conditional as unconditional hospitality is identified as impossible.

Postcolonial hospitality is identified as not reciprocal. There are also double standards of the nations regarding hospitality where emigrants should be honoured guests whilst immigrants are treated as being close to parasites. There are also undercurrents that hospitality is coming to be seen as an impossible luxury, with nations trying to restrict it. Although it is recognised that the guest and host must be open to the possibility of being changed by each other there is also the possibility of the hospitality being subverted by suspicion, with can lead to radical forms of distrust and exclusion.

The various philosophical perspectives, drawn from the philosophical writings, certainly indicate the potential complexities of the phenomenon of hospitality but the writings also provide examples of the potential for misinterpretation of the past, when applied to the present, and the potential for bias. Although the writings of philosophers reviewed in this chapter have clearly been influential, a clear and coherent philosophy of hospitality has yet to be proposed.

3 Judaeo-Christian Origins

The oldest collections of texts that refer to hospitality are from a literary genre known as Ancient Near East Texts. These texts belong to a large family of Eastern Mediterranean traditions from Mesopotamia, Asia Minor, Syria-Palestine, and Egypt. Normally these texts are seen in parallel with the Old Testament. These texts provide examples of Ancient Near East hospitality, where the host is attentive to those they have found in their house. A more readily and universally available collection of texts is the compilation known as the Old and New Testaments of the Bible.

3.1 The Old Testament

Within the Old Testament, numerous references exist to the practice of hospitality and serve as hosts, and to treating human life with respect and dignity. Janzen (2002) observes in the Book of Genesis, God offers the newly created world as living space and its plants and trees as food to all living creatures; they are to be guests in God's world and at God's table. In other words, while enjoying God's gracious provisions, God's human guests are to preserve awareness of and respect God's ultimate ownership. The story goes on to relate the 'fall of man' and the expulsion from Eden. Adam and Eve eating from the forbidden tree is an act of disobedience therefore sin in this situation can be defined as disobedience. Janzen then makes the challenging observation that Adam and Eve are saying 'we (humanity) want unlimited use and control of the world. In this light, sin can be described as the human attempt to be owners, rather than guests' (2002, p. 6).

In the Old Testament many laws specifically require hospitality and concern for strangers (see for example Leviticus 19:33-34). Other laws, often associated with those concerning strangers, assure good treatment of weak members of society, and laws concerning redemption are framed in accordance with the spirit of hospitality. Abraham was central to Old Testament hospitality; he showed unreserved hospitality to the strangers, only later seeing the true nature of his guests. Hospitality, and in particular, the treatment of strangers is then enshrined in the Old Testament: strangers have to be well treated, because the people themselves were strangers in a foreign lands.

Illustrative examples of the many hospitality events would include the story of Abraham (Genesis 18:2–8). The story of Abraham contains the classic hospitality event of Abraham and Sarah showing gracious receptiveness to three strangers at an oasis among the 'Oaks of Mamre'. This story is actually the occasion of God's appearance (a 'theophany') in anthropomorphic disguise; this is done to protect the host in response to the dictum of Exodus 33:20 'see God and you die!' The occasion of hospitality has become the occasion of divine visitation and revelation.

> *He (Abraham) looked up, and there he saw three men standing near him. As soon as he saw them, he ran from the entrance of the tent to greet them, and bowed to the ground. 'My lord,' he said, 'if I find favour with you, please do not pass your servant by. Let me have a little water brought, and you can wash your feet and have a rest under the tree. Let me fetch a little bread and you can refresh yourselves before going further, now that you have come in your servant's direction. They replied, 'Do as you say'. Abraham hurried to the tent and said to Sarah, 'Quick, knead three measures of best flour and make loaves.' Then, running to the herd, Abraham took a fine and tender calf and gave it to the servant, who hurried to prepare it. Then taking curds, milk and the calf which had been prepared, he laid all before them, and they ate while he remained standing near them under the tree.*
>
> *(Genesis 18:2–8)*

The text relates how when Abraham saw three simple nomads in the distance, he ran towards them to offer his hospitality. When he 'bowed to the ground' and washed their feet, he was not making a gesture of religious adoration, but simply a mark of respect. At first, Abraham sees his guests as humans, as their superhuman character is only gradually revealed. He welcomes them warmly and invites them into his tent, to rest a bit and to eat a little. When they followed him home, however, Abraham had a banquet prepared for them. Yet as great as Abraham's hospitality might have been, he had to contend with a society that was literally the antithesis of everything he represented. The cities of Sodom and Gomorrah were infamous for their cruelty and greed. When the angels journeyed to Sodom and Gomorrah, in search of a righteous man, only Lot and his family were set apart to be saved. Lot was deemed righteous, by the fact that he alone imitated Abraham's behaviour of hospitality.

> *When the two angels reached Sodom in the evening, Lot was sitting at the gate of Sodom. As soon as Lot saw them, he stood up to greet them, and*

3: Judaeo-Christian Origins

bowed to the ground. 'My lords', he said, 'please come down to your serv-
ant's house to stay the night and wash your feet. ... But he pressed them so
much that they went home with him and entered his house. He prepared a
meal for them, baking unleavened bread, and they had supper. They had not
gone to bed when the house was surrounded by the townspeople, the men
of Sodom both young and old, all the people without exception. Calling out
to Lot they said, 'Where are the men who came to you tonight? Send them
out to us so that we can have intercourse with them'. Lot came out to them
at the door and, having shut the door behind him, said, 'Please, brothers, do
not be wicked. Look, I have two daughters who are virgins. I am ready to
send them out to you, for you to treat as you please, but do nothing to these
men since they are now under the protection of my roof'. But they retorted,
'Stand back! This fellow came here as a foreigner, and now he wants to play
the judge. Now we shall treat you worse than them.'

(Genesis 19:1–9 abridged)

There are numerous legends about Sodom and Gomorrah. According to Arabic tradition, their ruins lie under the brackish waters of the Dead Sea (known in Arabic as, the Sea of Lot); this was raised up by the Creator to engulf these perverse cities. In relation to hospitality, there is another well-known legend: the people of the city had a special bed which they would offer to guests; when the guests were too tall for the bed, they would cut off their feet and when they were too short, they would stretch their limbs!

The Book of Exodus is one of travelling; God in various guises is leading His people on a journey from Egypt, out of slavery into the land promised to Abraham. That journey continues beyond the flight from Egypt, until Joshua conquers the Promised Land and distributes it to the tribes of Israel. The journey from Egypt is already marked by the hallmarks of hospitality, God's provision of food (manna and quails), water, and protection (Exodus 15–17). The latter part of Exodus (25–31; 35–40) tells of the construction of the tabernacle or sanctuary. This is the place where God is host and receives Israel as the guest; the tabernacle is a symbol of hospitality.

There is a breach of domestic hospitality identified in the Old Testament – it takes place in the Book of Judges. Sisera, running for his life, came upon the tent of a man named Heber and Jael his wife. Jael knew who Sisera was and she invited him into their tent; as a member of the Bedouin clan, Jael was bound by custom to extend hospitality to those she met. She gave him milk to drink and a mantle for covering, and apparently acquiesced in his request that she should stand guard at the tent and deny his presence to any pursuers. When Sisera was asleep 'Jael the wife of Heber took a tent-peg and picked up a mallet; she crept up softly to him and drove the peg into his temple right through to the ground. He was lying fast asleep, worn out; and so he died' (Judges 4:21). Thus she killed her guest while he was receiving her hospitality. There is no evidence that Sisera offered Jael any insult or violence, and little probability that she acted under any spiritual or divine suggestion.

There is an unusual example of peacemaking using hospitality in the second book of Kings. The prophet Elisha exhorts the king of Israel to treat his Syrian prisoners of war to a meal and then sends them home. Even prisoners are to be given the hospitality of the State:

> 'Offer them food and water, so that they can eat and drink, and then let them go back to their master.' So, the king provided a great feast for them; and when they had eaten and drunk, he sent them off and they went back to their own master. Aramaean raiding parties never invaded the territory of Israel again.
> (2 Kings 6:22–23)

In the book of Job the author swears an oath of innocence; in his defence of his exemplary life he lists all the sins he has not committed placing special emphasis on the practice of hospitality:

> Have I been insensible to the needs of the poor, or let a widow's eyes grow dim?
>
> Have I eaten my bit of bread on my own without sharing it with the orphan?
>
> I, whom God has fostered father-like from childhood, and guided since I left my mother's womb, have I ever seen a wretch in need of clothing, or the poor with nothing to wear…
>
> No stranger ever had to sleep outside, my door was always open to the traveller.
> (Job 31:16–19, 32)

Additionally the Prophet Isaiah looks ahead to the end of time; that is the coming of the day of the Lord in its fullness. He describes this coming of God in his glory as God's eschatological banquet:

> On this mountain, for all peoples, Yahweh Sabaoth is preparing a banquet of rich food, a banquet of fine wines, of succulent food, of well-strained wines.
> (Isaiah 25:6–9)

Thus, a banquet is used as the image of a redeemed humanity, which is entertained at the Lord's Table in a mood of fulfilment and rejoicing. This text has had particular influence on imagery in the New Testament and the concept of a messianic banquet was current in Jerusalem: Matthew 22:2–10, Luke 14:13, 16–24.

In the Old Testament, hospitality is central to virtually all of Old Testament ethics; God, the Great Host, invites His guests into His house, the created world, to enjoy its riches and blessings. However, the duties of the guest are clear too, the host expects these guests to follow His example and share their livelihood and their life, with their fellow guests on His earth.

3.2 The New Testament

The scholarly investigation of New Testament hospitality is both a recent and rapidly expanding phenomenon, Malina (1985) shows a discernible pattern to hospitality: testing the stranger, when one must decide if the stranger's visit is honourable or hostile, immediately followed by a transition phase, normally by foot washing. Then the stranger is now seen as a guest; the guest enjoys a full expression of welcome, becomes a part of the household, then the day comes when the guest must leave. In departure, the guest is transformed once again into friend or enemy. Koenig (1992) identifies a distinctive element in biblical hospitality; that of culture, in which God and/or Christ was often the host or guest. He also points out, that Luke seemed particularly interested in hospitality, since he alone in his gospel, included the stories of the Good Samaritan, the Prodigal Son, the rich man and Lazarus, Zaccheus, and the Emmaus appearance story.

At the beginning of John's gospel, an account is given into the treatment of Jesus by mankind:

He was in the world that had come into being through him, and the world did not recognise him. He came to his own and his own people did not accept him.

(John 1:10–11)

Even when he came to be born, there was no one who would take the family in. This, in a land where hospitality was considered so important, there was literally no room at the inn; mankind turned their backs and showed no hospitality to a pregnant woman.

Now it happened that, while they were there, the time came for her to have her child, and she gave birth to a son, her first-born. She wrapped him in swaddling clothes and laid him in a manger because there was no room for them in the inn.

(Luke 2:6–7)

Rather than 'inn' the Greek word καταλύμα (*kataluma*) can mean a room, and in this context most probably 'dwelling'. The beginning of Jesus' life on earth is rich with hospitality symbolism. The manger, where the animals ate, was probably fixed to a wall of the poor living space, which was so crowded that there was no better place for the child to safely lie. By mentioning the manger, Luke symbolises Jesus as the sustenance of the world; often, throughout his Gospel, Luke refers to eating and drinking as a symbol for close friendship and union with God.

Even towards the end of his life, Jesus remains dependent on the hospitality of others for two of his greatest acts. The Last Supper, which he celebrates with his disciples, takes place in a borrowed room (Mark 14:13–16 and parallels) and even after death, he is the guest of Joseph of Arimathea in his tomb (Mark 15:42–46 and parallels). Hospitality, in particular to the homeless, becomes the key to life eternal. The parable of the last judgement portrays Christ the king separating the sheep from the goats, based on hospitality extended or refused:

> *He will place the sheep on his right hand and the goats on his left. Then the King will say to those on his right hand, 'Come, you whom my Father has blessed take as your heritage the kingdom prepared for you since the foundation of the world. For I was hungry and you gave me food, I was thirsty and you gave me drink, I was a stranger and you made me welcome, lacking clothes and you clothed me, sick and you visited me, in prison and you came to see me.'*
>
> *(Matthew 25:32–7)*

He continues after his resurrection, to offer himself as guest. 'Look, I am standing at the door, knocking. If one of you hears me calling and opens the door, I will come in to share a meal at that person's side' (Revelation 3:20).

The images of God's kingdom that predominate overwhelmingly in Jesus' teaching are those associated with the production of food and drink or homelike refuge for God's creatures. Jesus takes the role of host to the multitude when he feeds the 5000 and then again 4000 people; he is portrayed as one like Yahweh, who fed the people in the wilderness as was seen in Exodus 16 and in the same style as the prophets of Yahweh, who fed his disciples and had food left over (cf. 2 Kings 4:42–44).

At the Last Supper, Jesus was the host directing the meal, and washing the disciples' feet (John 13:3–5), which was one of the great acts of hospitality in the Old Testament; moreover, he becomes the spiritually sustaining 'meal' himself:

*The blessing-cup, which we bless, is it not a sharing in the blood of Christ;
and the loaf of bread which we break, is it not a sharing in the body of
Christ? And as there is one loaf, so we, although there are many of us, are
one single body, for we all share in the one loaf.*

(1 Corinthians 10:16–17; Mark 14:12–26; John 6:30–40.)

By his auto-identification, with the symbolic elements of the Passover
meal, Jesus associated his body with the bread of affliction, which was
offered to all who were hungry and needy, and he associated his blood with
the third cup of wine, the cup of redemption. Moreover, by halting the meal,
before the traditional fourth cup, Jesus anticipates his role as eschatological host, when he will drink again at the messianic banquet, celebrating the
consummation of the kingdom of God 'Blessed is anyone who will share
the meal in the kingdom of God' (Luke 14:15; cf. Isaiah 25:6; Matthew 8:11;
Revelation 19:9). In his post resurrection appearances, the disciples perceive
the identity of Jesus, when he takes the role of host and says, 'come and have
breakfast' (Luke 24:13–43; John 21:1–14).

Jesus told his disciples to follow his example and 'take nothing for their
journey' (Mark 6:8 and parallels); thus, he presupposed that they were sure
of always finding hospitality. Further, it is assumed that they could even
make their own choice of hosts:

*Whatever town or village you go into, seek out someone worthy and stay
with him until you leave. As you enter his house, salute it, and if the house
deserves it, may your peace come upon it; if it does not, may your peace
come back to you. And if anyone does not welcome you or listen to what you
have to say, as you walk out of the house or town shake the dust from your
feet. In truth I tell you on the Day of Judgement it will be more bearable for
Sodom and Gomorrah than for that town.*

(Matthew 10:11–15)

In this case, however, the claims of the travellers to hospitality are accentuated by the fact that they are bearers of good tidings for the people. It is
in view of this latter fact, that hospitality to them, becomes so great a virtue,
the 'cup of cold water' becomes so highly meritorious, as it is given 'in the
name of a disciple' (cf. Matthew 10:41f). Rejection of hospitality to one of his
followers is equivalent to the rejection of Jesus himself.

Itinerant Christian ministers and refugees often found themselves in
need of sympathetic hosts. This was a particular characteristic of St Paul's
writings 'Help eagerly on their way, Zenas the lawyer and Apollos, and

make sure they have everything they need. All our people must also learn to occupy themselves in doing good works for their practical needs, and not to be unproductive' (Titus 3:13–14) and again in Philemon verse 22 'There is another thing, will you get a place ready for me to stay in?' (Romans 16:1–2, 23; 1 Corinthians 16:10–11; 3 John 5–8). Another characteristic of St Paul's writings, hospitality was clearly seen as a virtue, as one must 'contribute to the needs of the saints, practice hospitality' (Romans 12:13) and if one has been faithful, one 'must be well attested for her good deeds, as one who has brought up children, shown hospitality, washed the feet of the saints, relieved the afflicted, and devoted herself to doing good in every way' (1 Timothy 5:10). As a final admonishment is given, 'practice hospitality, ungrudgingly, to one another' (1 Peter 4:9). This is emphasised in the letter to the Hebrews; this refers all the way back in time to the hospitality of Abraham, when the Hebrews are told: 'Remember to show hospitality to strangers, by doing this, some people have entertained angels without knowing it' (Hebrews 13:3). In his commentary on Hebrews, Long (1997, p. 143) quotes the third century book on church order 'Didascalia', giving instructions to the bishop:

If a destitute man or woman, either a local person or a traveller, arrives un-expectedly, especially one of older years, and there is no place, you, bishop, make such a place with all your heart, even if you yourself should sit on the ground, that you may not show favouritism among human beings, but that your ministry may be pleasing before God.

The letter to the Hebrews, in its closing remarks, reflects the kind of hospitality in the early church, this can be contrasted with the concept of hospitality, as understood by the Qumran community:

And no man smitten with any human uncleanness shall enter the Assembly of God; no man smitten with any of them shall be confirmed in his office in the congregation. No man smitten in his flesh, or paralysed in his feet or hands, or lame, or blind, or deaf, or dumb, or smitten in his flesh with a vis-ible blemish; no old and tottery man unable to stay still in the midst of the congregation; none of these shall come.

(1QSa II:4–8, Vermes, 1997, p. 159)

Judaeo-Christian philosophy identifies that hospitality was necessary for the well-being of mankind and essential to the protection of vulnerable strangers. Therefore, it is not unsurprising that it was also to become a dis-tinctive feature of the early Christian church. This was due to two principal reasons: it was in keeping with the general continuity with Hebrew under-standings of hospitality that associated it with God, covenant, and blessing;

and partly in contrast to Hellenistic and Roman practices (as discussed in Chapter 4 and 5 respectively), which associated it with benefit and reciprocity. The Greek and Roman views of benevolence and hospitality stressed formal reciprocal obligations between benefactor and recipient. Because a grateful response from the beneficiary was key to the ongoing relationship, the Greek and Roman tradition emphasised the worthiness and goodness of recipients rather than their need; relations were often calculated to benefit the benefactor.

3.3   Biblical studies

In the field of biblical studies, hospitality in scripture has only been investigated during the last century. This was partly due to the Protestant analysis of the Bible and the development of Humanism. With this new movement history became a discipline in its own right rather than a branch of theology. Prior to the Renaissance, Biblical texts were treated as sacred and inviolable. This was then the first time that Biblical texts were to be critically evaluated; previously they were held as the divinely inspired word of God and beyond critical analysis.

Later one of the first writers to combine biblical anthropology and hermeneutical analysis was Robertson Smith (1927) who was trying to find, in contemporary Bedouin Arab practice, reflections on the notion of biblical hospitality portrayed in the behaviour of ancient Israel/Judah. He identified aspects of the hospitality encountered:

> The ger [stranger] was a man of another tribe or district, who, coming to sojourn in a place where he was not strengthened by the presence of his own kin, put himself under the protection of a clan or a powerful chief. From the earliest times of Semitic life the lawlessness of the desert has been tempered by the principle that the guest is inviolable. A man is safe in the midst of his enemies as soon as he enters a tent or touches a rope. To harm a guest or to refuse him hospitality is an offence against honour, which covers the perpetrator with indelible shame… The obligation thus constituted is one of honour, and not enforced by human sanction except public opinion, for if the stranger is wronged he has no kinsmen to fight for him.
>
> (Robertson Smith, 1927, p. 76)

From this quote it can be seen that biblical hospitality, like that of ancient Greece (which is cover in detail in Chapter 4), was embedded in the culture of the community. Hospitality at this stage brought protection from enemies, even to the extent it was the enemies that had to offer hospitality: Hospitality must not only be freely offered to strangers, but to enemies as well. Riddle (1938) in a hermeneutical study of early Christian writings, argued that biblically mandated hospitality was a central factor in the spreading of the Gospel amongst the early Christian community.

More recently, Crum (1976) published a supplementary volume to the long-time standard work *Interpreter's Dictionary of the Bible*, which did not make any reference to biblical hospitality. Later Malina (1985) wrote an article on hospitality in the *Harper's Bible Dictionary*. The biblical material is presented to show a discernible pattern to the provision of hospitality: testing the stranger (when one must decide if the stranger's visit is honourable or hostile); immediately followed by a transition phase, normally including foot washing. Only then is the stranger seen as a guest; the guest enjoys a full expression of welcome, and becomes a part of the household. Then the day comes when the guest must leave and in departure, the guest is transformed once again into friend or enemy.

Koenig's (1992) article on biblical hospitality was published in *The Anchor Bible Dictionary*. This is a more comprehensive overview than that provided by Malina (1985). It also contains the first list of biblical sources that detail hospitality. Koenig (1992) finds, amongst other things, that culture is a distinctive element in biblical hospitality, where God and/or Christ is often identified as the host or guest. He also identifies that Luke in his writings seems particularly interested in hospitality, since he alone, includes the stories of: the Good Samaritan; the Prodigal Son; the rich man and Lazarus; Zaccheus; and the Emmaus appearance of Christ, all of these passages have a significant hospitality perspective.

Other authors tend to over-simplify the concept of hospitality. Smith (1986, p. 277), for example, observes that 'the term means taking in strangers and travellers' and then goes on to interpret the Old Testamental examples of hospitality simply as acts of kindness. Similarly Field (1994) develops the somewhat romantic view of hospitality as being kind to strangers, going on to argue that the reference in Isaiah 58:6–7 to 'offering shelter to the homeless poor' is not connected to the traditional practice of hospitality, but is included in acts of righteousness to be the hallmark of the restored post-exilic community.

Hobbs (1993, 2001), Malina (1985) and Matthews (1991a, 1992) carried out an in-depth hermeneutical analysis into the concept of hospitality in particular pericopes or books of the Old Testament. Hobbs (2001) presents a summary of Matthews' (1991a, 1992) research into hospitality that is contained in the books of Genesis and Judges. This is summarised here as:

1   There is a sphere of hospitality within which hosts have the responsibility to offer hospitality to strangers. The size of the zone varies.

2   The stranger must be transformed from potential threat to ally by the offer of hospitality.

3   The invitation can only be offered by the male head of a household, and may include a time-span statement for the period of hospitality, but this can be then extended.

4   Refusal could be considered an affront to the honour of the host.

5   Once the invitation is accepted, the roles of the host and the guest are set by the rules of custom. The guest must not ask for anything, but is expected to entertain with news, predictions of good fortune, or gracious responses based on what he has been given. The host provides the best he has available, and must not ask personal questions of the guest.

6   The guest remains under the personal protection of the host until he/she has left the zone of obligation of the host.

This summary attempts to demonstrate that hospitality is not a simple concept; there are deeply rooted cultural norms that are not readily transferable from one culture to another. On the other hand, Malina (1985, p. 181) also attempts a detailed protocol of hospitality 'Hospitality is the process by means of which an outsider's status is changed from stranger to guest… [It] differs from entertaining family and friends.' The appearance of a stranger is regarded as an invitation from outside, and a local person takes on the role of testing the stranger. From the test three types of danger emerge: one who is recognised as better than the best of the community so that there is no problem with his precedence within the community; one who is vanquished by the local person and thus owes life and continued presence to their local patron; one who has no friends/kin within the community and is therefore treated as an outlaw – 'he could be destroyed or despoiled with impunity, simply because of his potential hostility' (Malina, 1985, p. 184). Finally, Malina (1985, p. 185) concludes by noting that when the stranger is transformed into a guest, 'The stranger will rarely, if ever, reciprocate hospitality', thus they are forever indebted to the host.

3.4   Patristic theology

Patristic theology is the study of early Christian writers, known as the Church Fathers or the Patristic Writers who are the early and influential theologians and writers in the Christian Church, particularly those of the first five centuries of Christian history. The term is used to classify and describe writers and teachers of the Church, not necessarily saints. It is generally not meant to include the New Testament authors, though in the early Church some writing of Church Fathers was considered to be canonical.

The earliest Christian writers, some of who were contemporaneous with the New Testament and others, in the century afterwards, make specific mention of hospitality. The earliest would probably have been from the letters by Clement of Rome to the Church in Corinth, when they are reminded to the hospitality shown by both Abraham and Lot:

> *And Abraham believed God, and it was counted to him for righteousness.*
> *On account of his faith and hospitality, a son was given him in his old age…*
> *On account of his hospitality and godliness, Lot was saved out of Sodom*
> *when all the country around him was punished.*
>
> *(Apocrypha, I Clement 5:11–6:1)*

These letters by Clement were included in the canons of scripture in the churches in Egypt and Syria and probably date to around AD 94. Contemporaneous with Clement was the 'Shepherd of Hermas', of whom very little is known; however, sometimes his writings were considered part of the canon of the New Testament and were read throughout the early church. His instruction on hospitality is clear:

> *There is nothing better than these things in the life of man… to be hospitable; for in hospitality there is sometimes great fruit.*
>
> *(Apocrypha, II Hermas 8:9–10)*

Ignatius of Antioch, the first-century Bishop of Antioch in Syria, retained the office for 40 years proving himself as an exemplary bishop. Whilst travelling he makes reference to the hospitality he has received:

> *My spirit salutes you, and so does the affection of the Churches that offered their hospitality to me, not as to a chance visitor, but in deference to Jesus Christ.*
>
> *(Apocrypha, Ignatius to Rome 3:11)*

The Patristic Writers do not include the New Testament authors such as St Paul; however in the early Church, others beside St Clement, mentioned above, were also considered canonical. According to Trevijano Etcheverría (1998) the Patristic Writers are generally subdivided into five groups:

◊ Ante-Nicene writers, those who lived and wrote before the Council of Nicaea AD 325;

◊ Nicene and Post-Nicene writers, those who lived and wrote after AD 325;

◊ Apostolic writers are the earliest of the writers considered to be the first two generations after the Apostles of Christ;

◊ Apologetic writers wrote in reply to criticism from Greek philosophers and in the face of persecution to justify and defend Christian philosophy and doctrine; and

◊ Desert writers were early monks living in the Egyptian desert.

Although the desert writers did not write as much as their literary predecessors, their influence on hospitality was surprisingly considerable. In addition to the five groups identified above, the division of the writers into Greek writers and Latin writers is also common. This division highlights the major issue in researching Patristic views of hospitality: they are not all translated into English.

There has been very little research undertaken on hospitality and the patristic writings, with the notable exception being Oden (2001) who presents a collection of early Patristic texts on hospitality and its practice. Within the texts that are quoted, one basis of Christian hospitality that is highlighted is the idea of the Christian as a sojourner. The readiness to welcome the stranger is a moral stance whereby one responds to the physical, social, and spiritual needs of the stranger, with the host benefiting as well. The biblical texts also narrate accounts of entertaining angels in the guise of travellers, such as in the story of Abraham (Genesis 18:3–9). Oden (2001) further observes that readers of these texts tend to identify with the hosts because of the hosts' greater power and the greater clarity of identity, whereas the guests are largely varied and undefined. Added to this are notions of common humanity of brothers and sisters, the human being as *imago dei* (in the image of God), in other words the host, and the church as God's household. In addition to obeying Jesus' command, and thus prospering at the final judgement, the practice of hospitality was seen as: imitating Jesus in washing the disciples' feet; as making a sacrifice to God; as giving hospitality as God does; and even with the expectation to have one's sins absolved.

Oden (2001) outlines the spiritual dynamics of hospitality and presents some ideas on how the host should be orientated ontologically when providing hospitality. These are summarised as:

1   The spirit not of hollow giving but of goodwill, which does not belittle or shame the recipient and which heals both the giver and the recipient;

2   A 'being with' the recipient just as Jesus wished to be present among us and a non-judgemental approach that does not do an outcomes or risk calculation;

3   A belief in miraculous abundance for all involved; and

4   An application of the Gospel injunction to give away life in order to gain it and to restore the *imago dei*.

What is unclear is exactly how Oden comes to these views. This highlights some methodological issues that arise when critically evaluating this book that include:

◊   The texts lack contextualisation or consideration of the socio-political background.

◊   There a lack of a clear methodology to show why the selection has been grouped in such a way.

◊   The texts have been gathered from over 50 English versions and translations; consequently as the author has not translated the texts, they could lack a constant translation philosophy or method.

◊   The standard classical referencing style has not been used, leading to difficulties in tracing some of the original sources.

These methodological anomalies lead to some confusion in the selection of texts. Throughout the compilation, hospitality texts are identified but often included with them are texts that in the original language actually discuss acts of charity and welfare. The texts are reflective of the eastern half of the Roman Empire, after Constantine (c.AD 320), whilst the western empire seems largely ignored, with no explanation or acknowledgment as to why. The sources that have been compiled address hospitality from a rather narrow perspective that has not been contextualised. Although all the texts and commentaries reflect Greco-Roman practices of friendship and hospitality, there is no significant reference or evaluation of the Greco-Roman roots of the Christian practice.

The Rule of St Benedict (c. AD 530) was recognised by Borias (1974) as the key focus for subsequent religious hospitality. This foundation was to become the basis of all western European religious hospitality. Within St Benedict's Rule, the main focus for religious hospitality is contained within Chapter 53 which is entitled 'De Hopitibus Suscipiendis' – 'The Reception of Guests' (*c.* AD 530). The rule has been lived by monks and laypeople from the last 1500 years and been commented upon and analysed by Böckmann (1988), Boiras (1974), Fry (1981), Holzherr (1982), Kardong (1984, 1996), Regnault (1990), Vogüé (1977), and Wolter (1880). Specifically the influence of Chapter 53 on hospitality provision has not been fully investigated by contemporary authors and this is critically reviewed in Chapter 8 of this book.

3.5   The Teleological Fallacy

When undertaking any historical textual analysis, care must be taken to avoid what Finley (1983, p. 110) characterised as 'the Teleological Fallacy'; the tendency to use ancient documents as 'a springboard for a modern polemic'. This is illustrated in the writing of Janzen (1994, p. 43) where he states:

> *Hospitality is an ethical component of the familial paradigm that is hard for modern western readers to appreciate in its full weight and significance. It may help us to remember that travel, in the ancient world, was only undertaken for grave reasons, often negative in nature, such as flight from persecution or search for food and survival. Hospitality, under those circumstances, has little to do with modern tourism, but embraces the biblical equivalent to our policies regarding refugees, immigrants and welfare.*

This quotation is also discussed by Hobbs (2001) when he notes that it incorporates two important elements: '(1) it has to do with travellers, that is, those who are away from their houses for one reason or another; (2) it is used as a parallel for modern ethical concerns.' Hobbs (2001) then highlights that the reader should be aware of the jump that has been made in the second point by discussing a small-scale society and comparing it to a western post-industrial society. Silberbauer (1993, p. 14) describes a small-scale society as 'one whose numbers are to be counted in tens of thousands, or even hundreds, rather than millions. Largely or wholly non-industrial, its technology is centred on agricultural or pastoral production or consumption within the society, or on hunting and gathering'. While ancient Israel/Judah became a monarchy with a centralised government, it remained agriculturally based; its later pattern has been likened by Sánchez Caro (1989, p. 79) to an 'advanced agrarian society' and they note that many, though not all, of the stories of hospitality in the First Testament are set in the premonarchic period. Caution against a westernising approach is also prompted by Silberbauer (1993), as detailed in Hobbs (2001, p. 8), and summarised as:

1 There is a clash between modern moral philosophy and alien cultural practices to the point where meaning cannot be assumed to be universal.

2 Comparison between cultures can be done only at the most general level.

3 Fundamental to small-scale societies is the notion of relationships symbolised by gift giving and reciprocity, which forms a milieu for its moral behaviour.

In effect, Silberbauer (1993) argues that in small-scale societies morality functions more as a means to an end, rather than as an end in itself. Therefore, it is important to bear in mind this functional aspect of hospitality when dealing with this topic in relation to the worlds of the Old Testamental and Homeric writings. This supports the idea that there is no reason why Old Testamental and Homeric writings cannot be considered as part of the corpus of knowledge for investigation as they are contemporaneous and similar in societal evolution and geographical location.

When biblical anthropologists make comparisons to Old Testamental times, they use the biblical writings for the basis of comparisons to modern-day practices; for example, De Vaux (1961, p. 10) observes current practices among the desert Bedouin of southern Israel and Jordan indicating the importance of the hospitality:

Hospitality is a necessity of life in the desert, but among the nomads the necessity has become a virtue, and a most highly esteemed one. The guest is sacred. The honour of providing for him is disputed, but generally falls to the sheikh.

Pitt-Rivers (1971, p. 59f) highlights the element of self-interest for the host:

There is no doubt that the ideal behaviour is very much opposed to closed-fistedness, but lavishness in one direction usually implies restrictions in another. Here people like to make gestures of generosity toward the friend, the acquaintance and the stranger, and they like to make a show of their generosity... it is more than a matter of individual disposition but a requirement of the system of friendship. The accusation of meanness is very damaging to a person's reputation, for such prestige as derives from money derives not from its possession, but from generosity with it.

These two quotes taken together demonstrate the use of the notion of prestige or honour is extremely important to the phenomenon of hospitality; it subsists in and is characteristic of many ancient and biblical societies.

Herzfeld (1987, p. 36) when researching the biblical lands observes that the guest is often made aware of the fact that they are on the territory of the host. This is designed to enhance the reputation of the host, and not necessarily to make the guest feel 'at home'. He states:

'As in your house' is a conventional hyperbole which underscores the poetic properties of the performance. The point is precisely that the visitor is not at home, but is indeed highly dependent upon his host. For many…the height of eghoismos (self-regard), is a lavish display of hospitality, since it speaks volumes about the social importance of the actor.

This further illustrates that hospitality given in a home setting is about the beneficence of the host, rather than the welcome given to the guest. In another work, Herzfeld (1991) draws a distinction between hospitality in taverns (public places) and in homes (private places). In taverns 'at one level it is the celebration of the ideological egalitarianism of the *parea* (company of friends), of all Cretans, and of all Greeks. At another it marks the possibility of subordinating a powerful guest!' Whereas Herzfeld (1991, p. 81) notes that in the home: 'Hospitality does not mark the acceptance of the stranger so much as the moral superiority of the host'. Hermeneutically analysing examples of biblical hospitality, then looking for examples of similar practices in traditional cultures in the world today, whilst being illuminating, can have its difficulties.

When examining the theological and biblical literature, an area where personal bias could emerge is in the analysis of the biblical and other texts from which the content of this and later chapters of the book have been derived. Other areas that may be open to bias are in the translation methodology and the textual selection. Clearly no interpreter can be a valueless interpreter; and it incumbent on any author, as suggested by Hall (2004) to maintain and adopt a personal research credo. It is also worth keeping mind the words of Benedict XVI (2005, p. 2) when he observes that today 'we are building a dictatorship of relativism that does not recognize anything as definitive and whose ultimate goal consists solely of one's own ego and desires.' Accepting this warning, the attempt being made in this book is to be as objective as possible. The exploration of the biblical writings and the issues identified take account of the potential for creating a Teleological Fallacy and have also attempted to avoid personal bias through the treatment of the biblical and other writings simply as literature to be critically analysed for evidence of hospitality events.

3.6   Summary of issues identified in the Judaeo-Christian literature

This chapter has explored the biblical origins of hospitality, which not only underpin the Judaeo-Christian hospitality traditions but also, as is demonstrated in the rest of this book, are similarly reflected in all the religions doctrines discussed. In all cases the provision of hospitality, and acting hospitably, is supported by the religious teachings of whatever denomination.

Within the Judaeo-Christian traditions, biblical hospitality has an ethical component that is often difficult for modern western readers to appreciate in its full weight and significance. Hospitality is essentially the process by means of which an outsider's status is changed from stranger to guest and the guest who is under the protection of host, is held as sacred in nomadic cultures. Hospitality requires protocols and transforms relationships and the biblical material shows a discernible pattern to its development. Hospitality is an extended system of friendship and is a complex concept with deep-rooted cultural norms and progresses through a stage-by-stage process. However in the biblical material the stranger rarely, if ever, reciprocates.

Prestige and honour can be gained through hospitality and it is also central to the self-interest of the host. The host operates within a zone of obligation (hospitality thresholds) and the guest is made aware they are on the territory of the host, not to make them feel at home but to reinforce the moral superiority of the host.

Biblically mandated hospitality was also a central factor in the spreading of the Gospel to the early Christian community, the first Apostles and the itinerant Christian ministers and refugees often finding themselves in need of sympathetic hosts. The claims of the travellers to hospitality are accentuated by the fact that they are bearers of good tidings for the people and the offering of hospitality to them is recognised as being of high virtue. Rejection of hospitality to one of his followers is equivalent to the rejection of Jesus himself.

4 Classical Greece

Just as Genesis set the foundations for the Judaeo-Christian practices of hospitality the Greco-Roman ones can only be understood in the context of the Homeric writings. In Chapter 1, section 1.4 it shows that ξένος *xenos*, had the interchangeable meaning of guest or stranger. Φιλόξενος *philoxenos*: the law/custom of offering protection and hospitality to strangers; its antithesis is still in common English usage today 'xenophobia'.

Within the texts related to the early period of Classical Antiquity, the writing is episodic; this is due to the nature of the texts themselves, which are pericopes taken from larger narrative sections and usually used to either highlight or illustrate a particular philosophic-religious point of view.

However, it is clear from the various texts that during the early period of Classical Antiquity that hospitality was regarded as one of the principal virtues: this is primarily shown by the centrality of hospitality in the religious/mythical writings. Both the Old Testament teaching (as discussed in Chapter 3) and the Homeric writings (which are explored in this chapter) expected the people to practise hospitality, by serving as hosts and treating guests with respect and dignity. The origins of hospitality to be found in Classical Greece are considered through the examination of domestic, civil and commercial hospitality.

4.1 Domestic hospitality: the nomad and the homestead

Throughout his journeys, Odysseus searches for *xenia* in the sense of 'hospitable reception' in a wide variety of situations; hospitality must be carefully balanced between two extremes, as explained by King Menelaus to Telemachos:

> *I would condemn any host who, receiving guests, acted with excessive hospitality or excessive hostility; all things are better in due measure. It is as blameworthy to urge a guest to leave against his wishes as it is to detain*

a guest who is eager to leave. One must grant hospitality to a guest who is present and grant conveyance to a guest who wishes to leave.

(Homer, Odyssey 15:69–74)

In these stories of primordial Greece, one never knew when the beggar knocking at the door might be a god, disguised or else watching from above, passing judgment. The deity could leave without being recognised:

They did not know who she was; it is hard for mortals to see divinity.
Standing near they addressed her with winged words.

(Homer, Demeter 1:111–12)

It does not matter who she is or that she had the appearance of an old homeless woman; she is still spoken to with great hospitableness. In this context hospitality should transcend; it does not matter who the person is, nor their apparent status in life. She is assured of hospitality towards her:

No woman there, when she first looks upon you, will dishonour your appearance and remove you from the mansion, but each will receive you, for indeed you look like a goddess.

(Homer, Demeter l:157–9)

The old woman was the goddess Demeter, and she accepts their invitation to return home with them; their kind words and hospitality draw the goddess out of her rage and hatred towards mankind.

Hospitality then was a way of honouring the gods:

...nor is it fitting
that the stranger should sit on the ground beside the hearth, in the ashes.
These others are holding back because they await your order.
But come, raise the stranger up and seat him on a silver-studded chair,
and tell your heralds to mix in more wine for us,
so we can pour a libation to Zeus who delights in the thunder.

(Homer, Odyssey 2:159–64)

Therefore, giving hospitality to a stranger was the same as offering it to a god. Hospitality towards a stranger is shown clearly in a scene where Odysseus' son, Telemachos, greets the goddess Athena, who is disguised:

...he saw Athene
and went straight to the forecourt, the heart within him scandalized
that a guest should still be standing at the doors. He stood beside her
and took her by the right hand, and relieved her of the bronze spear,
and spoke to her and addressed her in winged words: 'Welcome, stranger.

You shall be entertained as a guest among us. Afterward,
when you have eaten dinner, you shall tell us what your need is.
(Homer, Odyssey 2:118–24)

The Homeric writings show that hospitality brought expectations: food; a comfortable place to sit; charming company; and entertainment. Since the traveller would not usually be wandering out of their home into the dangers of the world, it was assumed they were on some sort of mission. The host then is expected to be able to provide some sort of assistance, as seen by the line in the above quotation 'you shall tell us what your need is'. Later in the scene there is celebration and revelry that the newcomer, Athena, would have been invited to join. The hospitality shown towards the goddess in this case demonstrates the importance of the accommodation and the correct attitude shown towards guests. In many of the stories, the honourable behaviour of the human hosts is rewarded with preferential treatment by the gods, as is the case with Telemachos and Athena. She clearly approves of Telemachos, as is demonstrated by all she does to help him, but expresses her displeasure with her suitors by saying:

I wish that such an Odysseus would come now among the suitors.
They would all find death was quick, and marriage a painful matter.
(Homer, Odyssey 2:265–6)

And her wish comes about: Telemachos is spared, and Athena's suitors are all killed, which happens as a direct result of their rudeness in their hospitality and of taking for granted the hospitality extended to them. At the end of the story, Odysseus returns to his house, to find only those who offered him hospitality on his journey, namely his son and wife, have not been killed. Finally, the rough outline of what all this meant for the people of ancient Greece, and what can be inferred about their society as a whole is perceptible. In these texts the gods, as well as legendary human characters, such as Telemachos and Odysseus, primarily served as role models for the ancient Greeks, who would have been expected to emulate their behaviour.

Hospitality brought obligations of friendship and duty; the failure to fulfil these hospitality obligations was viewed as both an impiety and a temporal crime. Any violation of the moral code or obligations of hospitality were likely to provoke the wrath of both mankind and gods; however, hospitality when properly conducted placates, pacifies, and delights the gods. The law and customs of hospitality were felt by the Greeks to be so central, and so fundamental to civilised life, that its patron was the god of gods, Zeus.

Zeus is the protector of suppliants and guests,
Zeus Xeinios, who attends to revered guests

(Homer, Odyssey 9:270–71)

Generally hospitality was considered sacred in nature and was not to be abused. For violations of the accepted code that did take place the Greeks had particular words for some of these breaches: ξενοδαίτης 'one that devours guests', a concept epitomised by the Cyclops, the notorious guest-eating monster; as Euripides (*Cyclops* 659) wrote 'Hurrah, hurrah! Thrust bravely, hurry, burn out the eyebrow of the guest-eating monster;' and ξενοκτόνος 'slaying of guests and strangers' (Liddell, et al., 1996). These breaches of the hospitality code were treated as some of the most serious crimes:

Proteus declared the following judgment to them, saying, 'If I did not make it a point never to kill a stranger who has been caught by the wind and driven to my coasts, I would have punished you on behalf of the Greek, you most vile man. You committed the gravest impiety after you had had your guest-friend's hospitality: you had your guest-friend's wife. And as if this were not enough, you got her to fly with you and went off with her. And not just with her, either, but you plundered your guest-friend's wealth and brought it, too. Now, then, since I make it a point not to kill strangers, I shall not let you take away this woman and the wealth, but I shall watch them for the Greek stranger, until he come and take them away; but as for you and your sailors, I warn you to leave my country for another within three days, and if you do not, I will declare war on you

(Herodotus, Historia 2:115)

Those who were guilty of these crimes against hospitality, such as the Cyclops, were generally condemned by mankind:

Perhaps among you it is a light thing to murder guests, but with us in Hellas it is a disgrace. How can I escape reproach if I judge you not guilty? I could not. No, since you endured your horrid crime, endure as well its painful consequence

(Euripedes, Hecuba 1247–50)

Violations of hospitality also brought the wrath of the Gods. Pausanias in his 'Description of Greece' warns that 'the wrath of the God of Strangers is inexorable' (Pausanias., *Ach.* 7:25); the Greeks were reminded of these words when Peloponnesians arrived and ransacked the city; before Zeus caused an earthquake and levelled it.

Hospitality was centred round the οἰκος *oikos* (home, household); this includes not only the resident 'family' in biological sense of the term, but also all those who live in the house as well as those who depend upon the household and contribute to its wealth and survival, including: slaves; illegitimate children (normally the offspring of the master and female slaves); resident in-laws; and 'adopted' persons who serve as retainers or 'squires'. Those who do not belong to a household, such as Odysseus, may be difficult to place: they could be valuable craftsmen who do not themselves own land but serve those who do, or they could be vagabonds or exiles, threatening instability, accepting the forgoing there is still a duty of hospitality. The master of the *oikos* distributes tasks and goods among its members and forms alliances with the masters of other *oikoi*. Thereby, through this tangible hospitality his house grows in wealth, strength and status as measured against other *oikoi*.

Solon, the most famous of all the ancient Greek lawgivers, was born in Athens about 640 BC; he is most famous for his repeal of the cruel laws of Draco (in which the term 'draconian' has its origin), by which the aristocracy had oppressed the people. He then remodelled the constitution and introduced the great body of the people to participation in the government. Solon placed great importance upon hospitality.

> *Anacharsis came to Athens, knocked at Solon's door, and said that he was a stranger who had come to make ties of friendship and hospitality with him. On Solon's replying that it was better to make one's friendships at home, 'Well then,' said Anacharsis, 'do thou, who art at home, make me thy friend and guest.' So Solon, admiring the man's ready wit, received him graciously and kept him with him some time. This was when he was already engaged in public affairs and compiling his laws.*

> *(Plutarch, Vita Solon 5:1)*

This is a direct continuation of the hospitality centred on the *oikos*, as shown in the writings of Homer.

Plato, in *Timaeus and Critias*, recounts a dialogue between Socrates and Timaeus showing the reciprocal nature of hospitality:

> *Socrates: One, two, three; but where, my dear Timaeus, is the fourth of those who were yesterday my guests and are to be my entertainers today?*

> *Timaeus: He has been taken ill, Socrates; for he would not willingly have been absent from this gathering.*

> *Socrates: Then, if he is not coming, you and the two others must supply his place.*

Timaeus: Certainly, and we will do all that we can; having been handsomely entertained by you yesterday, those of us who remain should be only too glad to return your hospitality'

(Plato, Timaeus and Critias 1:1)

As well as being reciprocal, hospitality can also be hereditary normally to three generations. Euripides refers to 'tokens' that were exchanged to show that two people were united in bonds of hospitality.

I am ready to give with unstinting hand, and also to send tokens, to my friends, who will treat you well. You would be a fool not to accept this offer.

(Euripides, Medea 613)

Aristotle, in the 'Athenian Constitution' gives examples of the duties leading from ties of hospitality. It is clear that hospitality brought with it obligations, not only of friendship but also of duty.

the house of Pisistratus was connected with them by ties of hospitality. The resolution of the Lacedaemonians was, however, at least equally due to the friendship which had been formed between the house of Pisistratus and Argos.

(Aristotle, Athenian Constitution 3:19)

Thereupon Isagoras, finding himself left inferior in power, invited Cleomenes, who was united to him by ties of hospitality, to return to Athens, and persuaded him to 'drive out the pollution', a plea derived from the fact that the Alcmeonidae were supposed to be under the curse of pollution.

(Aristotle, Athenian Constitution 3:20)

Odysseus was searching for *xenia*, in the sense of 'hospitable reception', in a wide variety of situations and various authors have examined how hospitable this reception actually was: for example, Levy (1963) and Webber (1989) look at the relationship between the host and the guest. Webber (1989, p. 47) notes that how the guests are identified is a central theme within the depictions of hospitality in the *Odyssey*, 'the society depicted in the poem is made up of a network of interdependencies, most strikingly realized in guest-friendships, in which reciprocal hospitality both creates personal ties and provides for a fair exchange of goods'. However on any single visit, the reciprocity is one-sided at the time; the guest arrives empty-handed, and the host must provide comforts and send the guest on their way with gifts. During the visit, the guest provides nothing in return but their name; the information that will enable the host to claim reciprocal hospitality at a later stage.

Levy (1963) argues that the reciprocal nature of hospitality is also evident in the duty of the guest not to overstay their welcome, and to have due regard for the substance of the host, who on their part must offer hospitality freely and without restriction. Levy (1963, p. 150) notes 'the Germanic proverb, 'After three days guests, like fish, begin to smell' has, as far as I have been able to discover, no counterpart in the Hellenic tradition.' If a guest abuses the hospitality offered by a generous host to the extent where the guest destroys the host's livelihood and sustenance, the guest is de facto destroying the host. Levy notes that in the *Odyssey* there is a definite indication of a concern that the guest should not overstep the limits of generosity and thus harm the host. Within the society in which the *Odyssey* is set, man is identified with his goods and chattels. Often when the host is harmed by the guest's abuse of hospitality, the gods are said to intercede and impose sanctions on the unreasonable guest. Levy (1963) illustrates this by imagining the first audience of the Homeric poems who were an:

> *audience of small farmers, shepherds, neatherds, and fisherfolk, listening with indignation to the recital of how the guests ate up the very essence of the host; each would hear in the tale an echo of his own inner conflict as, in his own home, he followed the dictates of hospitality on the one hand, but saw on the other his meagre stores, the fruit of his hard labour, his very self, in fact, consumed. The hearers would wait with grim anticipation and rising emotion for the denouement, in which the wasters were destroyed by the gods.*

This illustration highlights the importance of engaging with the bias of the audience; Homer was telling the story in the way that reflected the parlance of the audience that it was addressed to, whilst using a concept with which they were familiar: hospitality.

Pedrick (1988, p. 85) considers the provision of hospitality by noble women in the *Odyssey*, noting that 'the noble woman has three gestures of hospitality: when a guest arrives, she arranges a bed for him; before a grand feast, she supervises his bath; finally, when he departs, she gives him gifts of clothing.' Within the Homeric writings these gestures are so repetitive that this three-stage typology can be considered as standard part of the hospitality transaction. However, Pedrick (1988) goes on to observe that these gestures of hospitality do more than just provide simple domestic amenities for the guest, they begin the process of formalisation of the hospitality relationship (*xenia*) between the guest and the host (the husband of the noble woman), by elevating the stranger's status to that of an honoured guest. Burton (1998) further investigates the role played by women in the provision of hospitality in the Ancient Greek world in general, rather than just within the Homeric writings. This study highlights the centrality of women who are often playing a more important role than men; celebratory feasts were one of the few situations where women were on equal terms with men, or even presided over them. Wedding feasts offered other occasions on which Greek men and women could gather together and eat and drink on fairly equal terms. Burton (1998, p. 158) observes that Plutarch (*Quaestiones Convivales*) notes that a wedding guest list is often large because 'many or most of the activities relating to a wedding are in the hands of women, and where women are present it is necessary that their husbands also should be included'. Burton (1998) also observes that this situation is reflective of the long tradition of women's high visibility in Greek wedding processions and other activities, which are depicted in vase paintings dating from the 6th and 5th centuries BC.

Female gestures of hospitality that appear welcoming and generous can also have more sinister and deceptive qualities when, for example, in the absence of her husband the woman is the host in her own right. Hospitality gestures are not as innocuous in a matriarchal *oikos* (household) as they are in the context of a patriarchal *oikos*. Pedrick (1988, p. 85) argues that the offer of the noble woman's bed traps the guest 'eternally in a sterile, inglorious existence; the bath reveals too much about his person; and the clothing shapes his identity to her desires'. These gestures contrast two different visions of hospitality provided by women. On the one hand, hospitality is offered as a wholesome, welcoming gesture that will build a relationship; on the other hand, hospitality can be a useful medium from which the host can subordinate the guest and gain useful information about them.

4.2   Civic hospitality: communities and the emergent city

As civic life begins to develop, guests and strangers are still to be treated hospitably, but not all guests are to be treated equally. Plato, in his 'Laws' details types of strangers/guests who are to be welcomed but treated differently according to their rank and station:

> *There are four types of stranger which call for mention. The first and inevitable immigrant is the one who chooses summer… making gain by their trading… this stranger must be received, when he comes to the city, at the*

markets, harbours, and public buildings outside the city, by the officials in charge thereof; and they shall have a care lest any such strangers introduce any innovation.

The second type of stranger is he who is an inspector... for all such there must be hospitality provided at the temples, to afford them friendly accommodation, and the priests and temple-keepers must show them care and attention, until they have sojourned for a reasonable length of time and have seen and heard all that they intended...

The third type which requires a public reception is he who comes from another country on some public business: he must be received by none but the generals, hipparchs and taxiarchs, and the care of a stranger of this kind must be entirely in the hands of the official with whom he lodges...

The fourth type of stranger comes rarely, if ever: should there, however, come at any time from another country an inspector similar to those we send abroad, he shall come on these conditions: First, he shall be not less than fifty years old; and secondly, his purpose in coming must be to view some noble object which is superior in beauty to anything to be found in other States, or else to display to another State something of that description. Every visitor of this kind shall go as an unbidden guest to the doors of the rich and wise, he being both rich and wise himself; and he shall go also to the abode of the General Superintendent of Education, believing himself to be a proper guest for such a host, or to the house of one of those who have won a prize for virtue; and when he has communed with some of these, by the giving and receiving of information, he shall take his departure, with suitable gifts and distinctions bestowed on him as a friend by friends.

(Plato,*De Legibus* 12:952d–953e (abridged))

This typology of strangers can be summarised as in Table 4.1. The visitor's reason or purpose for the visit is given along with that the nature of the hospitality that must be provided to them, which is dependant on the reason/purpose.

Plato also indicated that there should be conformity with the 'Laws' for all guest/strangers from abroad, and that the 'Laws' also apply when sending out the state's own citizens to other states. The observance of these 'Laws' was doing honour to Zeus, Patron of Strangers, and was therefore seen as the only appropriate behaviour, rather than being unwelcoming to guest/strangers, which, by definition, is dishonouring Zeus. The 'Laws' also indicated that the relationships are formal ones, with legal obligations on both sides. In Homeric literature, hospitality was shown as a way of giving respect and showing honour; it was also non-judgemental of social status. However in Plato's 'Laws', although hospitality for the visitor/stranger from aboard is welcoming, it is codified to provide reference points for provision of hospitality.

Table 4.1: Plato's stratification of hospitality provision

Typology	Purpose/ reason for visit	Hospitality provision
Merchant	Trade/business	Received by the officials in charge of the markets, harbours and public buildings. Special care must be made to stop them introducing innovations.
Cultural visitor	To view artistic achievements	Hospitality at the temples, friendly accommodation. Priest and temple keepers are responsible.
Civic dignitary	Public business	Must be received by the generals and public officials at a civic reception. Home hospitality with a public official.
Occasional high-status cultural visitor	To view some unique cultural aspect	Over 50 years of age. A welcome visitor of the rich and the wise. Guest of those in charge of education or those with special virtue.

Plato's formal stratification of the hospitality provision and the growth of relations between the city-states gave rise to πρόξενος *Proxenos*, who was literally the 'guest-friend' of a city-state; looking after the interests of a foreign state in his own country; for example, the Spartan *Proxenos* in Athens was an Athenian citizen. The office of *Proxenos* was employed throughout the Greek world. The word ξενος implies 'guest' or 'foreigner' (as indicated in Chapter 1, section 1.4); however, in this context the προξενία *proxenia* (the relationship of the Proxenos) is one of hospitality. Domestic politics dominated the interests of citizens, who had little use for diplomacy since Greek city-states were essentially self-centred and insular; however, mutual ties of hospitality did exist between leaders of states and important families of other cities – these links brought about an informal diplomatic avenue of communication.

The office of *proxenos* was at first, probably, self-chosen (as Thucydides in *History of the Peloponnesian War* makes reference to volunteer *proxenoi*), but soon became a matter of appointment. These *proxenoi* undertook various functions including the reception and entertainment of guests; they would also represent the guest in courts of law if necessary. The earliest reference to an Athenian *proxenus*, is that of Alexander of Macedonia, who lived during the time of the Persian wars (Herodotus, *The Historia* VIII: 136). It was not until the middle of the 5th century BC that the term '*Proxenos*' became common throughout Greece; the establishment of the institution is documented by numerous inscriptions from the last third of the 5th century BC. There was however also a covert side to the *proxenia*; it could function as both an overt and a covert intelligence system, as representatives of this institution were indeed in an ideal position to collect and transmit political and military information or to organise political subversion and sabotage; they could also arrange the betrayal of besieged cities to the forces of their patrons.

The hospitable treatment of prisoners identified in the biblical writings (in Chapter 3) is also paralleled in the history of Greece. Xenophon, whose name means 'strange sound' or 'guest voice', was an Athenian knight, an associate of Socrates, and is known for his writings on Hellenic culture. While a young man, Xenophon participated in the expedition led by Cyrus against his older brother, the emperor Artaxerxes II of Persian. Cyrus hoped to depose his brother and gain the throne, but did not tell his mercenaries of the true goal of the expedition. A battle took place at Cunaxa, where the Greeks were victorious but Cyrus was killed, and shortly thereafter, their general, Clearchus of Sparta, was captured and executed. The mercenaries found themselves deep in hostile territory, far from the sea, and without leadership. The crossing of the high plateaus of modern day Armenia, whilst hasting to the rescue of Cyrus, offers the opportunity for Xenophon to describe the loyal and hospitable people they met on their way, during their campaign. The people offered them what they had: cattle, corn, dried grapes, vegetables of all sorts, and fragrant old wines. Details concerning the gifts of hospitality were:

> *Here they sent the Hellenes, as gifts of hospitality, three thousand measures of barley and two thousand jars of wine, twenty beeves and one hundred sheep.*

(Xenophon, Anabasis 6:1)

4.3   Commercial hospitality: the geneses of an industry

With the rise of cities and towns the importance of the commercial hospitality sector increases. Information about commercial hospitality in Greece is limited, however, Thucydides in his *History of the Peloponnesian War*, relates events from 431 BC to 411 BC. This text is also a significant departure from the literary style of historical writing. Thucydides wrote a military history; he is held to be scrupulous in his presentation of the facts as he abstains from commentary on social conditions, chronicles the events by seasons, and does not discuss state policy unless it refers to the progress of the war. Critically, he interprets mankind's nature and behaviour as a result of man's own actions rather than claiming that man's destiny is controlled by the Gods or other fates outside his influence.

In the text is the word καταγογιον *katagogion*, which is taken to mean inn or hostelry. From the context this can be understood in the commercial sense, and is one of the oldest references to large-scale hospitality.

> *The city the Thebans gave for about a year to some political emigrants from Megara, and to the surviving Plataeans of their own party to inhabit, and afterwards razed it to the ground to its very foundations, and built on to the precinct of Hera an inn two hundred feet square, with rooms all round above and below.*
>
> (Thucydides, History of the Peloponnesian War 3:68)

The same word, *katagogion*, appears in the writings of Xenophon, in this case they are to be constructed by the city-state for the ship owners, merchants and visitors; these inns bestow various benefits to the growing and developing city:

> *When [city] funds were sufficient, it would be a fine plan to build more inns for ship owners near the harbours, and convenient places of exchange for merchants, also inns to accommodate visitors. Again, if inns and shops were put up both in the Peiraeus and in the city for retail traders, they would be an ornament to the state and at the same time the source of considerable revenue.*
>
> (Xenophon, Ways and Means 3:12–13)

This was just one of a series of economic measures, proposed by Xenophon, that focused on attracting more foreign residents to Athens, both to strengthen and stabilise the Athenian economy and raise public funds.

Inns were clearly of different standards, some by no means unpleasant. One author whilst reflecting on a person's journey through life uses inns, comfortable and pleasing ones, as metaphor for a distraction to personal development.

> *What then is usually done? Men generally act as a traveller would do on his way to his own country, when he enters a good inn, and being pleased with it should remain there. Man, you have forgotten your purpose: you were not travelling to this inn, but you were passing through it. But this is a pleasant inn. And how many other inns are pleasant? And how many meadows are*

pleasant? Yet these are only for passing through. But your purpose is this, to return to your country, to relieve your kinsmen of anxiety, to discharge the duties of a citizen, to marry, to beget children, to fill the usual magistracies.
(*Epictetus*, Arrian 2.23)

By 400 BC, commercial hospitality was necessary to bring tourists or traders to the city and a key source of revenue. Commercial hospitality was a distinct and separate sector and it includes large-scale provision of food, beverage and accommodation. Commercial hospitality also existed for those who did not have a network of private hospitality or receive hospitality by the state. As well as attracting traders, the commercial sector was seen as a means of economic stimulus and an integral means of enhancing the influence of the state beyond its borders.

4.4   Summary of hospitality in Classical Greece

Hospitality was essentially organic and its evolution revealed a great deal about the cultural values and beliefs of the societies that existed in Classical Greece. Central to the process was the concept of crossing thresholds; hospitality was freely offered to a guest regardless of whether he had entered a tent, a house or a temple, and the guest was entitled to the hospitality of the host together with the sanctuary and security that came with it. However, the duties of the guest were clear too; the host (or gods) expected the guests to follow their example and share their livelihood and their life with their fellow guests on earth.

Strangers without exception, were regarded as being under the protection of the gods, and in general were treated as guests. Hospitality was central to virtually all the ethical and moral behaviour; the gods, the great hosts, led by example. Providing hospitality was a way of paying dutiful homage to the gods, and was enshrined as a worthy and honourable thing to do. Failure to provide hospitality was condemned in both the human and spiritual worlds.

The concepts of guest, stranger, and host are closely related but only when hospitality was based around the household, all guests/strangers were to be treated the same. However, as hospitality moved from being centred in and on the home into the civic domain, guests were no longer treated equally. Hospitality was still welcoming, but it was also stratified. This highlights the fact that as society was becoming more sophisticated, hospitality was no longer homogeneous and the codification of hospitality provided reference points as to how to treat a range of guests/strangers according to a variety of criteria.

Through practising hospitality, the household increased in strength and status; hospitality itself could be hereditary and reciprocal in nature. The formal linking of states by ties of hospitality led to civic receptions and the exchange of ambassadors. Civic and business hospitality developed from private hospitality but retained the key foundation: treat others as to make them feel at home even though they are not at home. There is also evidence of a distinct and rapidly developing commercial hospitality sector, which represented a key source of income for a city and as a necessary attraction to bring tourists or traders to the city. It was also seen as a means of enhancing the influence of the state beyond its borders.

Alliances were initially developed through hospitality between friends, households and states, and were strengthened through continuing mutual hospitality. This led to the use of hospitality networks as a communications system; visiting guests brought news from other city-states. Hospitality quickly became used as a political facilitator but there was also a darker side to the information exchange, hospitality networks could also be used for espionage, political subversion, and sabotage. The benevolent nature of the hospitality transaction was inverted and used for political gain.

Developments within the societies of Classical Greece led to the formal stratification of hospitality and three different typologies of hospitality had already clearly emerged: Private or personal hospitality based around the entire household; civic or public hospitality connected with the state; and an emergent, but important, commercial industry. Originally the home was symbolic of hospitality. The oldest accounts of the hospitality transaction are inextricably linked to and centred on the home; friendship established through hospitality began at home. These domestic principles of hospitality and the roles associated with them also provided the foundations for civic and commercial hospitality customs and practices.

5 Classical Rome

From the time of the earliest Hellenic civilisations, hospitality has been religiously sanctioned, with particular gods watching over strangers and travellers; this is also true of the Roman Republic. In the same way as Zeus presided over hospitality conducted by the Greeks, Jupiter was thought to watch over the *ius hospitia* (law of hospitality) in the Roman Empire. Similarly the violation of hospitality was also as great a crime and impiety in Rome as it was in Greece. This chapter explores the origins of hospitality to be found in Classical Rome, from its foundation, through considering domestic, civil and commercial hospitality.

5.1 Founding of Rome

Virgil's (*c.*40 BC) epic poem the *Aeneid* charts events from the fall of Troy (*c.*1200 BC) through to the establishment of the City of Rome (*c.*753 BC); in the first part of the poem the hero Aeneas flees from Troy to found a new home for his people. During the journey Aeneas and his people depend on the hospitality of Dido, Queen of Carthage (North Africa). Gibson (1999) notes that in the *Aeneid*, Virgil includes five major hospitality scenes: Dido and the Trojans; Aeneas and Helenus in Epirus; Aeneas and Acestes in Sicily, Latimis and the Trojans; Aeneas and Evander. To this may be added a number of minor episodes, such as Anchises and Anius on Delos and the Trojans and Achaemenides. Virgil will have been aware of the status of the hospitality episode in Homer as a type-scene with conventional elements as previously identified by Reece (1993). Wiltshire (1989) investigates hospitality in the *Aeneid*; highlighting five ways in which hospitality has an effect on the characters in the poem:

1. *Admitting a stranger may be disastrous to the public realm because they bring change and innovation;*
2. *Hospitality may provide a haven for those who can travel no further;*
3. *Hospitality may collapse in the wake of irrational behaviour on the part of the host or the guest;*

4.   *Reception of newcomers may foster political alliances; and*

5.   *Meeting strangers may free people to behave publicly in a new and more effective way.*

(Wiltshire, 1989, p. 89)

The hospitality that the main characters experience, either as guests or hosts, breaks down their isolated private world. Then they open their personal space to others and this enables the creation of shared public spaces, where the new community can evolve, or not, as the case may be. The effect of generous hospitality being freely offered and accepted is the creation of a world which at its best will turn all strangers into guests, however when hospitality is abused it can have devastating effects.

Ovid was the other epic poet for the Romans – his work *Ars Amatoria* also narrates the foundation of the city of Rome. Gibson (1999) observes that in the opening section of *Ars Amatoria*, Ovid records that Aeneas broke of the rules of *hospitium*. For the Romans, *hospitium*, like *xenia* for the Greeks, contained the ideals of duty, loyalty, and reciprocity (the reciprocal exchanges for hospitality). Gibson (1999, p. 184) confirms that *hospitium* included the idea of *pietas* 'a reference to the guest's sense of, or actual fulfilment of, the duty to pay a proper return on the hospitality received'. Throughout Virgil's *Aeneid*, Aeneas had a formidable reputation for doing his duty as a *hospes* (as someone who was conscientious about their reciprocal duty).

> *The erotic relationship between Dido and Aeneas in Book IV of the Aeneid evolves out of the hospitium relationship established between them in Book I. When Aeneas leaves Dido he asserts that their relationship is that of host and guest rather than of husband and wife, and that he has acted and will act well in this hospitium relationship (Aeneid 4.334–9). Dido, for her part, even after she has been forced to drop the argument that she and Aeneas are married (Aeneid 4.431), continues to attack Aeneas and the Trojans as bad or faithless hospites (Aeneid 4.538–41, 4.596–8), and ends by renouncing hospitium with them (Aeneid 4.622–9)*

(Gibson, 1999, p. 186)

In Ovid's *Ars Amatoria*, however, the reciprocal gesture made by Aeneas for the hospitality he received from Dido was to give her a sword and a reason for her to kill herself with it. Ovid presents an Aeneas who failed in his solemn duty to provide Dido with suitable reciprocity for her hospitality to him.

Gibson (1999, p. 185) argues that Virgil sets a problem for the reader of the *Aeneid:* 'how have Aeneas and Dido acted in the light of the values of *hospitium* to which they both appeal?' Virgil is using the criterion of hospitality to judge the respective guilt of Aeneas and Dido. Gibson (1999, p. 186) also argues that there is something intrinsically disordered about the very existence of a *hospitium* relationship between Aeneas and Dido, due to their background and history. Aeneas' mother and Dido's father were the gods Venus and Belus respectively, between whom enmity always existed (*Aeneid* 1.621f.); thus in Roman mythology there would have been corresponding enmity between Aeneas Prince of Troy and Dido Queen of Carthage. When Aeneas led his people from Troy they sought *hospitium* in Carthage. The whole question of *hospitium* between Carthaginians and Trojans was impossible until the gods intervened (*Aeneid* 1.297–300) when Jupiter sends his messenger Mercury to earth to intercede with Dido on behalf of the Trojans. It is only as a result of Mercury's intervention that Dido and the Carthaginians put aside their instinctive animosity (*Aeneid* 1.302–3) and develop a hospitality relationship with the Trojans (*Aeneid* 1.304). However, both Ovid and Virgil show that reciprocally enjoyed hospitality could lead to the establishment and development to alliances of state, for example between the Trojans and the Carthaginians, whereas its one-sided abuse could also lead nations to war as for example, the breach of hospitality that caused The Trojan War (waged against the city of Troy by the Achaeans (Greeks) after Paris of Troy stole Helen from her husband Menelaus, the king of Sparta – circa 12th century BC) that lead directly to the outbreak of lasting hostility and death.

Livy (*c.*59 BC–AD 17) wrote a monumental history of Rome, *Ab Urbe Condita*, from its founding, traditionally dated to 753 BC, through the reign of Augustus. Bolchazy (1993) investigated the portrayal of hospitality in the writings of Livy, and proposed two theses: Rome, like other societies, moved through seven stages of hospitality toward strangers, with the *ius hospitii* (those who are shown to be righteous by providing hospitality) playing an important humanising role in ancient Roman culture; and Livy in his writings appreciated this role and gave *hospitium* a primary place in his history of Rome. The centrality of *hospitium* is proposed by Bolchazy (1993) observations, summarised as:

◊ Livy introduces *hospitium* into Aeneas' escape from Troy, a tradition otherwise unattested in all other sources;

◊ *Hospitium* is also introduced or emphasised in other stories associated with the development of Rome; and

◊ Livy's Rome is hospitable above and beyond the call of duty, and words related to *hospitium* are scattered throughout all Livy's surviving books.

Therefore, according to Bolchazy (1993, p. 65), 'Livy appreciated the *ius hospitii* as a moral law dictating a friendly relationship between strangers and a peaceful solution to private and international differences', the altruism involved in the *ius hospitii* made it superior to the other virtues.

It is virtually impossible to either prove or disprove that a classical author had a particular theme in the front of their mind when writing; Livy nowhere explicitly states the thesis of hospitality attributed to him by Bolchazy (1993). However, there are a number of passages which are taken out of context: for example, a few lines after Aeneas and his countrymen escape from Troy, Aeneas is found slaughtering native Italians or driving them from their homes in return for their hospitality. Another example would be the reception of foreign ambassadors (Bolchazy, 1993, p. 60f); this was surely a matter of custom rather than altruism. Even Livy did not portray the Romans as unique in this respect, reception of ambassadors was a matter of custom (*Ab Urbe Condita* 39.55.4); whilst Livy's record of the speech by the consul to the Rhodian ambassadors in 167 BC indicates that hospitable treatment was reserved for friends (*Ab Urbe Condita* 45.20.7f.).

Bolchazy (1993) details seven stages of hospitality development, drawing on comparative evidence from Greece and modern 'primitive' societies. This, perhaps unintentionally, highlights that the use of comparative material can be highly illustrative, but without a sufficiently sophisticated methodology, it can be misleading. According to Bolchazy (1993) there are the seven stages of hospitality summarised as:

1 Avoidance or mistreatment of strangers;

2 Apotropaic hospitality (ritual neutralisation of strangers' magical powers);

3 Medea (named after the actions of Medea) category of hospitality (kindness to ensure the friendly use of strangers' magical powers);

4 Theoxenic hospitality (kindness to strangers who could be gods in disguise);

5 Kindness in accordance with divine law;

6 Contractual hospitality; and

7 Altruistic hospitality to anyone in need.

When considering this seven-stage evolution of attitudes toward strangers, Bolchazy (1993) discusses honour under the heading of altruism, suggesting that Livy viewed *hospitium* as an instrument of selfless peace. However, within Livy's writings there are many examples of how hospitality has been abused to the benefit of the abuser:

◊ Hospitality along with war to expand Roman domination (*Ab Urbe Condita* 21.2.5);

◊ Foreign guests and kinsmen were used to secure tyranny (*Ab Urbe Condita* 1.49.8); and

◊ Allegiances of hospitality were used to enlarge Carthaginian hegemony (*Ab Urbe Condita* 21.2.5)

From these examples the question arises over the justification for Bolchazy's (1993) thesis that Livy believes in the peaceful and humanising influence of hospitality. There are numerous other examples in Livy of cynical manipulation of guests for selfish ends (e.g. *Ab Urbe Condita* 42.17.3–5 and 42.43.3); in other words, it could be argued that hospitality to advance the host's honour and status is anything but altruistic. What is clear is that hospitality can be a useful means of control.

Bolchazy (1993) also makes use of modern anthropological studies to compare the evolution of hospitality in Roman times to the discoveries made by anthropologists in the early part of the 20th century. His bibliography shows that most of the anthropological sources come from the era of Frazer (see Frazer, 1911, 1923). Anthropologists in the late 19th and early 20th centuries combed through missionary and travellers' reports, collecting examples of quaint customs. The mass of data was then put together in a logical sequence to illustrate that human societies everywhere undergo a uni-linear development through parallel stages. Bolchazy (1993) has adopted this general overview to the extent that, when the Roman evidence for a particular category of hospitality is sparse or absent, he infers its existence by interpolation. However, since the writings of Evans-Pritchard (1965), Frazer's theory of stages has not stood up to rigorous scrutiny. The underlying reason is that when the reports of fieldwork rather than rhetorical anthropologies began pouring in after the turn of the century, the data did not conform to the stages of uni-linear, parallel evolution. This leads directly to the issue of what Finley (1983) describes as the Teleological Fallacy, which is the tendency to use ancient documents as basis for a controversial argument about a modern phenomenon; the Teleological Fallacy is discussed in greater detail in Chapter 3, section 3.3.

Although the idea of stages of hospitality evolution can be questioned, Bolchazy (1993) certainly stimulates ideas about guests, strangers and hospitality in classical Rome. However, rigorous translation and textual analysis is required; at one point Bolchazy (1993) rightly distinguishes between foreigners and strangers, and at another point he uses a passage about pilgrims resident in Rome as evidence of attitudes toward guests. It is argued that categories of hospitality should not be considered to be all encompassing, for example, Pitt-Rivers (1977) anthropological work has stressed honour as a motivation for hospitality. Bolchazy (1993) classes honour under the heading of altruism, however if a person's only reason for being hospitable is to gain honour, their intention can't be seen as altruistic. It would seem that honour and altruism are two quite different motivations and confusing the two fails to give adequate attention to the motivation for hospitality most relevant to the Rome of historical times.

The Roman Empire (27 BC to AD 467) was to become a vast centre of consumption, as André (1981) noted, importing much of its food from its many colonies under exclusive agreements and expected unusual food gifts for the aristocracy. In addition there was market expansion and the wholesale exportation of goods, services and cultural ideas through the colonisation process of the conquered lands. At its height (AD 117) Rome dominated Western Eurasia and northern Africa, and comprised the majority of the region's population; at this time the Roman Empire controlled approximately 6 million sq km of land. The Roman citizen could travel throughout the Empire and be protected by one legal system, speak one administrative language and needed only one currency.

Rome's influence upon the culture, law, technology, arts, language, religion, government, military, and architecture of Western civilization continues to this day, as does its influence on the commercial hospitality industry. Early forms of commercialisation did much to aid the growth of the Roman hospitality industry. The importance of the work/leisure dichotomy of Roman times was part of their approach to life and undoubtedly emerged as reward and in celebration for their successes in the expansion and growth of the Empire. Extensive commercial hospitality businesses existed for travellers, merchants, and sailors who came to trade and sell, or those who were stopping overnight along the way to other destinations.

5.2 Domestic hospitality: consolidation of power

The hospitality of the Romans was, as in Greece, either *hospitium privatum*, or *publicum*. Private hospitality with the Romans, however, seems to have been more accurately and legally defined than in Greece. The character of a *hospes* (a person connected with a Roman citizen by ties of hospitality) was deemed even more sacred, and to have greater claims upon the host, than that of a person connected by blood or affinity. There were various obligations, which the connection through hospitality with a foreigner imposed upon a Roman citizen – amongst those obligations was: to receive in his house his *hospes* when travelling:

> *They enjoyed the hospitality of private citizens whom they treated with courtesy and consideration; and their own houses in Rome were open to those with whom they were accustomed to stay.*
>
> (Livy, Ab Urbe Condita 42:1)

There were also duties of protection; and, in case of need, to represent him as his patron in the courts of justice. Private hospitality was established between individuals by mutual presents, or by the mediation of a third person, and hallowed by religion; for Jupiter was thought to watch over the *ius hospitii*, as Zeus did with the Greeks and the violation of it was as great a crime and impiety in Rome as in Greece (Cicero, *Pro Deiotaro* 6). The poet Ovid, who wrote on topics of love, abandoned women, and mythological transformations, also reinforced the role of the god Jupiter, when he told the story of the gods Jupiter and Mercury who came to earth in human form and travelled around looking for a place to rest. After being turned away a thousand times, they came upon the simple thatched cottage of Baucis and Philemon (Ovid, *Metamorphoses* 8:987). They had little to offer, but they generously shared what they had: a little bacon and...

> *double-tinted fruit of chaste Minerva, and the tasty dish of corner, autumn-picked and pickled; these were served for relish; and the endive-green, and radishes surrounding a large pot of curdled milk; and eggs not overdone but gently turned in glowing embers, all served up in earthen dishes. Then sweet wine served up in clay, so costly!*
>
> (Ab Urbe Condita 8:1026ff)

They were about to kill their only goose to feed their guests, when the gods revealed themselves. Jupiter and Mercury took Baucis and Philemon up the mountain to see the valley, in which the homes of all their neighbours who had turned away the strangers had been flooded. Their own simple home had been transformed into a temple. When asked what they wanted, Baucis and Philemon asked that they might be the priests of the temple, and that when their lives came to an end they might die together (Ab Urbe Condita 8:1095).

When hospitality was formed, the two friends used to divide between themselves a hospitality token *tessera hospitalis*, by which, afterwards, they or their descendants – the connection was hereditary – might recognise one another. Plautus examples this pratice in the dialogue between Hanno and Agorastocles in the play *Poenulus et Cistellaria*:

Hanno: If so it is, if you would like to compare the token of hospitality, see here, I've brought it.

Agorastocles: Come then, show it here. It is exactly true; for I've got the counterpart at home.

Hanno: O my host, hail to you right earnestly; for it was your father, then, Antidamas, that was my own and my father's guest; this was my token of hospitality with him.

Agorastocles: Then here at my house shall hospitality be shown you; for I don't reject either Hospitality or Carthage, from which I sprang.

Hanno: May the Gods grant you all you may desire.

(Plautus, Poenulus et Cistellaria *5:2:87ff)*

From an expression in Plautus and the corresponding description 'I have a token of hospitality, which I carry' (Poenulus et Cistellaria v.1.25), it has been concluded that this *tessera* bore the image of Jupiter. Hospitality, when thus once established, could not be dissolved except by a formal declaration and in this case, the *tessera hospitalis* was broken to pieces as in this situation:

Be gone! Go seek where there is confidence enough in your oaths; here now, with us, Alcesimarchus, you've renounced your title to our friendship.

(Poenulus et Cistellaria 2:1:27)

Hospitality in Rome was never exercised in the indiscriminate manner as in the heroic age of Greece, but the custom of observing the laws of hospitality was probably common to all the nations of Italy. It is clearly seen in the writings of Livy, who wrote during the Age of Augustus, a time during which Rome was powerful, prosperous, and still expanding. Much of what Livy included in his history was legend and epic drama.

A formal treaty was made between the leaders and mutual greetings exchanged between the armies. Latinus received Aeneas as a guest in his house, and there, in the presence of his tutelary deities, completed the political alliance by a domestic one, and gave his daughter in marriage to Aeneas.

(Livy, Ab Urbe Condita *1:1)*

In many cases, it was exercised without any formal agreement between the parties, and it was deemed an honourable duty to receive distinguished guests into the house. Public hospitality seems, likewise, to have existed at a very early period among the nations of Italy:

They were invited to accept hospitality at the different houses, and after examining the situation of the City, its walls and the large number of dwelling-houses it included, they were astonished at the rapidity with which the Roman State had grown.

(Livy, Ab Urbe Condita 1:9)*

and

It is stated that throughout the City the front gates of the houses were thrown open and all sorts of things placed for general use in the open courts, all comers, whether acquaintances or strangers, being brought in to share the hospitality.

(Livy, Ab Urbe Condita 5:13)*

These kind and generous acts of hospitality, lead to long-lasting friendships between the host and the guest. No doubt, it was from these personal bonds that the public ties of hospitality were later to be formed.

After recovering from their wounds, some left for their homes, to tell of the kind hospitality they had received; many remained behind out of affection for their hosts and the City.

(Livy, Ab Urbe Condita 2:14)*

Hospitality and the culinary arts were very much at the centre of Roman life. Feasts centred around the gods, some of whom were identified with hospitality, celebration, consumption, and hunting (providing the commodities to feast). These feasts provided much of the cultural impetus to reinforce the importance of indulgence and consumption of hospitality and events to the Roman way of life. Daily meals and routines added leisure values due to the social interactions and hierarchies of the time. Food and eating as part of the Roman hospitality function, was certainly an essential part of their daily life and was rich in semiology, artistic parallels and symbolism.

5.3   Civic hospitality: growth of an empire

The first direct mention of civic hospitality being established between Rome and another city is after the Gauls had departed from Rome, when it was decreed that Caere should be rewarded for its good services, by the establishment of public hospitality between the two cities:

Friendly relations as between State and State were to be established with the people of Caere, because they had sheltered the sacred treasures of Rome and her priests, and by this kindly act had prevented any interruption to the divine worship.

(Livy, Ab Urbe Condita 5:50)*

The public hospitality after the war with the Gauls gave to the Caerites the right of hospitality with Rome. In the later times of the republic, the public hospitality established between Rome and a foreign state is no longer found; but a relation, which amounted to the same thing, was introduced instead – that is, towns were raised to the rank of *municipia*:

> *Lanuvium received the full citizenship and the restitution of her sacred things, with the proviso that the temple and grove of Juno Sospita should belong in common to the Roman people and the citizens living at Lanuvium.*
>
> *(Livy,* Ab Urbe Condita *8:14)*

When a town was desirous of forming a similar relation with Rome, it entered into *clientela* to some distinguished Roman, who then acted as patron of the client-town. This hospitality when shared between states was applicable to individuals as well:

> *As they entered Capua the senate and people came out in a body to meet them, showed them all due hospitality, and paid them all the consideration to which as individuals and as members of an allied state they were entitled.*
>
> *(Livy,* Ab Urbe Condita *9:6)*

Nevertheless, the custom of granting the honour of *hospes publicus* to a distinguished foreigner by a decree of the senate seems to have existed until the end of the republic:

> *Servius had been careful to form ties of hospitality and friendship with the chiefs of the Latin nation, and he used to speak in the highest praise of that cooperation and the common recognition of the same deity.*
>
> *(Livy,* Ab Urbe Condita *1:45)*

Whether such a public *hospes* undertook the same duties towards Roman citizens, as the Greek *Proxenos,* is uncertain. Public hospitality was, like the *hospitium privatum*, hereditary in the family of the person to whom it had been granted:

> *Carthalo the commandant of the garrison, had laid down his arms and was going to the consul to remind him of the old tie of hospitality between their fathers when he was killed by a soldier who met him.*
>
> *(Livy,* Ab Urbe Condita *27:16)*

and

> *With a view to an alliance with Carthage he married a Carthaginian lady of noble birth, a niece of Hannibal's, and widow of Oezalces. He also sent envoys to Syphax and renewed the old ties of hospitality with him, thus securing on all sides support for the coming struggle with Masinissa.*
>
> *(Livy,* Ab Urbe Condita *29:29)*

and again

> *Close on this meeting came a deputation from Perseus. Their hopes of success rested mainly on the personal tie of hospitality which Marcius had inherited from his father.*
>
> (Livy, Ab Urbe Condita 42:38)

5.3 Commercial hospitality: diversified industry

The Roman Empire itself was a vast centre of consumption. It imported much of its food from its many colonies under exclusive agreements and expected unusual food gifts for the aristocracy. In addition, there was market expansion and the wholesale exportation of goods, services and cultural ideas through the colonisation process of the conquered lands.

Contemporary western cuisine still has evidence of the culinary practices and commodities of classical Rome (and others), included in the staple meat and vegetation, which was originally introduced to sustain the invading armies. The study of classical Roman food and cookery relies on an Apician viewpoint. Who or what exactly was Apicius is unclear; Apicius was the proverbial cognomen (nickname or later last name) for several connoisseurs of food. The most famous (and probably the second) was Marcus Gavius Apicius lived in the early Empire (*c*.30 BC). Much to the disgust of the moralist Seneca (*De Vita Benta* 8f), this Apicius is held to have kept an academy, in the manner of a philosopher. A third Apicius, or even a group of Apicii, lived in the late 4th or early 5th century and redacted the surviving Roman cookbook bearing his name.

Pliny the Elder (*Naturalis Historia* 19:137) and Tacitus (*Annales*) both note that the famous M. Gavius Apicius moved in the circles of Emperor Tiberius (AD 14–37). Pliny considered that Apicius was born to enjoy every extravagant luxury that could be contrived (*Naturalis Historia* 9:66). This Apicius invented various dishes and sauces in which the pursuit of the refined delicacy was taken to eccentric extremes. According to Athenaeus (*Deipnosophistae*, 1.5f), having heard of the boasted size and sweetness of the shrimps taken near the Libyan coast, Apicius commandeered a boat and crew, but when he arrived, disappointed by the ones he was offered by the local fishermen who came alongside in their boats, turned round and had his crew return him to his villa without going ashore. All of the subsequent translations of the Apician writings across the centuries concede that they were written to enhance the mysticism of the Roman cook and did not provide recipes that were easy to follow (no exacting measures, etc.). This could even be an attempt at self-preservation and the secret codes required to decipher the text were a way to protect the cook's earning power and place in society.

Roman celebrity cooks enjoyed notoriety and fashion leaders, such as Petronius (AD 27–66), provided much to the consumption gossip and trend setting of the day. The infamous Petronius was the *arbiter elegantiae* (arbiter of good taste) at the court of the Emperor Nero; Tacitus (*Annales* 16:17–20) describes Petronius as hedonistic and witty. Petronius also wrote the 'Cena Trimalchionis' ('Trimalchio's dinner') (*Satyricon* 26:6–78:8) which describes the typical food, drink and conversation of a Roman feast. The cook in Rome commanded the title of Artist; the social importance of the feast and the associated religious hospitality significance meant that the power of the professional cook was encouraged and indulged.

Extensive commercial hospitality businesses existed for travellers, merchants, and sailors who came to trade and sell, or those who were stopping overnight along the way to other destinations. Amongst the secondary literature, there is the general observation that women working in the hospitality trades were prostitutes. Inns and taverns were said to be 'hardly distinguished brothels which lived in constant fear of the police' (Balsdon, 1969, p. 153). Carepino (1940) said that inns were sources of seduction and prostitution and D'Avino (1967) stated that women who worked in inns were accused of working undercover as prostitutes. This idea is developed by Gardner (1991, p. 249): 'It was taken for granted that in many of these establishments, particularly the *cauponae*, which also had accommodation available; the women waitresses were also working as prostitutes.' Derogatory comments were not restricted to serving girls in the taverns; Cicero cites other occupations as *sordid* (dishonourable or vulgar).

> *First, those means of livelihood are rejected as undesirable which incur people's ill-will… Least respectable of all are those trades which cater for sensual pleasures: Fishmongers, butchers, cooks, and poulterers, and fishermen… Add to these, if you please, the perfumers, dancers, and the whole entertainment industry.*
>
> (Cicero, De Officiis 150)

This quote led to some authors to become obsessed with woman working and speculated that all working women were prostitutes. Lindsay (1960) and Pike (1965) hypothesised that women who worked in butcher shops and bakeries were often prostitutes. There is no other evidence in the primary sources to suggest this: *sordidi* means dishonourable or vulgar and should not be confused with sordid in the modern sense. There is, however, plenty of primarily literature portraying Roman bars as dens of iniquity.

> *Virtue is something elevated, exalted and regal, unconquered and unwary.*
> *Pleasure is something lowly, servile, weak and unsteady, whose haunt and*
> *dwelling-place are the brothel and the bar.*
>
> *(Seneca (the Younger),* De Vita Benta *7:3)*

However the clientele of a bar at least seemed to be interesting:

> *search for him in some big bar. There he will be, lying next a cut-throat, in*
> *the company of sailors, thieves, and runaway slaves, beside hangmen and*
> *coffin-makers, or beside a passed out priest:*
>
> > *This is liberty hall,*
> > *one cup serves for all,*
> > *no one has a bed to himself,*
> > *nor a table apart from the rest.*
>
> *(Juvenal,* Satires *8:168f)*

In Roman law there is certainly an indication that some women working in inns were prostitutes – the law code of Justinian lays down a clear mandate in relation to slave girls who have been sold:

> *A female slave, who has been sold under the condition that she does not*
> *make a shameful commerce of her body, must not prostitute herself in a*
> *tavern under the pretext of serving therein, in order to avoid a fraudulent*
> *evasion of the condition prescribed.*
>
> *(Justinian,* Codex Iustinianus *IIII:lvi:3)*

However, the law code of Theodosius, which dates from the time of Constantine, clearly differentiates between the wife of the tavern owner and a servant girl; it protects serving girls from prosecution and affords them safety under the law.

Commercial hospitality in Roman times indubitably included brothels (*lumpanar*); however, some evaluation of the culture behind brothels is necessary. It was assumed in Roman society that slaves were used as sexual partners for their masters; Seneca stated that sexual passivity was a crime for a free man, a necessity for a slave, and a duty for the freedman (Séneca (the Elder), *Controversiae* 4:10). Cato the Censor was famed for monitoring the behaviour of public officials and had a strong desire to return the people to conservative conduct and morality. Horace notes that Cato advocates when young men reach a certain age, it is only appropriate that they make the necessary arrangements.

> *When a well-known individual was making his exit from a brothel, 'Well done! Pray continue!' was the stirred verdict of Cato: 'as soon as libido has swollen their members, it's right for young men to come down here rather than drudging away with other men's wives'.*
>
> *(Horace, Satires 1.2:31–2)*

Other authors advance the observations of Horace: Prophyrio observes that libido must be kept in order, without committing crime; and Pseudo-Acro notes that young men should be praised for visiting brothels, not living in them.

> *Cato encountering him leaving a brothel; called him back and praised him. Afterwards when he saw him leaving the same brothel more frequently, he said: 'Young man, I praised you for coming here, not for living here'.*
>
> *(Pseudo-Arco, Pseudoacronis scholia 1:20)*

This is a rather dark and one-sided impression of the commercial hospitality industry; it can be contrasted with writings of Eunapius in his work *Vitae Sophistarum*. He tells the story of an unnamed barmaid, who whilst preparing a drink for a customer is interrupted and told that her friend is giving birth and in great danger. She drops everything and rushes to the aid of her friend; it transpires that she is also a midwife:

> *When she had relieved the woman in her travail and done all that is usual in case of child-birth, she washed her hands and came back at once to her customer.*
>
> *(Eunapius, Vitae Sophistarum 3.87)*

This text highlights that it was possible for a barmaid, in Roman times, to have an alternative profession, one not connected with prostitution. Another account tells of a man's attraction to the general character of a tavern keeper's wife, however dubious the surroundings might have been.

> *There, as the gods would have it, I fell in love with Terentius, the tavern-keeper's wife; you all knew Melissa from Tarentum, the prettiest of pretty wenches! Not that I courted her carnally or for venery, but more because she was such a good sort. Nothing I asked did she ever refuse; if she made a penny, I got a halfpenny; whatever I saved, I put in her purse, and she never chorused me. Well! Her husband died when they were at a country house. So I moved heaven and earth to get to her; true friends, you know, are proved in adversity.*
>
> *(Petronius, Satyricon 61)*

There is the affectionate inscription left by a husband, mourning for his wife (Figure 5.1).

DVICIS	... sweet
ATET HOC AMEMONE SEPVLCHRO	... in this tomb lies Amemone, a bar-maid known
PATRIAE POPINARIA NOTA	[beyond the boundaries] of her own country,
I TIBVR CELEBRARE SOLEBANT	[on account of whom] many people used to
AM DEVS ABSTVLIT ILLI	frequent Tibur. [Now the supreme] god has taken
AM LVX ALMA RECEPIT	[fragile life] from her, and a kindly light receives her
NVS COIVGI SANCTAE	spirit [in the aether]
SEMPER IN AEVOM	I, ... nus [put up this inscription] to my holy wife.
	[It is right that her name] remain forever.

Figure 5.1: Dedication from a husband to his barmaid wife
Source: Corpus Inscriptionum Latinarum XVI:3709

Although a great deal of information and insight can be gained from the analysis of the literature and individual artefacts, however archaeological investigation can provide a great deal more in terms of reinforcement and enhancement of understanding. As O'Gorman, Baxter, and Scott (2007) noted, there are many sites associated with commercial hospitality in classical Rome but amongst these, one of the most significant is Pompeii. For any analysis of Roman commercial hospitality, the sites of Pompeii and Herculaneum in Italy near modern-day Naples offer a unique perspective. The World Heritage Site designation documentation prepared by UNESCO states 'nowhere else is it possible to identify any archaeological site that even remotely stands comparison with these two classical towns' (UNESCO, 1996, p. 52). This is based on the circumstances surrounding the almost instantaneous destruction of the city in history by the eruption of Mount Vesuvius in AD 79, and its literal fossilisation as an archaeological site; at the time of its destruction the city of Pompeii had a population of approximately 10,000 people.

Pompeii is of importance to the examination of hospitality as it was a major centre of commerce and entertainment in the Roman world, and commercial hospitality existed in a highly organised fashion. Garnsey (2002) notes that for this large group of Romans, living accommodation typically did not have the basic utilities required to permit safe domestic preparation and consumption of food. Thus there was a significant requirement on commercial hospitality provision, which fuelled subsequent development, growth and entrepreneurial activity in the sector.

In the 1950s four principal categories of commercial hospitality establishments in ancient Roman times were defined by Kleberg (1957): *hospitiae;*

Plate 5.1: A bar counter at Pompeii

stabulae; tabernae; and *popinae;* these terms have become the standard for the archaeological categorisation of ancient hospitality businesses. In summary: *tabernae and popinae* had no facilities for overnight guests whilst *hospitia* and *stabula* usually did. *Hospitiae* were normally larger than *stabulae* and a *stabula* would have had accommodation to keep animals as well as guests. This list has been augmented with the inclusion of *cauponae* and other names for bars. The material remains of these different hospitality establishments make exact identification difficult. Not least because no two inns or taverns are exactly alike; the problem of certain identification is also compounded by the fact that many establishments are missing their second floors. These could have had apartments for rent, storage space, guest space or rooms for innkeepers and their families and staff.

Hospitiae were establishments that offered rooms for rent, and often food and drink to overnight guests. It would also seem that *hospitiae* were expressly fabricated for business purposes, although a number of them represent secondary uses of existing private homes in Pompeii. *Stabulae* were *hospitiae* with facilities to shelter animals; often found just outside the city, close to the city gates, the ancient equivalent of coaching inns. *Stabulae* had an open courtyard surrounded by a kitchen, a latrine, and bedrooms with stables at the rear. Businesses within city gates were smaller than those in the countryside, due to pressure of space.

In the first century AD, *taberna* referred to either a shop or a tavern – however, in many publications, the term *taberna* refers to almost any kind of shop, so there is a good deal of confusion when compiling a list of such establishments from literary sources alone. *Tabernae*, in their first century sense, served a variety of simple foods and drink. They usually contained a simple L-shaped marble counter, about six to eight feet long, with a simmering pot of water and shelves of other food on the back wall of a tiny room, often just large enough for the proprietor and several assistants. Ellis (2004) in a survey of Pompeii identifies 158 properties that could have been bars. *Cauponae* were establishments that provided meals, drink, and maybe lodgings; *Popinae* were limited to serving food and drink. Some may have offered sit down meals; this term was often used to describe public eating-houses. *Hospitiae, stabulae, tabernae,* and *popinae* should not always be understood as standalone businesses; often a *hospitia* or *stabula* would have a *taberna* or *popina* connected to it. What would seem to be important is that there were two basic types of establishment, one that dealt with accommodation, and one with food and drink. Table 5.1 is a summary of the various hospitality businesses and their facilities, and identifies modern equivalents.

Ellis (2004) argues that Pompeii has approximately 160 properties that could have been bars and restaurants, as well as numerous hotels. These have been found together with detailed kitchens and bakeries some with fossilised loaves of bread.

Plate 5.2: A bakery at Pompeii

From empirical archaeological evidence O'Gorman (2007) shows a cluster of hospitality establishments in the centre of Pompeii, less than two blocks from the busiest street and close to the administrative centre. The main building shown is a hotel, the largest *hospitium* identified so far in Pompeii; it is estimated that it could accommodate more than fifty guests and also had a large secluded garden. It was in the atrium that a graffito with the word 'Christianos' was found (*Corpus Inscriptionum Latinarum* (*CIL*) IV 679)

Table 5.1: Commercial hospitality establishments in Ancient Rome

Latin name	Description and facilities	Modern equivalent
Hospitium	Larger establishments that offered rooms for rent, and often food and drink to overnight guests; often specifically built for business purposes.	Hotel
Stabula	Buildings with open courtyard surrounded by a kitchen, a latrine, and bedrooms with stables at the rear. Often found just outside the city, close to the city gates; offered food, drink and accommodation.	Motels
Taberna Thermopolia Ganeae	Sold a variety of simple foods and drink. They usually contained a simple L-shaped marble counter, about six to eight feet long	Bar
Popina Caupona	Served food and drink, offered sit down meals; was often used to describe public eating-houses and sometimes included a few rooms	Restaurant
Lumpanar	Provided a full range of services of a personal nature.	Brothel

Adjacent but not internally connected to the hotel is a restaurant with a main dining room and a connecting smaller room with a latrine in back. One of the inscriptions in front attests to the fine wine served here (*CIL* IV 815). The name of the restaurateur was Drusus (*CIL* IV 814) who posted a sign in front of his bar that forbade loitering (*CIL* IV 813); of course this sign might be because this restaurant was it was close to lumpanar. Grand Lumpanar has ten rooms, five on each floor; from the layout it appears that only the first floor was devoted to sex for profit. Within each room on the first floor is the typical masonry bed used for sexual encounters, but not for sleep; there is even a concrete 'pillow' at the head of the bed. On the interior walls is the greatest cluster of *hic bene futui* graffiti in the city and above the door into each room is an erotic picture depicting a couple in the various positions of the sex act or foreplay. In each case the setting of the picture is in more comfortable surroundings than the cramped room behind it!

The bar shown at 8 in Figure 5.2 is a typical tavern; similar to another bar, shown in Figure 5.4. In level 1, a long counter took up most of the Room 1,

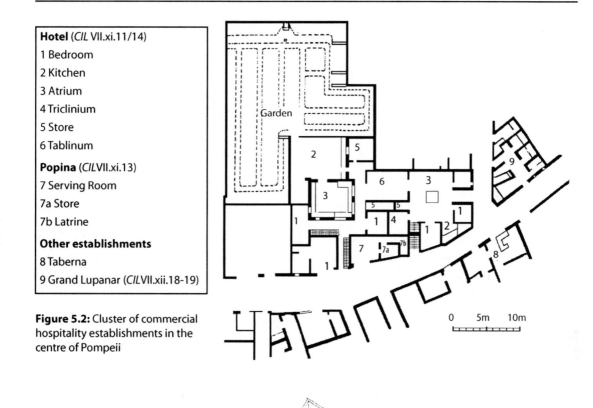

Hotel (*CIL* VII.xi.11/14)
1 Bedroom
2 Kitchen
3 Atrium
4 Triclinium
5 Store
6 Tablinum

Popina (*CIL* VII.xi.13)
7 Serving Room
7a Store
7b Latrine

Other establishments
8 Taberna
9 Grand Lupanar (*CIL* VII.xii.18-19)

Figure 5.2: Cluster of commercial hospitality establishments in the centre of Pompeii

Figure 5.3: Isometric view of the hotel at Pompeii; floor plan shown in Figure 5.2 (courtesy of Wylie Shanks Architects).

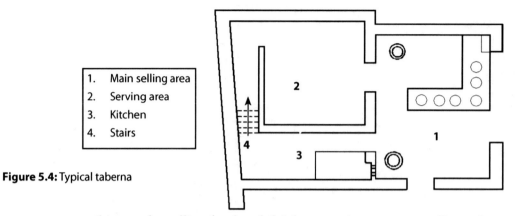

1. Main selling area
2. Serving area
3. Kitchen
4. Stairs

Figure 5.4: Typical taberna

this was for selling food and drink to passing customers; Room 2 contained stools for customers to sit on. Level 2 (destroyed), would have contained the Restaurateur's accommodation. An isometric drawing of the large hotel in Pompeii is shown in Figure 5.3.

Due to the reciprocal nature of private hospitality it is probable that not all travellers required such services. Accommodation in *stabulae*, along major roads and at city gates, gained a reputation for attracting lower classes who were too poor or socially insignificant to have developed a network of personal hospitality; Figure 5.5 shows the plan of a typical *stabula*.

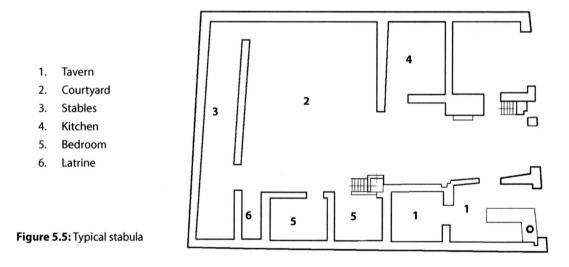

1. Tavern
2. Courtyard
3. Stables
4. Kitchen
5. Bedroom
6. Latrine

Figure 5.5: Typical stabula

Figure 5.6 shows the floor plan of Pompeii's largets brothel (The Grand Lupanar) which was able to cater for the needs of up to ten clients in individual rooms, and was strategiclly located next to the largest hotel.

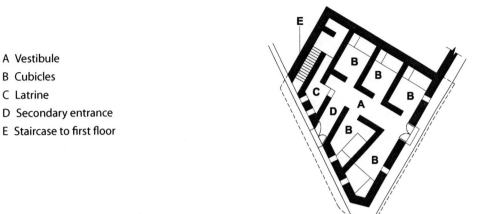

A Vestibule
B Cubicles
C Latrine
D Secondary entrance
E Staircase to first floor

Figure 5.6: The Grand Lupanar. (Courtesy of Wylie Shanks Architects)

Commercial hospitality businesses existed for travellers, merchants, and sailors who came to trade and sell, or those who were stopping overnight along the way to other destinations. Individual places of hospitality either offer associated services, or are located near other places of hospitality provision. Although originally at lower levels, the subsequent provision of higher levels of hospitality establishment and service was a direct consequence of the ability of the higher classes to afford to travel to lands where they were not known, but it enables them to be in environments which are commensurate with their wealth and status, without the need to establish a household there.

5.4 Summary of hospitality in Classical Rome

The emergent threefold typology of hospitality became more clearly focused on private, civic, and business/commercial hospitality, which increasingly became formalised as the societies developed. This included legal governance, more sophisticated approaches to codification of hospitality provision and the establishment of contractual relationships. Hospitality professionals emerged as civic and business hospitality developed, with particular individuals being recognised as having formal and defined responsibilities for hospitality. The importance of growth and flourishing of commercial hospitality was significantly changing everyday life and restaurants; bars and brothels were also common. The act of cooking became a popular pastime; however, the high-born woman of the household was not expected to cook. There were significant developments in civic hospitality, events such as civic receptions, or a distinguished person being given 'freedom of the city' came into being; formal hospitality, given by the state, was bestowed upon distinguished visitors. Civic hospitality was used to form strategic alliances between the nation states, this also brought an advancement of individual rights, and citizens of foreign states enjoyed certain rights and privileges if there was a bond of hospitality between their two states. A flourishing commercial hospitality industry existed for travellers, merchants and sailors who came to trade and sell, or those who were stopping overnight along the way to other destinations. In the cities, commercial hospitality establishments were often clustered in specific parts of the city.

During this period the hospitality customs reflect those of the Greek city-states. The hospitality process had the expectations of food, drink, accommodation and entertainment, etc. Domestic hospitality was of a more formal nature, in the style of a contract, entered into by mutual promise, the clasping of hands and exchange of an agreement in writing or of a token. The *tessera hospitalis* gave a hereditary character to hospitality and a reciprocal agreement, which could not be dissolved without a formal declaration. This formalised domestic hospitality was more binding and sacred in its nature than blood connections. The advantages thus obtained by the guest were the right of hospitality when travelling and, above all, the protection of his host in a court of law. Although hospitality was at the centre of existence, it was not to be entered into lightly – it was sacred and inviolable, undertaken in the name of the supreme god. One further development was when individuals, or states, were joined through a common bond of hospitality; this also required mutual recognition of their deities. Failure to undertake hospitality in an appropriate manner could cause the wrath of the gods on the offending city or household for generations.

Due to the reciprocal nature of private hospitality, not all travellers required the services of a commercial hospitality industry. Establishments along major roads and at city gates gained a reputation for attracting lower classes that were too poor or socially insignificant to have developed a network of personal hospitality. Although originally at lower levels, the subsequent provision of higher levels of hospitality establishment and service was a direct consequence of the ability of the higher classes to afford to travel to lands where they were not known; it enabled them to be in environments commensurate with their wealth and status, without the need to establish a household there.

Places offering commercial hospitality were frequented on a daily basis by the people within organised and structured social spaces. Inscriptions and illustrations, particularly from Pompeii, have been found that highlight both the mercantile nature of hospitality and level of service provision available. This is also symbolic evidence with regard to lifestyle and consumption statements indicative of branding and a sophisticated level of marketing. In addition, the strategic geographical concentration of hospitality services within cities suggests the synergised ease of hospitality provision and consumption. Commercial hospitality did not eclipse domestic and civic hospitality – there were still the associated spiritual and strategic benefits that properly given and received hospitality brought. The reciprocity of hospitality became legally defined and was used to foster and further develop relationships between the states of the time.

Domestic food consumption patterns generally centred on the provision of a light breakfast, normally a snack in the streets as they went about their business, a light lunch eaten at home or bought from the street vendors; for the higher classes usually in the cool of the bathhouse. Dinner was considered the most important meal, and almost a reward for the day's toil and would normally be eaten in a restaurant. Commodities and quantities eaten varied according to ritual and these were based on social standing, income, age and gender. Slaves were widely and cheaply used (but well-fed) and patronage of early forms of popular catering was the norm for the free citizens. For these people, living accommodation typically did not have the basic utilities required to permit safe domestic preparation and consumption. Large hospitable meals were a preoccupation of the upper classes; these meals took place in the home, public buildings and indeed commercial establishments. The lower echelons of society would aspire to attend banquets and would try to obtain the patronage of the elite.

The lifestyle, culture and consumption conclusions derived from the evidence provided from the examination of hospitality writings and tangible archaeological finds (with the attached importance of the proximity of associated facilities) indicates that the provision and consumption of hospitality in the Roman world was indeed regarded as a mark of civilisation. Commercial motives were evident in both the organisation of facilities and advertising efforts, menus of the day, etc. Early entertainments and events were highly organised activities, central to the leisure of the day and given prime geographical location to emphasise this importance. The skills involved in organising these mass spectacles are not to be overlooked. Pompeii in its role as a centre of leisure would have attracted and required the best hospitality employees that the Empire could offer, in order to maintain and improve its reputation. It was ultimately a place for mercantile and leisure activities with a correspondingly well developed and sophisticated commercial hospitality provision.

Although hospitality was still closely linked to its domestic roots, formal eating and feasting often moved to commercial hospitality establishments, partly due to many houses not having kitchen facilities. However, frequently, commercial establishments were homes that had been private houses and the bar owners often lived in a room above the bar. In some ways, commercial hospitality inverted the traditional domestic roles and men became famous chefs. As well as chefs the development of gendered hospitality roles included women working in the commercial hospitality sector.

In the cities, the centres of consumption, consumers demonstrated lifestyle perspectives by virtue of their engagements in the many aspects of hospitality, including symbolic hospitality, food and eating rituals. The hospitality process was much wider than the narrow product expectations of food, drink and accommodation. It included inherent symbolism centred on the idea that food and eating is an art form that punctuates everyday life.

6 Through the Middle Ages towards the Renaissance

The fall of the Roman Empire was to mark the beginning of the end of Classical Antiquity (for the timeline see page 7). It was also to mark the foundation of the Western monastic tradition and the beginning of the Middles ages that would eventually lead to the period known as the Renaissance. This chapter first considers the end of Classical Antiquity and then by way of summary, identifies the Five Dimensions of Hospitality, which have been determined from the literature of the previous five chapters. To mark the end of the Classical Antiquity period and to provide a foundation for the thematic exploration of charitable hospitality in Chapter 7 and monastic hospitality in Chapter 8, the chapter ends with a brief exploration of the Middle Ages up to the Renaissance.

6.1 Towards the end of Classical Antiquity

Throughout Classical Antiquity, hospitality was regarded as a fundamental moral practice; hospitality assured strangers at least a minimum of provision, protection and connection with the larger community. It also sustained the normal network of relationships on which a community depended, enriching moral and social bonds among family, friends and neighbours. It was necessary for the well-being of mankind and essential to the protection of vulnerable strangers.

It is not unsurprising that hospitality was to become a distinctive feature of the early Christian church. This was due to two principal reasons: it was in keeping with the general continuity with Hebrew understandings of hospitality that associated it with God, covenant and blessing; and partly in contrast to Hellenistic and Roman practices, which associated it with benefit and reciprocity. However, as has been shown in Chapter 4 and 5, Greek and Roman views of benevolence and hospitality stressed formal reciprocal obligations between benefactor and recipient. Because a grateful response from the beneficiary was key to the ongoing relationship, the tradition emphasised the worthiness and goodness of recipients rather than their need; relations were often calculated to benefit the benefactor. This is different from the hospitality that was practised by Christ; therefore, the practice of Christian hospitality is always located within the larger picture of his sacrificial welcome, to all who come to him. Christian hospitality was to turn that practice upside down – hospitality towards the weakest, those least likely to be able to reciprocate, was to become the practice.

Towards the end of Classical Antiquity, domestic hospitality was still held to be a personal duty – the head of the household would not delegate the duty to slaves, although they could carry out some of the laborious tasks. Hospitality in the home must be genuine and freely offered. Civic hospitality was to give rise to a growth of a hospitality network based around the churches and mutual bonds of hospitality between the churches. At the same time, the nature of the hospitality was to change in style. Charitable hospitality for the sick and pilgrims gives rise to organised, community-based hospitality networks. When Christians began to have organised communities with their own buildings, hospitality became a community practice. Hospitality was transferred from the house to various institutions which dealt with: the physical needs of the guest, whether stranger, travelling Christian or local peasant, and hosting and edification of the local assembly. The fall of the Roman Empire was to lead to the significant decline of the commercial hospitality industry as the unity of the empire was shattered. Monastic hospitality began to replace some forms of commercial hospitality because the industry had significantly declined after the break-up of the Roman Empire and the subsequent reduction in the need to travel.

Two areas are key in hospitality provision in late Classical Antiquity: treatment of guests and management practice. Sensitivity must be shown to the guests and their needs, they are to receive a cordial welcome, be led into the centre of community life, and given the opportunity to eat as honoured guests; the needs of the guests are of paramount importance. Everyone has to be treated with kindness, but not all are to receive equal treatment, i.e. greater honour is due to some, discrimination is based on ontological being; those who have configured themselves to be more like Christ have to be treated better – this could be reflected in a hierarchy of accommodation.

Hospitality should not be abused: it is a gift to be treasured by the guest who receives it; the guest must not abuse the host. Free hospitality should only be offered for a limited time, two or three days, those who wish to stay longer must not be idle; if they have a trade or be an artisan they must use their skills for the good of the community, thus the reciprocal nature of hospitality is again underlined. Those who abused the generosity of their host or breached hospitality in any way, were strongly and repeatedly condemned.

The principal motivations for Christian hospitality were Christological, humane, and eschatological; these were to guide and inform their hospitality practices. Within early Christian hospitality, and subsequently within Monastic hospitality (as discussed later in Chapter 8), there is tension between anchoritic informality and coenobitic order. There is a deeper polarity between monastic otherness and welcoming guests from the world from which the monks have distanced themselves. By leaving secular society, the monk sets up an alternative, if overlapping world, in which other people wish to share. At some point, too much sharing will destroy the very otherness which people admire, so care must be taken to avoid falsifying hospitality. The monk, by definition is one who has become a *xenos*, a stranger to the world. Hospitality within a monastery is welcoming but restrictive; this is not in any way intended to be disrespectful towards the guests, it has the intention not to falsify the hospitality that is offered.

The followers of Jesus did not expect earthly rewards for their hospitable actions, but expected metaphysical advantages after death. The early Christians would have been familiar with the theological anthropology of the Old Testament; Adam and Eve were guests in the Garden of Eden, humanity is a guest in God's creation. Mankind is a guest and stranger in the created order and therefore should be hospitable to fellow guests and strangers. Hospitality was seen as a societal need, something human beings owed to each other. This lead to the eschatological motivation, where those who are inhospitable to strangers here on earth, jeopardise their hopes of receiving hospitality in heaven.

The home was the primary location for hospitality, and a great deal of the practices of civic and commercial hospitality evolved from it. Encapsulated in the Christological motivation for hospitality was that in receiving strangers, one received Christ; this was an echo of Abraham, who did not know the identity of the strangers he received, nor did he ask, he received whoever came; the emphasis was placed on welcoming people into their space. Jesus himself was quite open to the world around him, especially to those who found themselves ostracised and marginalised by society. Despite the underlying ideal of domestic hospitality of being non-judgemental and open to all, society had become stratified to such an extent that people did discriminate.

Whereas the meal customs of Jesus were symbolic of this entire attitude; he accepted hospitality from the unacceptable. However he was eating, Jesus often chose to be hospitable to those who were alienated by society; his actions were a way of giving support to the estranged and protection to the vulnerable, both classical tenants of hospitality. Hospitality was held to be a moral practice, in which personal sacrifice was required for the sake of the guest, it was not enough to rely on third parties to carry out hospitable acts.

The treatment of guests often followed a ritualised pattern of welcome. After the welcome, the stranger became the guest and then the guest became a friend. The motivations that governed the performance of Christian hospitality caused the following characteristics that can be seen as central to early Christian hospitality: zeal, duty, sacrifice, courtesy, attentiveness and universality. The performance of hospitality emphasised sincerity and if hospitality was not offered and given in a sincere manner, it counted for nothing. Hospitality still had as the central purpose of providing food, drink and accommodation; however, there was a greater emphasis of meeting the spiritual needs of the guest.

Hospitality offered in the home was still indiscriminate and welcoming to all. The ideal behind religious hospitality was that the host should welcome the guest as if welcoming them into the house of God. In this way God was seen as the ultimate host, whereas in the past, the gods were also held as the ultimate guests. Civic and commercial principles already existed; Hospitality based around the home follows a symbolic transition that takes the visitor from stranger to guest to friend. Hospitality often focus on the relief of homelessness – however, this creates the paradox that without an actual home hospitality is impossible.

6.2 Identifying the Five Dimensions of Hospitality

This chapter together with Chapters 4 and 5 has presented explorations of the origins of hospitality, mainly within the Greek and Roman civilisations of the ancient and classical worlds, and also in the contemporaneous religious writings discussed in Chapter 3. From the exploration, clear parallels have been found between the texts, and a variety of common features of hospitality have been identified. Further evaluation of these outcomes leads to the identification of Five Dimensions of Hospitality.

Honourable tradition

Hospitality is initially concerned with the protection of others in order to be protected from others. Additionally within the ancient and classical worlds, often reinforced by religious teaching and practice, hospitality is considered as an inherently good thing to provide, without any immediate expectation of an earthly reward. The vocational nature of hospitality is established through the concept of the provision of hospitality as paying homage to a superior being, or pursuing a higher ideal. This may provide a basis for the view that hospitality management should be recognised as a true profession because of its strong vocational origins. Even with this vocational influence, the concept of reciprocity – monetary, spiritual, or exchange – is already well established, as is the concept of failure in providing hospitality being viewed as both an impiety and a temporal crime.

Fundamental to human existence

Hospitality is a primary feature in the development of the societies that have been considered. It is an essential part of human existence, especially as it deals with basic human needs (food, drink, shelter and security). It is also clear that the concept of the hospitality is being based on meeting the needs that the guests have at the time, rather than the type of people that they are, is already established. Relationships between households and friends were developed through mutual hospitality between the original partners, and then subsequently given to their descendants, and their wider circle of friends. This also establishes the concepts of loyalty systems and continuing shared benefits.

Stratified

Hospitality has never been homogeneous. Since the earliest time, hospitality provision is increasingly codified. As the societies become more sophisticated, the codification of hospitality provides reference points for how to treat a range of guests/strangers, according to a variety of criteria. Typologies of hospitality also become apparent: private, civic, and business/commercial. Other features identified, which increasingly become more formal as the societies develop, include legal governance, more sophisticated approaches to codification, and the establishment of contractual relationships. Hospitality professionals emerge as civic and business hospitality develops, with particular individuals being recognised as having formal and defined responsibilities for hospitality.

Diversified

The needs of the host and the guest have always varied; hospitality therefore has always had to be able to respond to a broad range of needs. The exploration of the ancient and classical worlds shows that the basis for a diverse range of types of establishments in order to meet the needs of the full spectrum of society is already developing. Although originally at lower levels, the provision of higher levels of hospitality establishment and service is a direct consequence of the ability of the higher classes to afford to travel to lands where they are not known, but it enables them to be in environments which are commensurate with their wealth and status, without the need to establish a household there.

Central to human endeavour

Since the beginning of human history, hospitality is the mechanism that has been central to the development of the societies, at both the individual and collective levels. It is the catalyst that is used to facilitate human activities, especially those that are aimed at enhancing civilisation. It is also identified as being the central feature of human endeavour and celebration, through until the end of time.

By way of summary, the Five Dimensions of Hospitality are given in Table 6.1 together with the principal aspects of each Dimension:

Table 6.1: Five Dimensions of Hospitality

A   Honourable tradition
◊   The concepts of guest, stranger, and host are closely related
◊   Hospitality is seen as essentially organic, revealing much about the cultural values and beliefs of the societies
◊   Reciprocity of hospitality is an established principle
◊   Providing hospitality is paying homage to the gods – a worthy and honourable thing to do – and failure is condemned in both the human and spiritual worlds
B   Fundamental to human existence
◊   Hospitality includes food, drink and accommodation and also is concerned with the approach to be adopted, e.g. welcoming, respectful and genuine
◊   Hospitality is offered and the extent or limitation of it is based on the needs and the purpose of the guests/strangers
◊   Alliances are initially developed through hospitality between friends, households and states, and are strengthened through continuing mutual hospitality

◊ Hospitality once granted between individuals, households and states is also granted to descendants and through extended friendships

C   Stratified

◊ Developments in the societies lead to the formal stratification of hospitality: the codification of hospitality being based on whether it was private, civic or business, and on the needs and purpose of the guest/stranger, and their nature or status

◊ Reciprocity of hospitality becomes legally defined

◊ Civic and business hospitality develops from private hospitality but retains the key foundations – treat others as if in their own home

◊ Hospitality management, in the civic and business sense, is established as being centred on persons responsible for formal hospitality, and also for the protection of the guest/stranger and ensuring their proper conduct.

D   Diversified

◊ Places of hospitality were initially differentiated primarily by the existence, or not, of overnight accommodation

◊ Individual places of hospitality either offer associated services, or are located near other places of hospitality

◊ Originally places of hospitality are for the lower classes that did not have established networks of hospitality enjoyed by the higher classes

◊ Increasing travelling amongst the higher classes created demands for superior levels of places of hospitality

E   Central to human endeavour

◊ Hospitality is a vital and integral part of the societies

◊ Shared hospitality is a principal feature in the development and continuation of friendships and alliances between persons, between communities, and between nations

◊ Hospitality is the focus for the celebrations of significant private, civic and business events and achievements throughout life

◊ Hospitality is also foreseen as a principal feature until the end of time

It is clear that the Five Dimensions of Hospitality identified so far, have been evolving since the beginning of human history. It also seems that it is inherent in human nature to offer hospitality, and that the societies, and the contemporaneous religious teachings, support and reinforce this trait. The identification of the Five Dimensions of Hospitality provides one way of interpreting the outcomes of the exploration that has been undertaken to date. Whatever the approach that might be used, it is certainly evident that hospitality has a long history, a honourable tradition, and a rich heritage.

6.3   The Middle Ages

The period of European history, from around the 5th century AD, to the beginnings of the Renaissance in the 15th century AD, has become known as the Middle Ages; and things of that period known as mediaeval. The term was probably first used by Flavio Biondo of Forlí, a historian and apostolic secretary in Rome, in his *Historiarum ab Inclinatione Romanorum Imperii Decades* (*Decades of History from the Deterioration of the Roman Empire*, 1483).

The Early Middle Ages

For the period known as the Early Middle Ages there is little literature. From what is known life had become relatively uncivilized following the fall of the Roman Empire (AD 476). For some 300 years, Western Europe was to consist of range of primitive cultures. Although various tribes came together to form kingdoms, which also provided the basis for the development of the feudal system, there was no real government as had existed in Roman times. The only major Western European institution was the Christian Church. Even though the Bishop of Rome, the Pope, initially had some pre-eminence, the majority of power was in the hands of local bishops. During this time however, it was in the monasteries where the recording and codification of knowledge was being undertaken, alongside the religious orders focussing on the standardisation of the liturgical rite, the calendar, and the principles of monastic rule.

By the 9th century, with the rise to power of the Carolingians (dynasty of Frankish kings who ruled a collection of territories in Western Europe from the 7th to the 10th centuries AD), the beginnings of a new European unity were founded. This dynasty was based on Roman traditions, much of which had been consolidated during the reign of the Emperor Charlemagne (AD 768-814).

The great households of Europe, whether they were ecclesial or not, were responsible for providing hospitality; the level of hospitality usually being governed by the status of the guest. Bishops have always enjoyed and enjoined a role in overseeing hospitality and directing poor relief. This has its basis in the New Testament 'A bishop then must be blameless, the husband of one wife, vigilant, sober, of good behaviour, given to hospitality, apt to teach' (1 Timothy 3:2). When St Augustine was sent to be the first Archbishop of Canterbury (AD 595), he corresponded with Pope Gregory on a great number of affairs. St Bede the Venerable, in his work *Ecclesiastical History of the English Nation*, records the correspondence between Augustine and Pope Gregory regarding how a Bishop was to run his household.

> *The First Question of Augustine, Bishop of the Church of Canterbury. Concerning bishops, how they are to behave themselves towards their clergy? Or into how many portions the things given by the faithful to the altar are to be divided? And how the bishop is to act in the church?*
>
> *Gregory, Pope of the City of Rome, answers. Holy Writ, which no doubt you are well versed in, testifies, and particularly St. Paul's Epistle to Timothy, wherein he endeavours to instruct him how he should behave himself in the house of God; but it is the custom of the apostolic see to prescribe rules to bishops newly ordained, that all emoluments which accrue, are to he divided into four portions; one for the bishop and his family, because of hospitality and entertainments; another for the clergy; a third for the poor; and the fourth for the repair of churches.*
>
> (Bede, Book I, Chapter 27)

The bishop's special role, is also emphasised by St Isidore, Bishop of Seville, in the early 7th century: 'A layman has fulfilled the duty of hospitality by receiving one or two; a bishop, however, unless he shall receive everyone ... is inhuman' (Isidore, *Patrologiae Latina* LXXXIII.786).

At the beginning of 10th century, new migrations and invasions were to take place, such as those of the Vikings from the north and the Magyars from Asia. The violence and dislocation of the times led to a reduction in land cultivation and the decline of populations. Moves towards European unity and expansion were weakened, and the monasteries became significant as the custodians of civilisation. Prior to this new period of unrest, cultural activity had been concentrated on recording and codifying the knowledge of the past. Encyclopaedic works, such as *Etymologiarum, seu Originum Libri XX* (*Twenty Books of Etymologies*, or *Origins*, AD 623) by St Isidore, which attempted to present the collected knowledge of humankind, had already been compiled and preserved.

The High Middle Ages

From the middle of the 10th century, Western Europe experienced the growth of a more settled population with town life, trade and commerce, and society became more developed. This was also the period of intellectual and cultural development. New educational institutions, such as cathedral and monastic schools, were founded, and universities were established with advanced degrees being offered in medicine, law, and theology. Literacy increased beyond the clergy, the subjects of literature broadened, painting styles developed, and the Romanesque style for architecture was perfected and moves towards the Gothic style had been established.

Within the Roman Catholic Church, the Decretum of Gratian (compiled just after the second Lateran Council in 1152) formed the basis of Canon Law in the Church; and was to do so until AD 1917. The Pope became recognised as its unequivocal head, and the Church was, through its elaborate hierarchy and extensive geographical coverage, to become the most sophisticated governing institution in Western Europe. The Papacy not only affected political control over the lands of central and northern Italy, it also exercised a directive power throughout Western Europe. Alongside these developments, the monastic orders grew and flourished, and also became more involved with the secular world. The Benedictine monasteries had become recognised as integral parts of feudal communities and alliances, together with those of the newer orders, such as the Cistercians (1098) and later the Franciscans (1208). However, hospitality was not forgotten. Within the Decretum of Gratin there was also a section dedicated to hospitality and the role of a bishop. In this section, it makes clear, that if any priest is found to be lacking in hospitality, he cannot be ordained a bishop (Gratian, Distinctio XLII). Tierney, in his work on the Medieval Poor Laws, notes the very close connection between clerical hospitality and the relief of the poor:

> The word 'hospitality' is of some importance because the phrase most commonly used by the medieval canonists to describe the poor relief responsibilities of the parish clergy was tenere hospitalitatem – they were obliged, that is, to 'keep hospitality'. The primary sense of the word referred to the reception of travellers, the welcoming of guests, but the canonists very often used it in a broader sense to include almsgiving and poor relief in general.
>
> (Tierney, 1959, p. 68)

During the 13th century the achievements of the 12th were codified and synthesized. The monarchical Church had become a great pan-European institution, and trade and commerce were supporting the economic unity of Europe. Travel, whether for pilgrimage, trade, or study, became easier and more common. The High Middle Ages also culminated in the great cultural achievements of Gothic architecture, and the imaginative vision of the totality of human life in, for example, Dante Alighieri's La divina commedia (The Divine Comedy, AD 1321) and the philosophic works of the Dominican monk

St Thomas Aquinas (1225-1274). He was a prolific author who combined Aristotelian science and Augustinian theology into a comprehensive system of thought that later became the authoritative philosophy of the Roman Catholic Church. He wrote on every known subject in philosophy and science and has about 80 works attributed to him the most famous being his *Summa Theologica* (*Summary Treatise of Theology*, 1265-1273).

The Late Middle Ages

During the Late Middle Ages the struggle for supremacy between Church and state became a central feature of European history. Towns and cities, which were continuing to grow in size and prosperity, began to strive for political self-control, and the urban conflict also became internal with various social classes, trade guilds, and interest groups vying for control. This period was also to see the emergence of the secular state in its own right, independent of the Church or community of believers. This consequence of the independence of social and political enquiry and thinking, brought to an end the endeavour of High Mediaeval philosophy, which had been an attempt to reach a synthesis of all human and spiritual knowledge and experience.

According to Kerr (2002) hospitality emerged in the High Middle Ages as a commonly accepted criterion of judgement, to receive guests is commendable, to be held in high esteem, you must be considered a good host. This is applied universally, whether to countries, towns or individuals, nobles, prelates or monastic communities. Illustrative examples would include Gerald of Wales (1146–1223) who notes the praiseworthy hospitality of the Welsh (Dimock, 1876). Robertson (1875) gives the examples of St. Thomas à Becket (1118–1170) was esteemed for his lavish and cheerful hospitality, and William FitzStephens (Biographer and contemporary of St Thomas à Becket) who listed amongst the virtues of Londoners their entertainment of strangers, their spread of feasts and cheering of guests. Abbess Euphemia of Wherwell, Hampshire (1226–57), was held in high esteem for her diligence in administering hospitality and charity (Kerr, 2002). However extravagant hospitality was also being criticised. William of Malmesbury (1090–1143) argued that hospitality should not be excessive and criticises those whom have resorted to prodigality (Mynors *et al.*, 1998). Roy Strong, in his book *Feast* (2003) makes reference to the overwhelming magnitude of some types of religious hospitality, observing, in particular, the scale of numbers involved in the coronation feast of Pope Clement VI at Avignon on 19 May 1344.

A hundred and eighteen cows, one thousand and twenty-three sheep, one hundred and one calves, nine hundred and fourteen kids, sixty pigs, sixty-eight barrels of lard and salted meat, fifteen sturgeon, three hundred pike, fifteen hundred capons, three thousand and forty-three fowls (poulets), seven thousand four hundred and twenty-eight chickens, one thousand four hundred and forty-six geese and fifty thousand tarts using three thousand two hundred and fifty eggs. For the same event three hundred jugs, five thousand five hundred pitchers, two thousand five hundred glass flagons, five thousand glasses and two thousand six hundred écuelles (drinking bowls) were hired. And in addition the pope co-opted all the cardinals' cooks and eighty boys to fetch water and serve.

(Strong, 2003, p. 88)

Thomas, Cardinal Wolsey, Chancellor of England, Archbishop of York, and successor of St Augustine, also seems to have taken the concept of religious hospitality to excess and beyond. Cardinal Wolsey's gentleman-usher, George Cavendish, gives an account, of dining in the cardinal's household, an example of conspicuous consumption:

Now to speak of the ordering of his household and offices, I think it necessary here to be remembered; first you shall understand that he had in his hall, daily three special tables furnished with three principal officers. That is to say, a Steward, who was always a doctor or a priest; a Treasurer, a knight; and a Comptroller, an esquire; these always carried their white staves within his house. Then had he a cofferer, three marshals, two yeomen ushers, two grooms, and an almoner. He had also in the hall-kitchen two clerks of his kitchen, a clerk-controller, a surveyor of the dresser, a clerk of his spicery. Also in his hall-kitchen he had two master cooks, and twelve other labourers and children, as they called them; a yeoman of his scullery, with two others in his silver scullery; two yeomen of his pantry, and two grooms.

Now in his private kitchen he had a master cook who went daily in damask, satin, or velvet, with a chain of gold about his neck; and two grooms with six labourers and children to serve that place; in the Larder there, a yeoman and a groom; in the Scalding-house, a yeoman and two grooms; in the Scullery there, two persons; in the Buttery, two yeomen and two grooms with two other pages; in the Pantry, two yeomen, two grooms, and two pages; and in the Ewery likewise; in the Cellar, three yeomen, two grooms, and two pages - beside a gentleman for the month; in the Chaundery, three persons; in the Wafery...

And in his chamber, all these persons; that is to say, his High Chamberlain; his Vice-Chamberlain; twelve gentlemen-ushers, daily waiters – besides two in his private chamber; and of gentlemen-waiters in his private chamber he had six; and also he had of lords nine or ten. ... Then had he of gentlemen, as cupbearers, carvers, sewers, and gentlemen daily-waiters, forty persons; of yeomen ushers he had six; of grooms in his chamber he had eight; of yeomen of his chamber he had forty-six daily to attend upon his person; he also had a priest there, who was his almoner, to attend upon his table at dinner.

(Cavendish, 1962, pp. 46-48)

Although hospitality being given in excess at one end of the spectrum, it was also being forgotten about at the other. At local level the clergy were working with minimal resources. In his work *Medieval Poor Law*, Tierney (1959) gives examples of exhortations in providing adequate hospitality and relief, emphasising that pastoral care includes the feeding of the hungry and also the reception of guests. Parishioners were expected, but not forced, to pay tithes to the church from which funds for hospitality and relief for the poor were taken. The clergy were required to provide hospitality, but the record of their work was mixed: In many parishes the clergy were simply absent.

Spirituality in the Late Middle Ages was also to register the social and cultural turmoil of the age. Heightened awareness brought with it a realisation that the Church, as an all-encompassing and worldly mediaeval institution, had become different from the original simplicity of the Church of Christ and the Apostles. Using the life of Christ as a model to be imitated, apostolic communities were formed. Two examples of these were to be The Brethren of the Common Life (AD 1376) and the (reformed) Spiritual Franciscans or Order of Friars Minor (AD 1517). These and other groups proliferated throughout Europe. Sometimes these groups focussed on the reform the Church from within, and sometimes they simply disengaged from it.

After the plague of the 1340s (which became known as the Black Death), that had killed nearly one third of the population of Europe, bands of penitents, flagellants, and followers of new messiahs and charismatic 'saints' could be found throughout Europe. Throughout this period the established Church found itself challenged and often marginalised. This process of spiritual unrest and innovation would end in the Protestant Reformation. New national identities would lead to the establishment of the modern, and secular, nation-state, and the continual expansion of trade and finance would contribute to the transformation of the European economy. The

Protestant Reformation itself was most manifest in British Isles, with the dissolution of the monasteries (brought about by the Acts of 1536 and 1539), which effectively ended monastic hospitality in Britain for a period of some 350 years. This event though, did not happen in isolation. In Germany and her Austrian dominions, the Treaty of Westphalia saw the confiscation of religious property to the benefit of Protestant princes, and in later centuries a similar situation was to arise throughout the Iberian peninsula, in France, and what would be considered modern day Italy.

The Protestant reformers were also attempting to redefine the practice of hospitality. They offered unrelenting critiques of the extravagance, indulgence, and waste associated with late medieaval hospitality. Heal (1990) emphasises that the clergy also were part of the ruling class, and had a particular role to play in affairs of state. Cardinal Wolsey was a bishop, but he was also King Henry VIII's Lord Chancellor, therefore his extravagance would have been expected as the King's principal minister. According to Pohl (1999) Luther and Calvin in their studies of Scripture, gave limited but explicit attention to hospitality and to how it should be practised in their own day. One of the beliefs of the Reformation was that there was supposedly an enhanced appreciation for the value of so-called ordinary life. The Protestant reformers did not see, in the ancient sources, an apposite understanding of the Church as an important location for hospitality; instead, they identified hospitality within the civic and the domestic spheres. Pohl (1999, p. 53) states that 'the sacramental character of hospitality was diminished and it became mostly an ordinary but valued expression of human care'. The Protestant Reformation consequently was to have a transforming effect on religious hospitality, hospitals, poor relief, and responsibility to refugees. These activities became separated from their Christian roots as the state increasingly took over more responsibility. Pohl confirms this by stating that 'At the same time, the domestic sphere became more privatised; households became smaller, more intimate, and less able or willing to receive strangers. With little attention to the church as a key site for hospitality, the institutional settings for Christian hospitality diminished and the understanding of hospitality as a significant dimension of church practice nearly disappeared' (1999, p. 53).

However the Catholic Church and the Counter Reformation within, was emphasising the importance of hospitality. In its 25th solemn session, the Council of Trent (which was convened in Trent, circa 1540, and in other towns for a period of about 40 years), decreed as a doctrine of faith 'all who hold any ecclesiastical benefices, whether secular or regular, to accustom themselves, as far as their revenues will allow, to exercise with alacrity and kindness the office of hospitality, so frequently commended by the holy Fathers; being mindful that those who cherish hospitality receive Christ in the person of their guests' (Tanner, 1990).

Towards the Renaissance

At the end of the 14th century the period, which was to become known as the Renaissance (or rebirth), had begun in Italy and was to spread to the rest of Western Europe by the 16th and 17th centuries. The Renaissance was a period of European history that saw a renewed interest in the arts and in the classical past. During this period the fragmented feudal society of the Middle Ages was transformed into one which was increasingly dominated by central political institutions, had an urban and commercial economy, and had lay patronage of education, the arts, and music.

The progress and achievements of the thousand years of the Mediaeval World had certainly established the solid foundations from which the Renaissance was to grow and flourish. In particular the monasteries had provided the blueprints for hospitality, the care of the sick and the poor, and responsibilities for refugees, which were to be adopted later within the nation-states and in secular organisations. The monasteries had also been the custodians of civilisation during the various periods of unrest during the Middle Ages. The *scriptoria* (writing rooms) of the mediaeval monasteries had been the centres for the production of copies of the works of Latin writers, such as Virgil, Ovid, Cicero, and Seneca. The legal system, which was to be the foundation of those adopted by the later nation-states, had its origin in the development of the civil and canon law of 12th and 13th centuries.

Whereas the mediaeval scholars had believed that they were living in the final age before the last judgment, and had considered the Greek and Roman Worlds as simply pagan, the Renaissance authors explored the rich history of the ancient and classical worlds, considered the Middle Ages as ignorant and barbaric, and proclaimed their own age as being the enlightened rebirth of Classicism. One of the most significant changes that had also emerged was the establishment of the humanist movement: history was to become a branch of literature rather than of theology and the critical analysis of the religious texts was to be undertaken with a secular view of history.

7 Charitable Hospitality

This chapter focuses on hospitality for the needy and considers how throughout history, even when religion is subjugated, there has always been recognition of the importance of hospitality *in necessitudine* or charitable hospitality. A brief historical summary is presented of the Abrahamic model of hospitality, which is shared by the three monothematic religions of Judaism, Christianity and Islam. It concludes by reflecting on the constantly evolving religious practice of providing hospitality to those in most need, through exploring this aspect of hospitality, which is often overlooked in the current hospitality management literature.

7.1 The Abrahamic model of hospitality

In the story of Abraham, there is the classic domestic hospitality event. Where Abraham and Sarah show gracious receptiveness to three strangers at their home and oasis among the 'Oaks of Mamre'. This story is actually the occasion of God's appearance (a 'theophany') in anthropomorphic disguise; this is done to protect the host in response to the dictum of Exodus 33:20 'see God and you die!' The occasion of hospitality has become the occasion of divine visitation and revelation. Abraham is central to any religious comprehension of hospitality; for example all three great monotheistic traditions consider his behaviour as the ideal model of hospitality. The following pericope is taken from the Torah, or the Christian Book of Genesis, (18:2–8) and parallels to this text are in the Qur'ān (15:51; 51:24):

> *Abraham looked up and saw three men standing nearby. He quickly left the entrance to his tent to meet them. He bowed low to the ground. He said, 'My lord, if you are pleased with me, don't pass me by. Let a little water be brought. All of you can wash your feet and rest under this tree. Let me get you something to eat to give you strength. Then you can go on your way. I want to do this for you now that you have come to me.' 'All right', they answered. 'Go ahead and do it'. So Abraham hurried into the tent to Sarah.*

Plate 7.1: Trinity by Andrei Rublev 15th Century Icon depicting the three angels who visited Abraham at the oak of Mamre. Source: Wikimedia Commons.

'Quick!' he said. 'Get about half a bushel of fine flour. Mix it and bake some bread.' Then he ran to the herd. He picked out a choice, tender calf. He gave it to a servant, who hurried to prepare it. Then he brought some butter and milk and the calf that had been prepared. He served them to the three men.'

This quote describes Abraham (Abraham in the Judaeo-Christian tradition and Ibrahim in the Islamic tradition) rushing from the door of his tent to meet the three visitors and bowing down before them in greeting. However when Abraham greets the strangers in this way, he was not making a gesture of religious adoration, but simply showing respect. At first, Abraham sees his guests as humans, as their superhuman character is only gradually revealed. He welcomes them warmly and invites them into his tent, to rest a bit and to eat a little, however, Abraham had a full course banquet prepared for them.

The Jewish commentaries (*midrash*) on the text elaborate aspects of Abraham's hospitality. A fairly common technique in *midrash* is to expand amounts and numbers when they help to make a point, for example, one account states that Sarah made honey cakes and other delicacies or Abraham slaughtered three calves so that each of the guests could have tongue and mustard sauce. In another example records that flour used to make the bread is further specified to be fine flour. A further tradition was that Abraham so enjoyed entertaining guests that he established a guesthouse in order that more travellers would stop. What is emphasised in all of these stories is the unconditional hospitality offered by Abraham and Sarah to their guests in their home. Yet as generous as Abraham's hospitality might have been, the scriptures compare his behaviour with a society that was literally the antithesis of everything he represented; the cities of Sodom and Gomorrah were infamous, amongst other things, for their cruelty, greed and inhospitableness to strangers and travellers.

Later (Qur'ān 11:78-82; Genesis 19:1–9) when the strangers journeyed to Sodom and Gomorrah, in search of a righteous man, Abraham's nephew welcomes the messengers and pleads with them to stay. Lut (or Lot in the Judaeo-Christian tradition) and his family were set apart to be saved. When the men of Sodom riot outside his house, demanding that the strangers be delivered into their hands, Lut opposes them: 'Guard against (the punishment of) Allah,' he urges them, 'and do not disgrace me with regard to my guests; is there not among you one right-minded man?' (Qur'ān 11:78). His generous hospitality helps protect him from the judgement visited on Sodom so graphically described in the same chapter: 'We turned them upside down and rained down upon them stones, of what had been decreed, one after another' (Qur'ān 11:82). Lut was deemed to be a good man, for he alone imitated Abraham's behaviour of hospitality.

There has always been a strong tradition of hospitality in the eastern Islamic world, based on earlier traditions often traced back to Ibrahim. Ibrahim is considered the first true Muslim and seen as a role model for hospitality, sharing of food makes the guest a temporary member of the host's family. Ibrahim became terrified when his guests' hands could not reach the food (Qur'ān 51:23), for the sharing of food normally proves that the guest's intentions are not hostile; in the case of Ibrahim his guests were divine messengers. Eating together confers both rights and duties; for example the host must protect the guests as if they were members of the host's family. Even in recent times, this hospitable relationship has been established through the sharing of bread and salt, and it lasts for two days and the intervening night, traditionally referred to as three days.

An Islamic tradition handed down by the Persian poets tells how Abraham, not wishing to eat alone, once sought to share his meal with an old man he met in the desert. When the time came to pray, he realized that his guest was a Zoroastrian and wanted to send him away. But an angel restrained Abraham, saying, 'God has fed this man for a hundred years, how could you refuse him a meal?' (Richard, 1990) Zoroastrianism is the oldest of the revealed world religions, and it has probably had more influence on mankind, directly and indirectly, than any other single faith. Zoroastrians are also linked to the birth of Christianity and indeed to the birth of Jesus: it is the Magi, the Zoroastrian priests or Wise Men from the East, who attended his birth of Christ in the New Testament.

In the Old Testament, there is the evolving relationship of God with his chosen people Israel and thus the whole of humanity. In the context of hospitality, there is the relationship of a divine host to his human guests; that the whole of mankind, is a guest in the host's house; the host's house is the created world, and these tests were held to be the history of creation. The challenge, placed before Israel in the Old Testament's covenant laws, is to live out in daily life, this understanding of being fellow guests in the Promised Land, after its occupation. Abraham, the father of the Jewish faith, is central to Old Testament hospitality; he shows unreserved hospitality to the strangers, only later does he see the true nature of his guest.

The hospitality portrayed in the Bible was centred on the household; however, it also has a universal application. It allowed the individuals to connect to the wider community, and just like Solon (most famous of all the Ancient Greek lawgivers who placed great importance upon hospitality, see Chapter 4, page 61), Jesus entertained in houses, through this act, he endeavoured to transform those who had been rejected by society through hospitality.

7.2 Hospitality to those in *necessitudine*

Throughout the last 2000 years the biblical instruction to be hospitable has been interpreted and developed in different ways, often at the forefront of medical as well as spiritual advances in hospitality. This began with the letter of St Paul to an apostolic delegate sent to oversee the Church in Ephesus. (1 Timothy 1:3 – the letter is datable to the year 60 or shortly thereafter if it is not by Paul's hand or dictation.) The instruction in the letter is: 'A bishop then must be blameless, faithful, vigilant, sober, of good behaviour, given to hospitality' (1 Timothy 3:2). Thus, the Bishop, as 'overseer' of the local Church, has been mandated from the beginning of the Christian faith to charitable hospitality.

The *Didache* or *The Teaching of the Twelve Apostles*, which is a manual governing community life probably codified in about AD 150, gives a clear indication on the reception of guests and how long they can expect to receive the public hospitality of the village or town.

> *Receive everyone who comes in the name of the Lord… If he who comes is a wayfarer, assist him as far as you are able; but he shall not remain with you more than two or three days, if need be. But if he wants to stay with you, and is an artisan, let him work and eat. But if he has no trade, according to your understanding, see to it that, as a Christian, he shall not live with you idle.*

> (Didache *12*)

Clement of Alexandria was born in the middle of the second century, probably in Athens, to an aristocratic pagan family. According to Trevijano Etcheverría (1998) he was to receive a traditional education in literature, in keeping with other young intellectuals; he travelled around looking for a mentor to satisfy his inquietudes. He eventually met Pantaenus, a Christian, and he then established the catechetical school of Alexandria. Clement taught that:

> *Akin to love is hospitality, being congenial and devoted to the treatment of strangers. And those are strangers, to whom the things of the world are*

strange… Hospitality, therefore, is occupied in what is useful for strangers; and guests are strangers; and friends are guests; and brethren are friends.
(Clement of Alexandria, The Stromata *2:9)*

Clement was an aristocrat, most probably writing to aristocrats who were unaccustomed to performing manual work or services; he uses the examples of Abraham and Sarah to show that performing physical services to guests, is required of all who live according to the teaching of Christ.

Let us fix our eyes on those who have yielded perfect service to His magnifi-cent glory. Let us take… Abraham, who for his faith and hospitality was called the friend of God… For hospitality and piety, Lot was saved from Sodom… Abraham, who for his free faith was called 'the friend of God,' was not elated by glory, but modestly said, 'I am dust and ashes.'
(Clement of Alexandria, The Stromata *4:17)*

Tertullian, who was the son of a Roman centurion rejected paganism and became a priest of the Church in Carthage. Trevijano Etcheverría (1998) notes that very little is known about his conversion; however, with a certain surety, his writings are dated from AD 196 to AD 212 – interestingly his rhetoric was Ciceronian in style. Tertullian in his *Prescription against Heretics* considers the importance of mutual hospitality between the churches as one of their great bonds of unity:

Therefore the churches, although they are so many and so great… and all are apostolic, whilst they are all proved to be one, in unity, by their peace-ful communion, and title of brotherhood, and bond of hospitality, privileges which no other rule directs than the one tradition of the selfsame mystery.
(Tertullian, De Praescriptione haereticorum, *20)*

On 14 September 258, St Cyprian, Bishop of Carthage, suffered martyr-dom during the persecutions conducted under the authority of Emperor Valerian; the night before he was to enjoy the hospitality of the village he was staying in:

The proconsul Galerius Maximus ordered Cyprian to be reserved for him until the next day… and he stayed… enjoying his hospitality in the village… Thither the whole company of brethren came; and, when the holy Cyprian learned this, he ordered the maidens to be protected, since all had remained in the village before the gate of the hospitable officer.
(Acta Proconsularia Cypriani 1900:25)

According to Trevijano Etcheverría (1998) Origen lived in Alexandra and Caesarea and is considered one of the most prolific Christian writers. In his work *Contra Celsus*, he condemns those who breach hospitality, by 'partaking of a man's table' and then conspiring against their host:

> *Observe also the superficiality and manifest falsity of such a statement of Celsus, when he asserts that he who was partaker of a man's table would not conspire against him; and if he would not conspire against a man, much less would he plot against a God after banqueting with him. For who does not know that many persons, after partaking of the salt on the table, have entered into a conspiracy against their entertainers… numerous instances can be quoted showing that they who shared in the hospitality of others entered into conspiracies against them.*
>
> (Origen, Contra Celsus, 2:21)

History credits Emperor Constantine with the conversion of the Roman Empire to Christianity after his victory, over his stronger rival Maxentius, at the Milvian Bridge on 28 October 312. With Constantine's public support of the church, it became richer and undertook substantial responsibilities not least in hospitality through the care of need. In AD 362, the Emperor Julian was attempting to suppress the Christian Church and reintroduce paganism across the Empire, however, he explicitly urged his governors to maintain the Christian practice of the *xenodochein* or hospice. In a letter to the (pagan) Archpriest Arsacius, he writes:

> *If Hellenism [paganism] is not making the progress it should, the fault is with us who practise it ... Do we not see that what has most contributed to the success of atheism [Christianity] is its charity towards strangers...? Establish numerous hospices in every city, so that strangers may benefit from our charity, not only those of our own number, but anyone else who is in need ... For it is disgraceful that not a single Jew is a mendicant, and that the impious Galileans [Christians] maintain our poor in addition to their own, and our needy are seen to lack assistance from us.*
>
> (Browning, 1975, p. 179)

He then goes on to give the specific command 'Teach those of the Hellenic faith to contribute to public service of this sort.' Thus, in his attempt to reintroduce paganism, Emperor Julian gave clear witness to the significance of Christian institutions, to care for society as a whole. Christians carried on to established many more *xenodochia* in the fourth century, to care for strangers, but particularly for poor strangers who had no other resources, and for the local poor. Gradually these were differentiated into separate institutions according to the type of person in need: orphans, widows, strangers, sick and poor.

Patlagean, the eminent Byzantine historian states that the *xenodochia* lead to 'a social classification built on poor versus rich with poverty not only a material and economic condition, but also a legal and social status'. An arrangement which constituted 'a privileged establishment for the Church' endowing 'it with the means of sustaining the burden of relief which the Byzantine Emperor could henceforth devolve on it' (Patlagean, 1981, p. 71). Mollat (1978), in his study *Les pauvres au Moyen âge*, shows that beggars and travellers were treated by the law as total strangers and therefore did not enjoy protection. Unlike slaves, who were some citizen's property and, as such, enjoyed the protection of the law. The *xenodochia* treated these legal non-persons as legitimate inmates, forcing Emperor Justinian to grant them legal status, sometime around AD 530.

Two fourth-century writers were to articulate the unmistakably Christian concept of hospitality. Lucius Caecilius Firmianus Lactantius was a Christian apologist of the fourth century and was friendly with Emperor Constantine; Constantine raised him from penury and though very old, he was appointed tutor in Latin to his son Crispus. Lactantius explicitly contrasted Christian hospitality with classical practices. He used the classical example of the gods assuming human form to go into the world to exercise their right to hospitality:

Jupiter himself, after that he received the government, erected temples in honour of himself in many places. For in going about the world, as he came to each place he united the chiefs of the people to himself in friendship and the right of hospitality; and that the remembrance of this might be preserved, he ordered that temples should be built to him, and annual festivals be celebrated by those connected with him in a league of hospitality.

(Lactantius, Epitome Divinarum Institutionum 24)

Recognising hospitality as a 'principal virtue' for philosophers and Christians alike, Lactantius criticised those philosophers who tied it to advantage. Noting that Cicero and others urged that the 'houses of illustrious men should be open to illustrious guests' he then rejected the argument that our bounty must be bestowed upon suitable persons, he reasoned instead that a Christian's house must be open to the lowly and abject.

Therefore hospitality is a principal virtue, as the philosophers also say; but they turn it aside from true justice, and forcibly apply it to advantage. Cicero says: 'Hospitality was rightly praised… it is highly becoming that the houses of illustrious men should be open to illustrious guests'. He has here committed the same error which he then did, when he said that we must

bestow our bounty on 'suitable' persons. For the house of a just and wise
man ought not to be open to the illustrious, but to the lowly and abject. For
those illustrious and powerful men cannot be in want of anything, since
they are sufficiently protected and honoured by their own opulence. But
nothing is to be done by a just man except that which is a benefit. But if the
benefit is returned, it is destroyed and brought to an end; for we cannot pos-
sess in its completeness that for which a price has been paid to us. Therefore
the principle of justice is employed about those benefits which have remained
safe and uncorrupted; but they cannot thus remain by any other means than
if they are bestowed upon those men who can in no way profit us. But in
receiving illustrious men, he looked to nothing else but utility; nor did the
ingenious man conceal what advantage he hoped from it. For he says that he
who does that will become powerful among foreigners by the favour of the
leading men, whom he will have bound to himself by the right of hospitality
and friendship.

(Lactantius, Epitome Divinarum Institutionum 4:12)

St John Chrysostom was to be one of the leading voices within the Christian community, encouraging them to live their lives according to the teachings of Christ. He was to describe exactly how a Christian was to comport himself:

He must be well awake, he must be fervent in spirit, and, as it were, breathe
fire; he must labour and attend upon his duty by day and by night, even
more than a general upon his army; he must be careful and concerned for all.
Sober, of good behaviour, given to hospitality.

(Chrysostom, Homily on Timothy 1:10)

This was not prearranged hospitality, Christians were to be ready at all times to receive and welcome guests, due preparations were always to be in place.

Make for yourself a guest-chamber in your own house: set up a bed there,
set up a table there and a candlestick. For is it not absurd, that whereas, if
soldiers should come, you have rooms set apart for them, and show much
care for them, and furnish them with everything… This do: surpass us in
liberality: have a room, to which Christ may come… Be not uncompassion-
ate, nor inhuman; be not so earnest in worldly matters, so cold in spiritual.
Let also the most faithful of thy servants be the one entrusted with this office,
and let him bring in the maimed, the beggars, and the homeless.

(Chrysostom, Homily on Acts 45)

Taking up the teaching of Clement of Alexandria and others, this hospitality was not to be left to the servants; the masters of the household must do it:

Observe, the hospitality here spoken of is not merely a friendly reception, but one given with zeal and alacrity, with readiness, and going about it as if one were receiving Christ Himself. The widows should perform these services themselves, not commit them to their handmaids. ... And though a woman may be very rich, and of the highest rank, vain of her birth and noble family, there is not the same distance between her and others, as between God and the disciples. If you welcome the stranger as Christ, be not ashamed, but rather glory: but if you receive him not as Christ, receive him not at all.
(Chrysostom, Homily on Timothy 1:14)

Chrysostom was a realist and he recognised the earthly benefits Christians could gain from entertaining persons of high status but he criticised such a practice:

Whereas if thou entertain some great and distinguished man, it is not such pure mercy, what thou doest, but some portion many times is as signed to thyself also, both by vain-glory, and by the return of the favour, and by the rising in many men's estimation on account of thy guest.
(Chrysostom, Homily on 1st Corinthians 20)

He develops his teaching by showing that generous hosts, as long as they are not seeking gain, would nevertheless find themselves blessed in the hospitality relationship. Central to his teaching was the idea, that by offering hospitality to a person in need, one ministered to Christ, and in this context, the discrepancy between small human acts of care and the extravagance of divine hospitality was underscored.

If you show me hospitality,' He said, 'in your home I treat you hospitably in the Kingdom of My Father; you fed me, so I will take away your sins; you saw me captive, I will free you; I was a stranger, I will make you guest of heaven; you gave me bread, I will give you an entire Kingdom'.
(Chrysostom, Homily on Acts 45)

In the Fourth Council held at Carthage in AD 419, the duties of hospitality were given precedent over the use of church buildings. Canon 42 was entitled 'Concerning the not having feasts under any circumstances in churches' and it stated:

That no bishops or clerics are to hold feasts in churches, unless perchance they are forced thereto by the necessity of hospitality as they pass by. The

people, too, as far as possible, are to be prohibited from attending such feasts.
(*Council of Carthage,* Canon *XLII*)

In the Coptic 'Gospel of Thomas', written about AD 200, the alleged words of Jesus are found, when he is giving his disciples instructions on how to be good guests when they receive hospitality:

Jesus said to them... when you go into any land and travel in the country places, when they receive you eat whatever they serve to you.
(*Trevijano Etcheverría, 1997, p. 58*)

St Benedict's Rule (*c.* AD 530), written at the end of Classical Antiquity, and is recognised as one of the key foci for Christian and subsequent Western European hospitality provision. By the 6th century, St Benedict had codified the provision of hospitality within the monastic guesthouse (as detailed in Chapter 8), these rules were to underpin hospitality provision in Europe for at least the next 900 years, until the Protestant reformation. The Benedictine Rule stated that monasteries were to incorporate infirmaries within and the following should be observed:

The Benedictine Rule states that 'the care of the sick is to be placed above and before every other duty, as if indeed Christ was being directly served by waiting on them'.
(*Poter, 1858, p. 111*)

The practice of hospitality to those in the most need was being practised in the Britain too. St Bede the Venerable (*c.700*), in his work *Ecclesiastical History of the English Nation*, records the correspondence between St. Augustine of Canterbury and Pope Gregory regarding how a Bishop was to run his household.

The First Question of Augustine, Bishop of the Church of Canterbury. Concerning bishops, how they are to behave themselves towards their clergy? Or into how many portions the things given by the faithful to the altar are to he divided? And how the bishop is to act in the church?

Gregory, Pope of the City of Rome, answers. Holy Writ, which no doubt you are well versed in, testifies, and particularly St. Paul's Epistle to Timothy, wherein he endeavours to instruct him how he should behave himself in the house of God; but it is the custom of the apostolic see to prescribe rules to bishops newly ordained, that all emoluments which accrue, are to he divided into four portions; one for the bishop and his family, because of hospitality and entertainments; another for the clergy; a third for the poor; and the fourth for the repair of churches.
(*Bede, Historica I:27*)

This was not unique to Canterbury; it was also common all across Europe. Early seventh century St Isidore, Bishop of Seville, emphasises the bishop's special role: 'A layman has fulfilled the duty of hospitality by receiving one or two; a bishop, however, unless he shall receive everyone ... is inhuman' (Isidore, *PL* LXXXIII.786). Before AD 800 Latin documents tended to refer to houses of public hospitality and charity using the Greek term *xenodochion*, after this period, however, the Latin word 'hospital' became more common although some confusion can arise from a number of writers who still used the Greek term.

In around AD 700 the Christian community in Damascus aided the local Islamic community in the construction of a hospital; probably the first prominent Islamic hospital (Dols, 1987). Muslims actively engaged in alms giving, with the *waqf* system allowing for pious gifts as part of a contract between Allah and the *waqif* (donor). Founding a hospital or a caravanserai (accommodation for travellers as discussed in Chapter 9, page 143) allowed prominent Muslims to display their prosperity and benevolence and the flourished in some of the most important Islamic cities: Cairo (874), Baghdad (918) and even Granada (1366) (Imamuddin, 1978). This meant that by the time that great urbanisation and population growth occurred, Eastern civilisations appeared far greater equipped to deal with the changing demographics. So much was this the case, that 'by the Twelfth century a hospital was an essential feature of any large Islamic town' (Conrad, 1995, p. 136). Eastern hospitals seem to be far superior to the Western countries, at that time, as they included separate areas for men and women, wards for different ailments and even the creation of psychiatric units.

Within the monasteries, the *xenodochia* were not as elaborate as the newer Islamic hospitals a twofold provision began to appear (Miller, 1978). The plans for the monastery at St Gall were due to include not just a much valued hospital for the monks, it was also to provide some sort of public *xenodochion*, which would operate under more traditional values offering rest and respite to the needy, travellers and pilgrims.

The Benedictines were not the only religious order to concentrate on hospitality. Orders such as the Knights Hospitaller of St John of Jerusalem were largely given up to works of charity and hospitality. The hospitality of the Hospitallers is based around hostels, or pilgrim hospices, and caring for the sick, for spiritual reward. In the seventh clause of their Statutes, adopted in 1181, they decree:

Commanders of the houses should serve the sick cheerfully, and should do their duty by them, and serve them without grumbling or complaining, so

*that by these good deeds they may deserve to have their reward in the glories
of heaven.*

(Hume, 1940, p. 29)

Among the customs of the Order, the ceremony of initiation provided for
the usual vows of poverty, chastity, and obedience, and then spoke of the
respect due to the sick:

*Also we make another promise, which no other people make, for you promise
to be the serf and slave of our lords the sick. And to each of these things he
should reply: 'Yes, if it please God'.*

(Hume, 1940, p. 33)

Raymond du Puy, who according to King (1931) succeeded Brother
Gerard in 1118, further developed the Order and increased its role from a
defensive hospitaller one, to that of also defending the invalids and pilgrims
against the Saracens. The statutes adopted by the Order, during the master-
ship of Raymond du Puy, included detail on reception. The reception of a
sick person arriving in the community was not dissimilar to that experienced
by a guest on arrival at a Benedictine monastery. Importance was given to
prayer, welcome, accommodation, and a meal. The Constitution of the order
states as one of its rules:

*How Our Lords the Sick should be Received and Served. And in that Obedi-
ence in which the Master and the Chapter of the Hospital shall permit when
the sick man shall come there, let him be received thus: let him partake of the
Holy Sacrament, first having confessed his sins to the priest, and afterwards
let him be carried to bed, and there as if he were a Lord, each day before the
brethren go to eat, let him be refreshed with food charitably according to the
ability of the House.*

A hostel for pilgrims was already in existence in Jerusalem by 1070, probably under the control of a community of Benedictines, held to be founded
by Pope Gregory, in the ninth century. It was supported by funds sent out to
Jerusalem by various supporters. The members of the Order became known
as Knights of St John or Hospitallers. The hostels of Jerusalem fitted into a
pattern of flexibility and adaptability of religious life, where the emphasis
was not only on spirituality but also on making a positive impact in the
world through practical service and hospitality for others.

A chronicler, Rabbi Benjamin from Navarre, who visited Jerusalem in 1163,
described the hospital in Jerusalem 'which support four hundred knights,
and afford shelter to the sick; these are provided with everything they may

want, both during life and death' (Wright, 1848, p. 83). He also described the hostel of the Knights Templar in Jerusalem. Theodorich visiting Jerusalem in 1187, before the Order's expulsion from the city, wrote:

> *Here on the south side of the church, stands the Church and Hostel of St.*
> *John the Baptist. As for this, no one can credibly tell another how beauti-*
> *ful its buildings are, how abundantly it is supplied with rooms and beds,*
> *and other materials for the use of poor and sick people, how rich it is in the*
> *means of refreshing the poor, and how devotedly it labours to maintain the*
> *needy, unless he has had the opportunity of seeing it with his own eyes...*
> *but we saw that the beds numbered more than one thousand. It is not every*
> *one even of the most powerful kings and despots who could maintain as*
> *many people as that house does every day.*
>
> *(Hume, 1940, p. 15f).*

In 1187 when Saladin recaptured Jerusalem he allowed a small number of Hospitallers to stay behind and care for their sick until they could travel; he then enlarged the hospital and appointed a staff of Moslem physicians (Hamarneh, 1974).

The Medieval Poor Laws, highlight the very close connection between clerical hospitality and the relief of the poor:

> *The word 'hospitality' is of some importance because the phrase most com-*
> *monly used by the medieval canonists to describe the poor relief responsibili-*
> *ties of the parish clergy was tenere hospitalitatem – they were obliged, that*
> *is, to 'keep hospitality'. The primary sense of the word referred to the recep-*
> *tion of travellers, the welcoming of guests, but the canonists very often used*
> *it in a broader sense to include almsgiving and poor relief in general.*
>
> *(Tierney, 1959, p. 68)*

The importance of hospitality was emphasised and enshrined in church law with the *Decretum Gratiani*. This code of laws compiled just after the second Lateran Council in 1152, formed the basis of Canon Law in the church until 1917. It has a section dedicated to hospitality and the role of a bishop. In this section, it makes clear, that if any priest is found to be lacking in hospitality, he cannot be ordained a bishop (Gratian, *Distinctio* I:xlii).

As the population grew within Europe, the need for following the Islamic model of providing hospitality for travellers and care for the sick based on public charity was emphasised; by around AD 1250, civil hospitals started being built across Western Europe. The designs for these were mainly taken from the stories past down from pilgrims, crusaders or travellers; about the vast and impressive hospitals in the East. It is ironic how one of these hospitals, which influenced Western building, was built by a group of Westerners in the East. This highlights, in particular, the importance on Western hospitals of Eastern cultures, in particular, Byzantine and Arab influences.

As Eastern European nations were expanding their hospitals grew rapidly during the 12th and 13th centuries, Western civilisations started to build more and more civil hospitals. Many travellers, pilgrims and crusaders were returning from the East, therefore the growth of the hospital became more apparent. Monasteries started to become considerably more important in the surge of medical learning, until the rise of universities in the mid-fourteenth century. As Nutton (1995) notes, added to this was that hospitals were vast in comparison to the *xenodochia* of centuries gone by and included more specialist medical requirements. Furthermore, according to Porter (2003), during the early part of the 13th century these special hospitals included those to combat the threat of the plague and leprosy, in fact there were almost '19,000 leprosaria within Europe' and these had the ability to be altered into units for fatal diseases once this particular threat appeared to die down.

The role of the monk and monastic houses also started to change, within this time period. Retief and Cilliers (2005) note that during the 12th century, bishops in Germany started building new *xenodochia* outside any form of monastic rule. As well as these changing roles came the greater need for the expansion of medical learning, therefore there was no coincidence in the fact that universities started to be developed and expanded, in line with the growth of the hospital. Although the running of hospitals was taken out of monastic hands, the new hospitals were still staffed, throughout by monks and nuns.

The diminished responsibility of monasteries for medicine stopped abruptly in the 16th century, with the spiritual unrest and innovation that lead to the Protestant Reformation, which effectively ended monastic hospitality in Britain for a period of some 300 years (as identified in Chapter 6). Although the monastic mediaeval hospitals had smaller capacity in terms of the medical treatment, they still offered a place of shelter for the old and the needy. However, Porter (1997) records during the Reformation many of the mediaeval hospitals were being closed and sold on to others. This event though did not happen in isolation. In Germany and her Austrian dominions, the Treaty of Westphalia in 1648 saw the confiscation of religious property to the benefit of Protestant princes, and in later centuries a similar situation was to arise throughout the Iberian Peninsula, in France, and in what would now be considered Italy. The Protestant Reformation had a transforming affect on religious hospitality, hospitals, poor relief, and the responsibility to refugees not least because the sacramental character of hospitality was diminished and it became mostly an ordinary expression of human care. Hospitality thus became separated from its Christian roots as the state increasingly took over more responsibility.

7.3 The evolving but unchanged essence of charitable hospitality

What is evident, from this short historical summary of hospitality for the needy, is that even when religion is attacked there has always been recognition of the importance of hospitality *in necessitudine*. Emperor Julian when attempting to suppress the Christian faith, emphasised the importance of preserving and adapting for use by the state the Christian institutions of charitable hospitality. Emperor Justinian had been forced to give legal status to beggars and travellers because of the protection that they received through the same institutions of hospitality. The Protestant reformers of the Late Middle Ages had also moved them out of religious control into the secular realm of society just as Julian had attempted to do 1100 years earlier. However, most recently, instead of trying to subsume charitable hospitality, governments generally chose to support and partially fund the religious efforts. In every case the influence of the underpinning ethos remains even although the governance of the institutions may have changed.

In the early stages, any medical treatment was hard to come by as the old *xenodochia* were converted into monastic houses that only treated their own. This changed over time as the Arab-Islamic influences became more recognised in the West. By the end of these times medicine advanced further with the importance of anatomy and surgery becoming more apparent.

Hospitality provision for those *in extremis* has always continued to change and develop. Undeniably society has changed and evolved over the last 2000 years. Despite the continually evolving practice of providing hospitality to those in most need, the Abrahamic Model of Hospitality and St Paul's subsequent mandate of hospitable behaviour is still being interpreted and followed. As people's needs continue to change it remains the various religion faiths and orders, and now for society in general, to care for those needs in a practical and compassionate manner.

8 Monastic Hospitality

At the end of Classical Antiquity the Roman Empire fell and Europe entered a period of decline; at the same time the sophisticated network of commercial hospitality that had been established fell into disuse. For the considerably fewer people that needed to travel, the monasteries filled the vacuum that had been left. In contemporary literature, for example *Acta Ionannis*, the few remaining contemporaneous commercial establishments had a reputation for bedbugs, discomfort, violence and danger; these only existed in the towns and there was no provision in the countryside or along roads.

This chapter explores the Western European monastery traditions of the Middle Ages, starting with the Rule of Benedict, who was writing in about AD 500. Benedict's Rule is analysed and the chapter identifies how, during the 1000 years of mediaeval times up to the beginning of the Renaissance, the monastic traditions were affected at the time and subsequently. The chapter concludes with an identification of the principles of hospitality that had been established by the traditions of western monasticism.

8.1 The Origins of Western Monasticism

The teachings of the New Testament provide the basis for the western monastic tradition. There are also parallels to be found in early Buddhist and Hindu writings, and it is known that there was considerable contact between India and Alexandria, which was, at that time (*c*. AD 200), the principal commercial and intellectual centre in the Mediterranean. Hindu merchants had formed a permanent and prosperous colony in Alexandria (Clement, *The Stromata* 1.71). Other forms of monasticism such as the Syrian and strictly Oriental monasticism, were to have no direct influence on that of Europe.

The growth of Christian asceticism (self-denying way of life) coincided with the last of the great Roman persecutions of Christians to take place in Egypt; when many Christians fled from the cities to avoid martyrdom. The followers of St Anthony were purely eremitical (Christian hermit-like), whilst those who followed the Rule of St Pachomius more nearly approached the coenobitical (communal living within a monastery) ideal. Under the Antonian system, the austerities (regime of self-discipline) of the monks were left entirely to their own discretion; under the Pachomian system though, there was an obligatory rule of limited severity, and the monks were free to add to it what other ascetical practices they chose. In addition, the prevailing idea in both sets of followers was that they were spiritual athletes and as such they rivalled each other in austerity. In the 4th century AD, when St Basil organized Greek monasticism, he set himself against the eremitical life and insisted upon community life, with meals, work, and prayer, in common. With him the practice of austerity, unlike that of the Egyptians, was to be subject to control of the superior of the community. His idea of the monastic life was the result of an amalgam of the ideas existing in Egypt and the East, together with European culture and modes of thought.

8.2 The rule of Benedict and rise of Western monastic hospitality

St Benedict is considered the founder of western monasticism. He was born at Nursia, about AD 480 and died at Monte Cassino, AD 543. The only authentic life of Benedict of Nursia, is contained within the second book of St Gregory's *Dialogues*, where St Benedict is introduced as:

> *a man of venerable life, blessed by grace, and blessed in name, for he was called 'Benedictus' or Bennet: who, from his younger years, carried always the mind of an old man; for his age was inferior to his virtue.*
>
> (*Dialogues II, Migne, P.L. LXVI*)

For Benedict, a monastery was nothing more or less than 'A school for the Lord's service'. Benedict had lived the life of an eremite in the extreme Egyptian pattern. Instead of attempting to revive the old forms of asceticism, he consolidated the coenobitical life, emphasised the community spirit, and discouraged all private ventures in austerity. Benedict did not write the Rule for clerics; nor was it his intention to found a worldwide order. His Rule was meant to be for the governance of the domestic life of lay individuals who wanted to live, in the fullest possible way, on the path that led to God.

In Benedict's Rule, the main focus for religious hospitality is contained within Chapter 53 which is entitled *De Hopitibus Suscipiendis* (*The Reception of Guests*). In Benedict's chapter, there is a polarity between the closed monastic world and the secular world in general. By leaving the secular society, the monk sets up an alternative world in which people from the secular world might wish to share. Therefore the ritual reception of guests was to play an important role by being both the bridge and the barrier between the two worlds. An English translation (from the original Latin) of Chapter 53 is given in Figure 8.1. There are however texts from other abbeys and congregations, which also highlight certain aspects of monastic hospitality. These texts have been collected by Wolter (1880) in his book, translated by Sause (1962), and some are also presented here to further illustrate the text of Benedict's Chapter 53.

In verse 1 of Chapter 53 is the central feature that 'all guests are to be received as Christ'. From the original Latin used in the opening phrase it could be concluded that the chapter is dealing as much with those travellers who arrive unexpectedly, as those who come for a planned visit. The Latin word used for guests is *hospites*. Kardong (1996) emphasises that the same word is used in the Bible (Matthew 25:35) for 'strangers', showing clearly that hospitality should be offered to those who are in need of it, as well as to those who command shelter by power or prestige. When he quotes Matthew 25:35, Benedict changes the latin words *collegistis* 'you welcomed' to *suscepistis* 'you received', and *suscipiantur* 'be received'. This is the key concept in the Chapter. Kardong (1996) shows that this echoes in the profession of a monk: he is 'received' in to the monastery, so he can then 'receive' others in hospitality.

The stratification of the hospitality is evident in Verse 2, 'proper or due honour' (*congruus honor*), means that not all receive the same honour. There are two categories of person due particular honour: in Latin these are *domesticus fidei* and *peregrinis*. Fry (1981) indicates that *domesticus fidei* literally 'those who share our faith', would apply to other clerics and monks, who are to be received with greater honour. The latin word *peregrinis* can mean 'pilgrim', 'visiting', 'strange', and 'foreign'. The context seems to favour the more technical meaning of' 'pilgrim'; who could possibly be understood as another type of the *domestici fidei* who would then be due same honour. Later in Verse 15, Benedict is also recognising the fact that people who were on a holy journey would single them out for special attention. Leclereq (1968) asserts that pilgrimage, as a form of popular spiritual exercise, peaked after St Benedict's time. However there is evidence for pilgrimage to the tombs of the martyrs and saints, especially at Rome, and to the Holy Places before Benedict wrote his rule.

[1.] All guests who arrive should be received as if they were Christ, for He himself is going to say: 'I came as a stranger, and you received Me'; [2.] and let due honour be shown to all, especially those who share our faith and those who are pilgrims. [3.] As soon as a guest is announced, then let the Superior or one of the monks meet him with all charity, [4.] and first let them pray together, and then be united in peace. [5.] For the sign of peace should not be given until after the prayers have been said, in order to protect from the deceptions of the devil. [6.] The greeting itself, however, ought to show complete humility toward guests who are arriving or departing: [7.] by a bowing of the head or by a complete prostration on the ground, as if it was Christ who was being received. [8.] After the guests have been received and taken to prayer, let the Superior or someone appointed by him, sit with them. [9.] Let the scripture be read in front of the guest, and then let all kindness be shown to him. [10.] The Superior shall break his fast for the sake of a guest, unless it happens to be a principal fast day; [11.] the monks, however, shall observe the customary fasting. [12.] Let the Abbot give the guests water for their hands; and [13.] let both Abbot and monks wash the feet of all guests; [14.] after the washing of the feet let all present say this verse: 'We have received Your mercy, O God, in the midst of Your church'. [15.] All guests should be received with care and kindness; however it is when receiving the poor and pilgrims that the greatest care and kindness should be shown, because it is especially in welcoming them that Christ is received.

[16.] There should be a separate kitchen for the Abbot and guests, so that the other monks may not be disturbed when guests, who are always visiting a monastery, arrive at irregular hours. [17.] Let two monks who are capable of doing this well, be appointed to this kitchen for a year. [18.] They should be given all the help that they require, so that they may serve without murmuring, and on the other hand, when they have less to occupy them, let them do whatever work is assigned to them. [19.] And not only in their case but a similar arrangement should apply to all the jobs across the monastery, [20.] so that when help is needed it can be supplied, and again when the workers are unoccupied they do whatever they are required to do. [21.] Responsibility for the guest house also shall be assigned to a holy monk. [22.] Let there be an adequate number of beds made up in it; and let the house of God be managed by wise men and in a wise manner. [23.] On no account shall anyone who is not so ordered associate or converse with the guests, [24.] but if he should meet them or see them, let him greet them humbly, as we have said, ask their blessing and pass on, saying that he is not allowed to converse with a guest.

Figure 8.1: Rule of Benedict, Chapter 53

In verse 3, Benedict talks about the nature of the greeting and Kardong (1996) emphasises that Benedict is probably referring to cordial words and facial expressions, rather than concrete acts of hospitality. The acts are described in the succeeding verses, but the nature of the greeting is extremely important for the morale of the guest. The key point here is that the duty of caring for the physical needs of the guest actually counts for little if it is carried out in an insensitive manner. The desired reception of a guest is further illustrated in the quote from the Swabian Congregation of St Joseph:

> *Our holy Father desired that guests arriving at the monastery be received with every manifestation of politeness and benevolence. As soon as a guest comes to the door of the monastery, therefore, the porter, after having acquainted himself with the guest's name and the general purpose of his visit, will request him to wait briefly in a properly appointed room. He will forthwith make the visitor's presence known to the abbot or his representative, who will permit nothing to delay him in greeting the guest in a polite and friendly manner, according to his state in life. He will welcome him in a proper and becoming manner and accompany him to the guest quarters.*
>
> *(Sause, 1962, p. 601)*

Benedict now (Verse 4 and 5) gives further instruction on how a guest has to be received. Primacy of the spiritual in the dealings of monks with outsiders is emphasised, making clear that the guest is received on the monastery's terms. If the monks put aside their religious character to deal with all guests at their level, then the cloister is breached and true monastic hospitality is falsified. These quotes serve to illustrate some of the considerations further:

From the 14th century Congregation of Strasburg:

> *In performing the duties of hospitality superiors will keep specially in mind that with due regard for the person's social rank and dignity they show those evidences of charity, considerateness and politeness which will edify them and make them well disposed toward the superiors personally, their monasteries, and the order. But above all else they are to see to it that the signs of respect are given in the true spirit of charity and out of love of Christ whom they receive and worship in the person of the guests.*
>
> *(Sause, 1962, p. 600)*

And from the Swabian Congregation of St Joseph:

> *Superiors are to perform all duties of hospitality promptly and willingly according to the rank and dignity of each guest and in keeping with the means of the monastery.*
>
> *(Sause, 1962, p. 601).*

In verse 6 the phrase 'the greeting itself, however' (*in ipsa autem salutatione*) would seem to indicate that only after the status of the guest is determined, are they actually greeted, and that despite the initial wariness, all humility must now be displayed. In verse 7 'a complete prostration on the ground' (*prostrato omni corpore in terra*) is clearly an echo of the greeting Abraham (Genesis 18:2ff) gave to the strangers, and for the monks shows their general submission to the power of God and the benevolence of the community. This is reinforced in the quote from the 14th century Congregation of Strasburg:

> *Abbots are to guard against treating guests by imitating worldlings, and on*
> *the pretext of hospitality or regard for dignity, entertaining them lavishly*
> *or extravagantly. Toward all there should be proper consideration for the*
> *guest's state in life, as well as for monastic poverty and sobriety.*
>
> (Sause, 1962, p. 600)

In Verses 8 and 9 there is rich symbolism as the guest is being led deeper into the building and into the life of the community. Although guests are not allowed into the cloister, if the guests are allowed to pray with the monks then this demonstrates the fullness of the welcome that the monks offer to the guests; praying with the monks is to penetrate to the very centre of their life. From its earliest origins, monasticism considered hospitality so important as to override asceticism. In verses 10 and 11, it is clearly shown however, that the bending of the Rule when there are guests to be accommodated should not be allowed to disrupt community life. The washing of feet (verses 12–14), is a mark of hospitality, not uncommon in the early Church (1 Timothy 5:10; cf. Luke 7:44–45). Verse 15 reminds the monks that special care must be shown to those in greatest need of hospitality, and closes with a specific mention of the poor; those in most need of hospitality.

The rest of the Chapter 53 (verses 16 to 24) is pragmatic, and even restrictive, although certainly practical. It would seem that guests are never in short supply and can arrive at any time, but the monks need to try to minimise the disturbance to the community. In recognition of this there are three specific matters that are dealt with in these verses: the guests' kitchen; their accommodation, and their communications with the monks.

In verse 16 Benedict allows for a separate abbot's kitchen, this is to provide for the times when the abbot is eating with the guests, while the rest of the monks are fasting (cf. verse 10). The running of the guesthouse is entrusted to two monks, who may even need help, indicates that guests 'are never lacking'. The two monks 'who are capable of fulfilling this office' (*qui ipsud officium bene impleant*), are appointed for a year and must be competent.

Another preoccupation characteristic of Benedict is indicated by the use of the words 'giving help to those in need of it and keeping them from grumbling' (*murmuratione and solacium*). Kardong (1996) observes that if people are not given what they need to carry out their duties, they are not at fault: It is their superiors who fail to train or resource them who are culpable. The following text, from the 11th century Abbey of Cluny, further illustrates how a guest should be received:

> *The guest master receives with all politeness guests who are pilgrims or those who come to the monastery simply for their spiritual welfare... When a guest is led to the entrance of the enclosure at meal time, he waits there until presented to the abbot, who will pour water over his hands and accompany him to the head table... Whatever has been prepared for the brethren is to be served generously to the prior and the guest... If guests request to be shown the various departments of the enclosure, the guest master will obtain the prior's permission and take them through the monastery during the time of one of the Masses while the community is in church. He will take them to the alms house, the store rooms, kitchen, refectory, novitiate, dormitory, and infirmary. When they encounter brothers who have no permission to speak, these brothers are not to break the silence.*

> *(Sause, 1962, p. 601)*

Verse 22 has two practical suggestions. The first is 'let there be sufficient beds made up' (*ubi sint lecti strati sufficienter*). The guesthouse should always be ready for travellers arriving fatigued from the journey. Long delays in preparing the guesthouse would therefore be a hardship for them. The second is that the guesthouse should be 'wisely managed by wise persons' (*sapientibus et sapienter administretur*). In other words those who are managing the guesthouse should be practically competent. However this is not to deny, that in a given monastic situation, the Guest Master may give spiritual counsel. The term 'managed' (*administretur*) is important, for it contrasts with proprietorship: within this context God is the owner of the house; the monks merely manage it. This need for careful management is also exampled in the quote from the 15th century Congregation of Bursfeld:

> *In the guest rooms everything is to be kept clean, but simple, lest in striving too hard lo please we displease. Without explicit permission, none of the brethren is to visit guests; permission is not granted to anyone for visits after Compline.*

> *(Sause, 1962, p. 600)*

Chapter 53 concludes with a strict instruction to the monks about contact with the guest, 'not to visit or speak with them' (*ullatenus societur neque colloquatur*). This, seemingly harsh restriction, appears quite out of harmony with the spirit of the first half of the chapter. Kardong (1996) defends this by showing on the one hand monasteries that are overrun by guests need to protect their monks from the curious, whilst on the other hand there are garrulous monks in need of a sympathetic ear. Guests who come to the monastery for solitude should not have to provide that kind of listening service.

Benedict's rule also provides the basis for the organisation of large-scale hospitality. The most obvious principle is emblazoned at the very head of the chapter in the saying of Jesus, quoted from Matthew 25: 'I was a stranger and you took me in'; an encounter with Christ has to be expected in encounters with strangers and wayfarers. Benedict is very practical in his rules. The administration of large-scale hospitality must be 'wisely managed by wise persons'. Good oversight is necessary, and help given to those entrusted to a department, when needed, is of paramount importance. The guest-director, in particular, should be marked by fear of God and by wisdom. Multi-tasking is seen as important: monks must not become so specialised in a particular sphere of work that they will be unable to help in others when required. Preparation is the key to the running of the guesthouse, which must be kept primed and ready. Benedict makes it clear that murmuring or petty moans will not be tolerated. They are neither good for the guest nor are they edifying to the life of the community. If the monks are not given what they need to carry out their duties, it is not their fault but the fault of those who instructed them to undertake the tasks failing to provide suitable training, skills, or tools for the job.

8.3 Basis for religious hospitality

St Benedict's Rule of monastic life was later to be adopted by most Western monasteries. This foundation was also to become the basis of all western European religious hospitality. It would influence the monastic approaches to caring for the sick (hospitals), the poor (hospices and charities) and the provision of education (the establishment of the first universities), all of which were originally part of the monastic tradition. The Rule, which stressed communal living and physical labour, was also concerned with the needs of the local people, and the distribution of alms and food to the poor. During the lifetime of St Benedict, his disciples spread the order throughout the countries of Central and Western Europe. As Vogüé (1977) and Regnault (1990) note, the Benedictines were also to have wide influence both within the Roman Catholic Church and later within the secular society.

The monks distance themselves from the distractions of the outside world as much as is possible; their life is one of solitude and separation that should lead to spiritual enlightenment. By leaving the secular society, Böckmann (1988) notes that the monks sets up an alternative world in which people from the secular world might wish to share.

The monasteries have always been peaceful retreats for scholars and were the chief centres of Christian piety and learning. During the Middle Ages the monasteries (as well as being the custodians of civilisation, knowledge and learning) had provided detailed and formalised rules for religious hospitality. Chapter 7 showed that they were also centres for the care of the sick and the poor, and had responsibilities for refugees. The Middle Ages was also the period of intellectual and cultural development. New educational institutions, such as cathedral and monastic schools, were founded, and universities were established with advanced degrees being offered in medicine, law, and theology.

The spread of Western monasticism (primarily based on the Rule of St Benedict for monastic life) together with its influence on religious life generally, and also throughout society, led to generally accepted and well-understood principles of hospitality. These principles were to become the foundations of the provision of hospitality that were later to be adopted and modified within the nation-states and by secular organisations as they took over greater responsibilities for the full range of hospitality activities.

8.4   The legacy of mediaeval monasticism

Following the fall of the Roman Empire at the end of the 5th century the monks were writing about and providing hospitality that would easily be recognised today. St Benedict established the rule of monastic life that was to be adopted by most Western monasteries. The Rule, which stressed communal living and physical labour, was also concerned with the needs of the local people, and the distribution of alms and food to the poor. During the lifetime of St Benedict, his disciples spread the order throughout the countries of Central and Western Europe. It soon became the most important order, until the founding of the Augustinian Canons in the 11th century and the mendicant orders (those religious orders that forbad the ownership of property and encourage working or begging for a living) in the 13th century. The Benedictines were also to have wide influence both within the Roman Catholic Church and in the secular society. St Augustine of Canterbury, for instance, the disciple of Gregory the Great, took the Benedictine rule to England in the late 6th century, and was to be the first of a long list of Benedictines who would become Archbishop of Canterbury. By as early as 1354 the order had also provided 24 popes, 200 cardinals, 7000 archbishops, 15,000 bishops, and it had also included 20 emperors, 10 empresses, 47 kings, 50 queens, and many other royal and noble people. The order reached a peak of around 37,000 Benedictines in the 14th century.

Early in the 6th century, the first 12 Benedictine monasteries had been founded at Subiaco, near Rome. The monastery, founded by St Benedict in 529, was situated on the hill of Monte Cassino overlooking the town of Cassino, Italy, northwest of Naples. It was for many centuries the leading monastery in Western Europe. Monte Cassino had a chequered history and was remodelled and re-built several times, with the present buildings being in the style of the 16th and 17th centuries. During the 11th and 12th centuries it was a centre of learning, particularly in the field of medicine: Monte Cassino monks established the famous medical school at Salerno. Abbeys were to become typical of Western monasticism. These self-contained communities have within the abbey walls: the abbey church; the dormitory; the refectory, or dining hall, and the guesthouse for travellers. The buildings enclose a large courtyard that is usually surrounded by a cloister, or sheltered arcade. The abbeys of the Middle Ages were peaceful retreats for scholars and were the chief centres of Christian piety and learning. They were also centres for religious hospitality, the care of the sick and the poor, and had responsibilities for refugees.

In the centuries that had immediately followed after St Benedict, the hospitality afforded by monasteries was comprehensive. It included lodging for travellers, accommodation and treatment for the sick, and charitable services for the poor. The usual period, during which hospitality was freely provided, was two complete days; and some similar restriction, upon the abuse of hospitality, seems to have been prescribed by most of the orders, friars, as well as monks. When there were few urban centres, the monasteries represented the most stable and well-endowed institutions in the countryside. Lenoir (1856) observes that the prominence of the guesthouse in all monastic buildings, beginning with the famous plan of St Gall (Switzerland) in the ninth century, attests indirectly to how scrupulously this tradition was respected. This is highlighted by *The Rites of Durham*, written in 1593 (Fowler,

1964), where there is an account of the splendour of their guesthouse and of the hospitality practised therein.

However Holzherr (1982) states that monks have historically not always been completely faithful to Benedict's demand that all guests be accorded full respect. Society was much more sharply stratified in mediaeval times, and it was virtually impossible to host nobles and peasants in the same manner: a clear example is given in Horn and Born (1979) when they demonstrate that the plan of the monastery of Abbot Adalhard (c. AD 760) shows completely separate guest quarters for rich and poor.

The Benedictines were not the only religious order to concentrate on hospitality. Orders such as the Knights Hospitaller of St John of Jerusalem, were largely given up to works of charity and hospitality. The Knights Hospitaller founded a centre, dedicated to care and hospitality in Jerusalem in 1195. The hostel for Latin pilgrims, founded by Pope Gregory, in the 9th century AD was supported by funds sent out to Jerusalem by the Emperor Charlemagne (in Latin *Carolus Magnus* (Charles the Great) (742–814), King of the Franks (768–814) and Emperor of the Romans (800–814)). King (1931) records that the hostel was placed in charge of a community of Benedictines. According to Hume (1940) the hostel, from its very beginnings, adopted the policy of receiving all those who were in need: Christians; Moslems; and Jews, irrespective of religion. The monk in charge broke away from the Benedictines and organised a religious order under the protection of St John the Baptist. The members of the order became known as Knights of St John or Hospitallers. The order was formally recognised by Pope Paschal II in 1113.

> *Paschal, bishop, and servant of such as are the servants of God, to his venerable son Gerard, founder and Master of the Hostel at Jerusalem, and to his lawful successors for evermore...*
>
> *We, therefore, much pleased with the pious earnestness of thy hospitality, do receive the petition with our paternal favour...*
>
> *Furthermore, all dignities or possessions which your hostel at present holds, either on this side of the water, to wit in Asia, or in Europe, as also those which hereafter by God's bounty it may obtain; we confirm them to thee and to thy successors, who shall be devoting themselves with a pious zeal to the cares of hospitality, and through you to the said Hospital in perpetuity.*
>
> (Poter, 1858, p. 490ff)

The hospitality of the Hospitallers is based around hostels, or pilgrim hospices, and caring for the sick, for spiritual reward. Charitable hospitality is discussed more fully in Chapter 7.

There were many other orders that flourished around the same time. The military order of St Lazarus of Jerusalem originated in a leper hospital that was founded in the 12th century, by the Crusaders of the Latin Kingdom; there had been, before this date, leper hospitals in the East, of which the Knights of St Lazarus claimed to be the continuation. The inmates of St John were merely visitors, and changed constantly; the lepers of St. Lazarus, on the contrary, were condemned to perpetual seclusion. In return, they were regarded as brothers or sisters of the house that sheltered them. They also observed the common rule, which united them with their religious guardians.

Other orders, included the Knights Templar or the Order of the Temple (c.1100) who according to Barber (1994) gave hospitality to pilgrims in Jerusalem, by escorting them around the various sites. These orders were more militaristic in their nature. At the same time the Antonites founded the first centre consecrated by perpetual rule to the care of the sick, in Europe. This group followed the Rule of St Augustine. It was more flexible than that of Benedict and thus better suited for a community organised for service, rather than for prayer (Chaumartin, 1946). Hospitals as institutions of public service increased in importance during the Middle Ages. Care was more impersonal, but also more predictable, and increasingly separate from the Church. In the 13th century, there were Church laws forbidding clerics to practise medicine; the fourth Lateran Council also forbade clerics to practise surgery. The provision of charitable services and lodgings, as discussed in Chapter 7, had remained monastic ministries throughout the Middle Ages, but gradually municipalities and their citizens sponsored not only hospitals, but also other charitable services. By the 14th and 15th centuries, many hospitals in European cities had come under municipal control; a change that further distanced the hospital from its origins in Christian hospitality.

Throughout the epoch of the Middle Ages, trade had all but ceased, and travel was mainly for religious reasons only: pilgrimages; crusades; and education. Sources from this period of time are somewhat limited; Aeneas Sylvius, who was to become Pope Pius II, was visiting Scotland in the 1440s. Whilst on his return to Rome he stayed at a private farmhouse in Northumberland; a visit that prompted his famous description of the barbarity of the border inhabitants. According to Sylvius, these people had never seen either white bread or wine; he was adamant that Northumberlanders had no idea of how to act as hosts (Gabel, 1960).

By the High Middle Ages, hospitality emerged in as a commonly accepted criterion of judgement of esteem at all level of society; to receive guests is commendable, to be held in high esteem you must be considered a good host. This is applied broadly, whether to countries, towns or individuals, nobles, clergy or monastic communities.

Although commercial hospitality was not born out of the decline of the monasteries (as summarised in Chapter 6), its growth and development has been inexorably linked to religion. As has been shown in Chapter 3, Section 3.2, in the gospel of Luke, κατάλυμα *kataluma* can mean a room or 'dwelling' (Luke 2:7), there is also the word πανδοκεῖον *pandocheion* used for an inn, a tavern, or even a brothel. In the Gospel of Luke, for example, the 'Good Samaritan' brought the man, whom he had rescued, to a *pandocheion* (Luke 10:35). The parable makes clear that this *pandocheion*, was a 'for profit' hostelry, as the Samaritan left money with the innkeeper, to pay for the care of the invalid guest. Texts and archaeological data suggest that such hostelries were quite common alongside the roads, in the late Roman world. Remains of a somewhat later *pandocheion* lie along the route between Batnae and Edessa, though no record survives of its fees. Greek and Latin inscriptions by its door, note that in the late third century 'Aurchus Dassins ... prefect and governor of Osrhoene... made in this place a *pandocheion*... so that travellers may enjoy refreshment and repose' (Mango, 1986, p. 227).

The term *pandocheion* continued to be used later, in the Byzantine world, though it appears less frequently than the word ξανοδοχεῖον *xenodochein*, which referred to a charitable hostelry for lodging strangers and the poor. Some of the *xenodocheia* association with good works, seem to have been incorporated into the understanding of the Byzantine *pandocheion*, since, unlike those from antiquity, later *pandocheia* sometimes provided charitable hospitality. Others, however, continued to function as ordinary inns. Many Byzantine *pandocheia* were privately owned, though some were built in conjunction with churches or monasteries to lodge needy travellers (Constable, 2001, p. 146).

Whilst it would be incorrect to make a claim for commercial hospitality to be the world's 'oldest profession', there is certainly some link. The Emperor Theodosius, writing his laws against adultery and prostitution in AD 430, made an important exemption for women working in the early hospitality industry exempting them from juducal proceedings (*Codex Theodosius* 9.7.1). Polybius, whilst travelling in southern Italy, gives an early example of the perceived good value associated with commercial hospitality as 'travellers in this country who put up in inns, do not bargain for each separate item they require, but ask what daily charge is per person' (Polybius, *Historia* 2.14:5–5). Polybius also observes that the innkeepers had a reputation for fairness and generosity, coupled with quality and abundance of food.

8.5   Summary of the principles of hospitality

This chapter has explored the development and regulation of hospitality in the Western European monasteries, from towards the beginning of the Middles Ages through to the dawn of the Renaissance period. From their foundation through the Mediaeval period, the monasteries (as well as being the custodians of civilisation, knowledge and learning) had provided detailed and formalised rules for religious hospitality, the care of the sick and the poor, and responsibilities for refugees.

The monastery, the home of the monk, has elements of domestic, civic and commercial hospitality. The posture of the monk, before the guest, is one of humility and receptivity. It is clear that the monk is there to aid the guest, who must not be seen as a hindrance to the lifestyle of the monastery. The reception of guests must not disrupt community life for those not directly involved with their care. Guests will be received on the community's terms; however, the rule of life of the monks may be altered slightly to accommodate the needs of the guest. More paradoxically, the cloister is the avenue to the world. In a monastery, there was the outer cloister surrounding the courtyard, i.e. guest facilities; the inner cloister marked the monk's own buildings; and the innermost cloister, the cloister walk with its garden. Often there was a fountain in the middle of the innermost cloister, from which the water flowed in the four directions of the compass. The cloister became an Eden; not a closed Eden, but an Eden flowing into the whole world.

It is clear that the prima-facie purpose of a monastery was not to offer hospitality; it is to house the monks in a community environment so that they can dedicate their lives and live their vocation to the service of God. Monastic hospitality, as well as being an extension of early Christian hospitality, also was to filled part of the void left by the decline in the commercial industry. Monastic hospitality, and in particular the concept of the guesthouse, has its roots in the home. Although the monastery could be perceived as a home, it was not entirely. The separation of the monks from their guests (and by definition the separation of the monks from the world in general) is not an act of inhospitableness; rather it is mandated by the Rule and necessary for the monastery to function. Therefore, the ritual reception of guests and the provision of hospitality play an important role by being both the bridge and the barrier between the monastic and secular worlds.

The spread of Western monasticism (primarily based on the Rule of St Benedict for monastic life) together with its influence on religious life generally, and also throughout society, had led to generally accepted and well-understood principles of hospitality. From the analyses of St Benedict's Rule 53, and reviewing this together with the rise of monasticism and the parallel developments during the Middle Ages, a taxonomy of principles of hospitality has been identified. These principles, in their original form, were also to become the foundation of the provision that would also be adopted and modified within the nation-states and by the secular organisations as they took over greater responsibilities for hospitality.

It may be worth reflecting that the principles of hospitality identified within the monastic tradition, essentially based on the Rule of Benedict, are as relevant today as they were 1500 years ago. To demonstrate this further, a revised taxonomy of those principles of hospitality, in a secular and more modern terminology, is presented in Figure 8.2.

Business principles
◊ Guests are central to the purpose of the business
◊ When providing service the management and staff are separate from the society that they are providing service to.
◊ The level of service offered is determined by the type of the business
◊ Businesses have a responsibility for the health, safety and security of the guests
◊ Management and staff should display personal integrity and be practically competent
◊ The business, its management and staff must maintain a professional relationship with guests at all times

Guest principles
◊ Guests are to be treated with respect
◊ Welcoming gestures and language are as important as the acts of service.
◊ Delays in the provision of hospitality are a hardship for the guests
◊ Guests should not feel that the provision of service is an inconvenience to the business
◊ The difficulties in providing the service are of no interest to guests
◊ Providing service and improving it is more important to guests than providing additional hospitality

Hospitality provision principles
- ◊ All guests are welcome
- ◊ Service is offered at different levels
- ◊ Hospitality is offered based on the needs of the guests at the time
- ◊ There must be provision of hospitality for guests with special needs
- ◊ Provision must be for basic needs (food, drink and accommodation) as well as other needs as required
- ◊ Food and drink should be available at all times for guests as they arrive

Staffing principles
- ◊ The person providing the service is seen by the guest as representing the business as a whole
- ◊ Personal characterises of staff must be genuinely disposed to providing service
- ◊ There is a need for specialised staff as well as multi-skilled staff
- ◊ Staff roles should be clearly defined to indicated which staff interact with guests and how
- ◊ The level of staffing needs to match the business demand
- ◊ Staff should maintain their dignity in providing service: service not servility
- ◊ Staff must not cause the guests unnecessary disturbance

Management principles
- ◊ Hospitality managers must be professional and competent
- ◊ Managers have a responsibly to balance the provision of service the requirements of the business
- ◊ Managers as well as having responsibly to manage the business also have to be seen by the guests as the host
- ◊ Both expected demand and unexpected demand need to be prepared for
- ◊ Guest and staff areas should be separated and access controlled
- ◊ Staff who are providing hospitality must be fully resourced and supported by the management team
- ◊ The management is to blame if staff do not have the skills or equipment to carry out their duties
- ◊ Teamwork is important for efficient service

Figure 8.2: Principles of hospitality derived from monastic traditions

9 Along the Silk Routes

The Silk Routes or Silk Road is one of the best known of the world's historical trading routes, traditionally running from Xian in northern China through Iran and on to Istanbul. This ancient route had a regular supply of traders and travellers. This chapter first considers the provision of caravanserais (hostels for travellers) and then looks in more detail at the provision of hospitality in Iran and Mongolia.

9.1 Caravanserais

From at least the 7th century AD there is a strong Middle Eastern literary tradition based around hospitality, particularly that of the Bedawīn. The collection of poems gathered together in the 9th century AD, known as the *Hamāsa al-sughrā*, make frequent references to hospitality (Hamāsa, 1970). The poets observe that at night the fires attract travellers, without inquiring about the stranger, or even when the stranger is known to be an enemy, a meal is prepared for the guest; then he is given a place to sleep; sometimes they sleep with the family, at other times a special tent is erected. Even if they are a timid and gentle household, they will endure any hardship or inconvenience and are always ferocious in defence of their guests. Hospitality is frequently mentioned in Islamic traditions known as *hadīths*, one such tradition notes that if the guest stays longer than the 'three days' it becomes charity, and it is forbidden for a guest to stay when he becomes a burden to his host (ibn Anas, 1999).

Caravanserais were hostels for travellers, where accommodation was often given for free for the traditional three days, although in reality most travellers would continue with their journey after just the one night. In contrast to the mediaeval western monasteries, caravanserais could also be used as commercial centres for merchants. Establishing caravanserais to provide hospitality for travellers is often reflected among the traditions and writings, for example the historian al-Tabarī (c. AD 910) records how the governor of Samarqand (now called Samarkand, Uzbekistan) in AD 719 was ordered to:

establish inns in your lands so that whenever a Muslim passes by, you will put him up for a day, and a night and take care of his animals; if he is sick, provide him with hospitality for two days and two nights; and if he has used up all of his provisions and is unable to continue, supply him with whatever he needs to reach his hometown.

(al-Tabarī, 1989)

There are other evidences from the seventh and eighth centuries: ibn Abd al-Hakam (1922), who died in AD 860, described caravanserais built by the governor of Egypt; and there is evidence from AD 710 when the ruler of Damascus was roundly criticised for funding the construction of a Mosque rather than maintaining the roads and building caravanserais (al-Muqaddasī, 1877). In the ninth and tenth centuries there was a well established record of hospitable works for travellers in Bukhara, Uzbekistan (al-Narshakhī, 1954) and in the 11th century, a governor in Western Iran had 'built in his territories three thousand mosques and caravanserais for strangers' (ibn Abd

1	Gate
2	Watch towers
3	Office
4	Entrance lobby
5	Courtyard
6	Stables
7	Basic room
8	Standard room
9	Prestigious room
10	Suite
11	Stairs to roof
12	Mill
13	Private courtyard
14	Mosque
15	Bath house
16	Toilets
17	Corner tower room

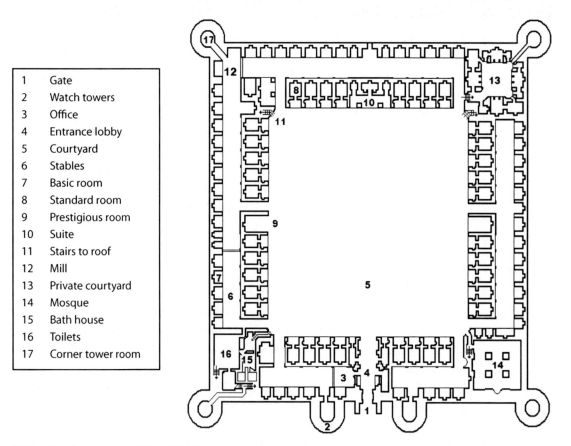

Figure 9.1: Caravanserai at Dayr-i Gachin, Iran

al-Hakam, 1922, p. 113). Provided for sound theological reasons, the building of caravanserais would make the ruler renowned for ever and gather the benefits in eternal life (al-Mulk, 1994).

A comprehensive system of caravanserais existed throughout the whole Islamic world, providing hospitality and care for travellers both pilgrims (Petersen, 1994), and merchants (Yavuz, 1997). Some caravanserais still exist in various states of repair. Some have been redeveloped and are used as hotels, others still operate like the caravanserais of old, and a great number of others unfortunately suffer from inappropriate restoration and are now in an advanced state of decay and disrepair. One example is at Dayr-i Gachin, two hours south of Tehran. After a detailed archaeological and historical survey, Shokoohy (1983) argues that this *caravanserai* dates back to the 3rd century AD. It was originally established by the Sasanian Emperor Ardashir I (AD 224–41). Throughout the last millennium and a half it has had many uses including a Zoroastrian sanctuary, however it had always provided accommodation for travellers. It was abandoned in the late 19th century when the alignment of the road was significantly altered. From the plan (Figure 9.1) the full extent of the caravanserai can be seen including stratified accommodation, bathhouse and a mosque.

9.2 Iranian hospitality

Iran is a country that is incredibly diverse and rich in cultural and historic terms, representing a recorded human history that stretches back some 10,000 years. Following a short background to Islamic hospitality, this chapter presents a contrast between the ancient and contemporary hospitality offered in Iran, in particular focusing on the operational complexities of running the one of the highest hotels in the world.

There has always been a strong tradition of hospitality in the Islamic world, as with the mediaeval western monastic tradition, this Islamic practice is emulating Ibrahim; Ibrahim in the Islamic tradition is Abraham in the Judaeo-Christian tradition. He is considered the first true Muslim and seen as a role model for hospitality; the sharing of food makes the guest a temporary member of the host's family. Ibrahim became terrified when his guests' hands could not reach the food (Qur'ān 51:23), for the sharing of food normally proves that the guest's intentions are not hostile; in the case of Ibrahim his guests were divine messengers. Eating together confers both rights and duties; for example the host must protect the guests as if they were members of the host's family. Even today, this hospitable relationship is established through the sharing of bread and salt, and it lasts for two days and the intervening night, traditionally referred to as three days.

Provision for travellers

A comprehensive system of caravanserais existed all across Iran. Today 120 of these caravanserais still exist in various states of repair. Some have been redeveloped and are used a city centre hotels, others still operate like the caravanserais of old. At Zein-i-edin in the desert, about 100km outside Yazd in the direction of the Afghan border, there is the restored caravanserai, referred to in section 9.1, located on the route of the Great Silk Road and shown in Plates 9.1 and 9.2. It is owned by the Iran Cultural Heritage and Tourism Organisation, and was, until recently, neglected and derelict. In 2006 it was secured on a 12-year lease by three brothers with an agreement to renovate the site as a hotel designed in a style sympathetic to its original origins. They employ a professional Iranian hotelier to manage and operated the project. It attracts international visitors, mainly from Spain but also elsewhere in Europe, domestic tourists and also provides meals for passing tour groups.

Tochal Hotel and recreational complex

Today, the capital city, Tehran has a population of around 12 million people and is principally situated at an altitude to 800–1600m. Taking a cable car from the north of the city, the intrepid traveller can reach one of the world's highest hotels, located near the summit of Mount Tochal at approximately 4000 m (13,000 feet) in the Alborz mountain range and adjacent to the metropolitan area. The area was first used as a ski resort in 1975 until the Islamic Republic of Iran was declared after the revolution of 1979, when the regime of the last Shah was overthrown, and the hotel was closed.

However 2002 saw the reopening of the Tochal Hotel and recreational complex. The lower altitude parts of the complex consist of various amenities, including: restaurants; coffeehouses; ski slopes; tennis club; health and fitness club; paintball; archery; and designated running paths. It also contains three ski slopes, and three separate chair lifts; one of which offers approximately 4.5 km of continuous decent. The slopes are opened from the beginning of November through until the end of the June, these ski slopes are unique in location, nowhere else in the world are there ski slopes of such magnitude, situated in a capital city.

Plate 9.1: The caravanserai outside of Yazd Zeni-i-edin.

Plate 9.2: Inside view of the Yazd Zeni-i-edin caravanserai.

The hotel itself is reached by a gondola style cable car that starts at 1800m (the highest point of metropolitan Tehran) and reaches the summit of 4000m, 7.5 km or 45 minutes later. Alternatively there are hiking roots that reach the summit where, en route, walkers can stop at the various restaurants and coffeehouses located on the mountain side. After reaching the summit there is the option of a 2km ski run or a 10-minute chair lift down to the hotel in the Tochal mountain valley (3600m).

The hotel is built in the style of a typical Swiss three-storey mountain chalet, with 30 suites and rooms, these are all equipped with the standard amenities of minibar, satellite television; air conditioning, triple glazing; three layer windows; clothes warmers and dryers; and an interior design that is intended to inspire a sense of warmth. By European standards the facilities are incredibly cheap, with a (2010) rate of $35 for a single room to $150 for the royal suite that can sleep up to four people; these prices include bed, breakfast, unlimited skiing and a fast-track pass for the ski-lifts and cable cars; the rates are not seasonally adjusted. The guests can be generally divided into two groups: young skiers, snowboarders and climbers; and those who wish to relax and unwind in a calm and more liberal environment.

The hotel is run by about 20–25 members of staff that have to contend with working and sometimes living at high altitude, and struggle against the associated climatic conditions. The hotel facilities include a lounge and bar area located on the first floor of the hotel, which offers a magnificent view over the snowy Tochal mountain peak. The lounge also contains a wide screen television that seemed to be constantly tuned to BBC News 24; the next plan is to offer wireless Internet throughout the hotel. The main restaurant has the capacity for 120 guests and serves both Iranian and international food; it doubles a conference and seminar venue when required. There is also a self-service restaurant that, during the height of the season, serves over 1,000 snack meals to skiers and snowboarders every day. Additionally, a ski-school offers tuition and equipment hire and the staff patrol the slopes.

The hotel is located in a mountain valley at 3600m it has to deal with some extremes of weather, which lead to considerable operational challenges. It is located in snow fields from October till the end of June and during this period there is no vehicle access; everything must be brought by cable car. The temperature varies from + 25°C in the summer to below –30°C in winter, in winter the wind-chill can lower the temperature to around –50°C and the wind can reach speeds of 60 km per hour.

Most of the guests are residents of Tehran who live at 1000m, and have travelled to 4000m in only 45mins. This rapid ascent to an altitude over 2500m can induce high-altitude illnesses; these are medical conditions that can develop in un-acclimatised people shortly after an ascent to a high altitude. According to Basnyat and Murdoch (2003), these conditions include: acute mountain sickness; cerebral oedema; and pulmonary syndromes, the most common symptoms are: headaches; loss of appetite; nausea; fatigue; dizziness, and insomnia all of which usually appear within 8–16 hours of arrival at high altitude. Acute mountain sickness tends to develop in about 50 per cent of the guests within the first 24 hours of their stay, in accordance with the best medical advice the hotel recommends preventative medication 48 hours before the guests arrive.

Comprehensive medical facilities are also provided by the hotel, in order to assist both resident guests and day visitors, the hotel is equipped with a heli-pad for evacuation to Tehran hospitals; there is a doctor on call in the hotel 24 hours a day. During check-in guests are also given a brief medical examination, their personal health and physical ability, the hotel only accepts guests aged between 5 and 60 years of age. As one of the hotel physicians reported, the hotel clinic normally has several trauma patients each day; mostly originated from mountain climbing and ski accidents. The most serious accidents have to be stabilised and evacuated to Tehran hospitals for specific diagnosis and management; the hotel is delighted to report that there have been no fatalities so far!

There is a power supply that is meant to serve the hotel from the city, however this sporadic at best and most the time it has to relay on generators provide electricity of the hotel, the staff accommodation, and chair lifts. Water is supplied from a deep borehole well, this provides the drinking water of the entire hotel, and is closely monitored for purity. The waste water drains into septic tanks, which are considered to be harmless to the mountain environment of the hotel; all other refuse must be transported back to the city on specially designated gondolas. Tankers supply most of the gasoline required of the hotel during the summer period, however, sometimes during the winter deliveries are required by cable car. Liquid gas for the kitchen is delivered in pressurised bottles by cable car and chair lift.

For eight months of the year the hotel's entire delivery system is dependent on a cable car and chairlift system that was constructed in 1975. The gondolas are not climatically controlled and often the adverse weather and

149

change in atmospheric conditions experienced on the journey causes caned drinks to explode and fresh produce to freeze. In an attempted to combat some this, the hotel attempts to stock up on imperishable stock during the summer, when some supply trucks can reach the hotel by road. The hotel also controls the level of wildlife: rabbits and foxes during the winter and scorpions during summer.

Although the Tochal complex has opportunities for skiing for eight months of the year, and a hiking and climbing market for the other four, the hotel has an occupancy rate of roughly 12 per cent. This is partly due to the dependency on the cable car that can only operate from dawn to mid afternoon but cannot be used in adverse weather conditions, however, the staff feel it is also due insufficient and ineffective marketing.

Tourism potential in modern Iran

Despite Iran's turbulent reputation, the Iranians are some of the most hospitable people on the planet, and Iran's tangible cultural assets include seven ancient locations recognised by UNESCO as World Heritage Sites as well as a range of renowned Islamic shrines and cultural sites. The cultural assets range from the era of the great Persian empires, extending back some 10,000 years. Particularly notable among them is the renowned site of the tomb of Cyrus, which held the first charter of human rights and the nearby Palace of Darius at Persepolis, sacked by Alexander in 320 BC. Iran is also home to the Zoroastrian religion and sites in Isfahan and Yazd provide unique insights into the first of the monotheistic religions.

However the country is in close proximity to highly sensitive political and religious neighbours, including Iraq and Afghanistan. As a result, of the geopolitical uncertainty in the region, over 50 per cent of the tour groups that were expected in the next two years have cancelled. This evident reluctance on the part of international markets to visit Iran is denying many people the chance to experience traditional hospitality and the unique cultural and heritage opportunities that this wonderful country has to offer.

9.3 Mongolian hospitality

In 2006 the Mongolian people celebrated the 800th anniversary of the unification of the Mongol tribes, the foundation of the Great Mongol Empire under Chinggis Khaan. Although there seem to be many transliterations of his name into English, the quasi-official version seems to be Chinggis Khaan. On 21 December 2005, Ulaanbaatar airport was renamed to Chinggis Khaan International Airport to celebrate the 800th anniversary of the establishment of a Mongolian State. At its zenith, this empire covered a 12 million-square-mile expanse that stretched 7000 miles from the Pacific Ocean to the Baltic Sea. It is entirely landlocked and held to be the nation furthest from the sea. Historically, its isolation combined with its terrain of high-altitude steppes, deserts and mountains produced a small, but hardy population of horse-riding nomadic herders. Today Mongolia has a population of fewer than three million people in a country about the size of the whole of Western Europe. Roughly half of this population still pursue a traditional nomadic lifestyle on the steppe, while the rest live in the cities, mainly in the capital Ulaanbaatar.

Today approximately 300,000 tourists visit Mongolia per year (Ministry of Road Transport and Tourism, 2005). It is seen as a mysterious, spellbinding destination, with great natural beauty: a visit to Outer Mongolia is often the ultimate goal for any intrepid backpacker. Mongolia is synonymous with remoteness and wilderness and 'stirs up the nomadic, exotic and mystic images of an international tourism destination'(Yu and Goulden, 2006, p. 1332). This is in marked contrast to the view presented to the Royal Geographical Society on 8 June 1903:

> *Mongolia has not received much attention from Englishmen. Nor do I wonder. It has little or no charm for the tourist; no scenery, no sport. Mongol life is simple and not beautiful, and the few objects of interest are archaeological relics, unattractive in form, and not easily accessible… but there is still a good deal of blank space on the map – blank space which hardly contains any secrets of moment.*
>
> *(Campbell, 1903, p. 485)*

The twin appeals of Mongolia for the tourist are seen as its natural resources and the traditional, semi-nomadic culture of the Mongolian people, showcased at events such as the Ulaanbaatar Naadam. A central feature of the rich nomadic tradition is hospitality, in particular the warm and sincere manner in which the traveller is welcomed into the Mongolian home. Very little commercial hospitality exists in Mongolia outside the capital Ulaanbaatar and the other main towns. This lack of commercial hospitality provision means that, when travelling outside the main cities, tourists have the opportunity to integrate themselves more fully into Mongolian society and can be provided with a profound hospitality experience; crossing the vast open countryside the traveller has to depend on the home hospitality.

Basis of Mongolian hospitality

Hospitality has been a fundamental part of Mongolian culture and heritage for centuries and can only be understood in the context of the lived experience of the people. As Heissig (1980) notes it has been influenced by many different religious customs and practices including Nestorianism, Manichaeism, Christianity, Taoism, Confucianism, Chinese and Tibetan Buddhism, and Shamanism. Mutual hospitality is central to Mongolian life and pervades the way the people think and behave; a traditional Mongolian proverb states:

> *Happy is he whom guests frequent, joyful is he at whose door guests' horses are always tethered.*
>
> *(Rinchen, 2005, p. 5)*

The customs of offering warm hospitality have evolved from the centuries old nomadic life on the vast steppe and Chinghis Khaan's 13th century legal code, the 'Ikh Zasag'. Any herder may have had to cover hundreds of kilometres on horseback in search of herds or camels driven off their pastures by a storm. Even today in the vast Gobi Desert, when families travel away from their homes they will leave out food and drink for any guest that may call by in their absence. For their part, the guest has to observe hospitality customs and practices so as not to offend the host or bring bad luck on the household.

The home is the focus of hospitality

Hospitality for Mongolians is based around the home. Outside Ulaanbaatar, the vast majority of Mongolians still live in a *ger*, a large round white felt tent that travellers have long considered to be evocative of the Mongolians. The *ger* acts as a one roomed house, where the family, eat, sleep, cook and live. In Mongolian the word *ger* simply means 'home', in Russian these round felt tents are known as *yurta*, hence they are more commonly known in English as 'yurts'. The *ger* exists as a traditional dwelling not only in Mongolia, but equally within other areas of Central Asia and Siberia that are home to traditionally nomadic peoples such as the Kazakhs, Kirghiz, Tuvans, Tatars, Yakuts and Buryats. The most commonly known kind is the traditional nomads' *ger*, which is used by almost all Central Asian nomads, including the Mongols.

Plate 9.3: Nomadic ger erected in the steppe outside Ulaanbaatar

Plate 9.4: Typical tourist ger camp.

The traditional nomads' *ger* is easily assembled and disassembled, and its components can be loaded onto a yak cart, although a truck tends to be more commonly used today. The *ger* is made of a wooden framework covered by large pieces of felt; decorative cloth covering may be laid over the felt. The wooden framework consists of collapsible lattice walls, topped by poles radiating from a central smoke hole. The entire *ger* is covered by a layer of thick felt held in place by ropes made of hair and wool. During the summer, one layer is sufficient, but during the winter, two or three layers are necessary. The bottom of the felt is arranged so that it can be raised about 30 cm from the ground to allow for more ventilation during warm weather. During the winter, wood is stacked against the *ger* as insulation from the cold and the rain.

Many customs and practices are associated with the *ger* and the provision of hospitality. As Humphrey (1974) describes, for Mongolians the *ger* is not only the centre of their universe, but also a kind of microcosm of the social world of the Mongols within it; it is a map of the universe at large, the vault of the heavens reflected in the arched shape of the interior of the roof. The entrance is south facing, whenever possible and the north side (*xoimor*), located behind the central fire or cooking stove is the most honourable spot in the *ger*. It is here that sacred objects, *ongon* spirit dwellings and other religious images are placed on a table. The sitting place next to the *xoimor* is the most honoured and is occupied by elders, chiefs, lamas, or other honoured guests. Traditionally the right, west, side is the male side, and is the sitting place for men and storage place for men's tools, saddles, bows, and guns. The left, east, side is the sitting place for women, where cooking utensils, cradleboards, and other women's objects are placed. Since the southern side is the least honoured spot, young people are usually seated there.

9.4   Customs and practices of hospitality

Before entering a *ger* the traveller must leave any weapons outside. It is also customary when entering to cough loudly or make some kind of noise to alert the host and demonstrate that there is no evil intent. Custom dictates that a male guest should keep his hat on, but must always take his gloves off to shake hands, even when it is 50° C outside. Visitors should always bring a small gift, which should never be placed on the floor, but left on a table or ideally the *xoimor*, since putting things on – the floor is considered disrespectful to the host. Gifts are expected to be of a practical nature. A good guest should make sure that he is not a burden on the host and gifts of tinned or packet food, soaps or detergents are particularly useful. On arrival, the guest should tell the host where they have travelled from and the purpose of their journey. It would, however, be considered rude for a host to ask if the guest did not offer the information freely. Another arrival custom is the exchange of snuff and Mongolian men traditionally offer each other their snuffboxes – it is rude to refuse!

Whenever guests arrive they will always be offered a place to sit, something to drink, and some food. If the host has nothing to offer his guests, the neighbours will always give everything he needs to entertain his guests. The guest will always be shown where to sit. It is common practice to sit on the floor and the guest should either squat or kneel or, if seated on a stool, should tuck his feet underneath him and take particular care not to not stick them straight out in front. After being welcomed and received into the *ger* the guest is free to walk about, however it is important to always move around the central fire/stove in a clockwise direction. Whistling inside the *ger* or leaning against the upright supports is considered to bring bad luck on the host and the household.

Beverages in the hospitality ritual

Central to any act of hospitality in Mongolia is *airag* (fermented mare's milk) and its use is recorded throughout history. Herodotus (*Historia*), in the 5th century BC, records that, during milking, tubes were inserted into the mare's vulva and air was blown in to force the teats down whilst blinded slaves stood in a circle churning the milk to ferment it before distillation. During his travels to Mongolia in the 13th century, the Franciscan Friar William of Rubruck, refers to the consumption of fermented mares' milk at banquets in the Khaan's court in Mongolia. Friar William goes on to describe how it is made:

> the mothers stand near their foal, and allow themselves to be quietly milked; and if one be too wild, then a man takes the colt and brings it to her, allowing it to suck a little; then he takes it away and the milker takes its place. When they have got together a great quantity of milk, which is as sweet as cow's as long as it is fresh, they pour it into a big skin or bottle, and they set to churning it with a stick prepared for that purpose, and which is as big as a man's head at its lower extremity and hollowed out; and when they have beaten it sharply it begins to boil up like new wine and to sour or ferment, and they continue to churn it until they have extracted the butter. Then they taste it, and when it is mildly pungent, they drink it. It is pungent on

the tongue like vinegar when drunk, and when a man has finished drinking,
it leaves a taste of milk of almonds on the tongue, and it makes the inner
man most joyful and also intoxicates those with weak heads. It also greatly
provokes urine.

(William of Rubruck, 1990, p. 147)

The process of milking and fermentation today remains remarkably similar to that described by Friar William, rather than the colourful version of events presented by Herodotus. *Airag*, stored in large hide bags, is sold at the 'roadside' in recycled plastic bottles which have an unfortunate tendency to explode due to continuing fermentation: *airag*, like Guinness, does not travel well. Mongolians have long extolled the medicinal qualities of *airag*. It is said to give strength and cheerfulness, destroy microbes in the intestines, and improve the metabolism. A guest, when offered a bowl that they do not wish to drink can either just take a sip and pass it to the next person, or make a libation offering by dipping the ring finger of their right hand in the bowl and flicking it three times towards the sky. Undeniably *airag* is an acquired taste as President George W. Bush discovered on his visit to Mongolia in 2005. According to the Washington Post doubt exists on whether Bush actually drank:

No word on whether Bush actually swallowed or not, but some of his aides
evidently did, judging by the looks on their faces afterward.

(Baker, 2005, p. 25)

Another and stronger dairy based alcoholic beverage is distilled from *kefir* (a thin yoghurt) or *airag*. Mongolian *arkhi* is a clear spirit which is consumed undiluted. The popularity of *arkhi* among Mongolian males can be attributed to the days when it was the strongest available alcohol in Mongolia, rather than to its pungent flavour, which resembles rancid milk. *Tsagaan Arkhi*, or white vodka, introduced under the Russian influence, is a popular gift for the host. Often bottles change hands several times before they are finally drunk.

The main non-alcoholic drink, also consumed in copious quantities, is *suutei tsai* (milk tea), which frequently contains hot water, mare's or yak's milk, a generous spoonful of fresh or rancid butter, rice, lots of salt, very little tea and possibly some *borts* (dried meat). It is considered to aid digestion. Some Mongolians also hold sacred the bowl in which the tea is served, because it is through this bowl that the fire communicates with the people surrounding it. Bowls of food and drink will be offered by the host using their right hand, or both hands, and the guests should receive them in a similar manner.

The traditional Mongolian barbeque

Mongolian cooking is generally very simple and does not use many spices, flavourings or sauces. Common dishes include *buuz* (steamed meat-filled dumplings), *guriltai shul* (mutton soup with noodles) and *khuushuur* (fried meat pasties). The most common meat is mutton, in various forms – boiled, stewed, cooked with fat and flour, or served with noodles. Mutton is the staple national food, to such an extent that the smell is inescapable, particularly in *gers*, and travellers often complain of smelling of it for weeks after their return. Horsemeat is also particularly popular in Western Mongolia, as is roasted marmot. Marmots were traditionally hunted as a nomadic past time. When caught, they are killed and cooked whole from the inside out by stuffing with hot rocks, taking care to avoid puncturing their skin and letting the fatty juices escape; simultaneously fur is often singed off with a blowtorch. The animal puffs up and the arms and legs extend as steam and the stones cook the marmot from the inside. This cooking technique – the real Mongolian Barbecue – is also used for sheep, and it is considered lucky to sleep with one of the stones used in cooking underneath one's pillow. A recent Western craze of 'Mongolian Barbeque' restaurants appears to have very little to do with either Mongolian food or true Mongolian hospitality.

Culinary traditions and practices date back at least 800 years; as the Venetian explorer Marco Polo reported in the 13th century, the Mongolians:

> *live on the milk and meat which their herds supply, and on the produce of the chase, and they eat all kinds of flesh, including that of horses and dogs, and Pharaoh's rats [the name Marco Polo gave to marmots], of which last there are great numbers in burrows on those plains.*

> (Latham, 1958)

One particular danger with Mongolian marmots is they can be carriers of bubonic plague. Most years there is a summer outbreak of this plague somewhere, people die and an area is quarantined but this does not deter people from hunting them for food. However Mongolians will never eat an animal that that they found already dead or could catch and kill with their bare hands, as this is an indication that the creature could be infected with the plague. Meat products are often supplemented during the summer with a variety of dairy products made from yak or horse milk, including the dubious delicacies of dried milk curd, and fermented cheese.

Service and etiquette

At any Mongolian meal, guests are served according to gender and status. Sheep are divided in a symbolic manner with male guests and men of high status given meat from the back, whereas women are offered the breast bone and rib. Small slices are taken from the lower back and offered to the goddess of the fire. The fire situated in the middle of the *ger*, literally in the centre of the Mongolian home, is considered to be one of the oldest religious concepts for the Mongols. Rinchen Yöngsiyebü (1984) notes that the spirit of the fire has given life to all the clan's fires, and is held sacred. The fire god can be evoked on many occasions that are central to the hospitality process, e.g. in spring for blessings upon the animals (Mostaert, 1962), which are depended upon for food throughout the year. Likewise libation offerings are made to the fire god: in spring; at the summer solstice; during the preparation of meat; and at wedding ceremonies (Mostaert, 1956). When receiving hospitality it is important to treat the fire in a respectful manner: the most common ways of transcending this custom are throwing rubbish into the fire or sitting with feet pointing to the fire; both of these are considered disrespectful.

Another custom to be wary of is that tucking up of the cuffs of a *deel* (traditional Mongolian gown, still commonly worn outside Ulaanbaatar), which is associated with death; if a person had touched a dead body he had to tuck up his cuffs, and if he had no cuffs he had to tuck up his sleeves instead. Old people, especially if they are ill, become very troubled and visibly upset if someone comes to visit with their sleeves rolled up, there is a genuine fear that the visitor has come to bury them alive.

Even after only one night living in a *ger* with a Mongolian family the departure can be an emotional experience as despite the stay having been so short a level of closeness and affection has developed which is rarely experienced outside one's own immediate family. On departure hosts will traditionally wish their guest a safe journey; a customary reply is to wish that their sheep will fatten or their horses grow up to be strong and swift.

9.5 The future of Mongolian hospitality

For tourists visiting the Mongolian countryside it is still common to stay with a family in their *ger*. However, an extension of this traditional hospitality within the Mongolian home can be found in the commercial *ger* camps that have been constructed at popular tourist sites throughout this vast country.

These camps generally consist of a collection of smaller *gers* for sleeping, along with a toilet block and a larger *ger* used for the restaurant and communal areas. Although demand is highly seasonal, the camps are permanent in location and the *gers* often have concrete bases to increase the visitors' comfort. Within both the larger *ger* where guests are received for their meals and the smaller ones where they sleep, many of the customs and practices relating to traditional Mongolian hospitality are increasingly being diluted, a function of the commercialisation of the host/guest relationship. Whilst the potential for profitability spillovers is welcomed, there is a real fear that the arrival of international conglomerates will detract from Mongolia's appeal as a unique destination.

Since the 1903 presentation to the Royal Geographical Society, Mongolia has encountered both political revolution and significant social turmoil. Given that the country experienced both Chinese and Soviet rule before finally gaining independence after the fall of communism in Mongolia in 1990 and adopting a new, democratic constitution in 1992, it is remarkable that hospitality customs and practices have survived in a form that would be recognised by Marco Polo or even Herodotus. Today, Mongolians remain a profoundly hospitable people and this is consistently shown in their hospitality to strangers, who very quickly feel a genuine and deep sense of welcome as they are treated like honoured guests. The steady increase of tourists to Mongolia is in danger of changing the dynamics of the host/guest relationship, as much through the behaviour of the tourists as though the development of a commercial hospitality sector. Travelling in Mongolia is still challenging, both physically and emotionally, but it is a rich, rewarding and wonderful experience, with a great responsibility on the guest to behave hospitably to his host. Just as the Mongolian host is hospitable towards his guests, guests must be aware of their host's circumstances and not place an undue burden on him. How the development of the commercial hospitality industry within Mongolia will affect the tourist experience is, as yet, unclear. Indeed, given the practical difficulties of travelling to and from Mongolia, and the current climatic and infrastructural limitations on visitor numbers, there must be a question over the scope for such development. Moreover, there are certainly those who would argue that commercialising Mongolian hospitality by separating it from the home and from the traditions on which it is based will deprive the country of its unique selling point.

10   The Dynamic Model of Hospitality

The phenomenon of hospitality is becoming recognised as a field of study to which this book is intended to contribute. Aspects of hospitality found in Classical Antiquity had already been constructed into the Five Dimensions of Hospitality, as presented in Chapter 6. This chapter considers the implications of the publication of *Hospitality: A Social Lens* (Lashley *et al.*, 2007) and brings into the framework the aspects of hospitality identified throughout the writings of Classical Antiquity. The chapter then continues to presents a Dynamic Model for Hospitality and ends with the overall reflection of the origins of hospitality and tourism within Classical Antiquity.

10.1 Hospitality: a social lens

The study of the phenomenon of hospitality has recently been supported further with the publication of *Hospitality: A Social Lens*, where Lashley *et al.*(2007) argue that hospitality research has gained an increasingly multidisciplinary perspective, primarily caused by:

◊ Maturity within the hospitality management field, intellectually advancing through engagement in a broader spectrum of enquiry, emancipating the previous closed system, reductionist, and unitary approaches through criticism and liberation, reflecting on existing knowledge;

◊ Belief that more critical perspectives drawing on the breadth of the social sciences can better inform the management of hospitality; and

◊ A challenge to the orthodox, conventional wisdom and rhetoric, and challenge to complacent mind-sets, drawing attention to novel and previously peripheral hospitality associated areas worthy of study, and bringing in to the mainstream of social sciences debate.

The editors observe that the chapters in the book 'explore hospitality and the relationship between guests and hosts as a phenomenon in its own right' with this being achieved by investigating the relationship from different academic perspectives. Lashley *et al.* (2007, p. 174) judge that the different perspectives presented 'challenge conventional wisdom by bringing to bear multiple 'eyes' all focused on the same phenomenon that is hospitality, but arriving from diverse intellectual starting points and ways of seeing the world'. These academic perspectives of hospitality and the different concepts of hospitality contained within *Hospitality: A Social Lens* are summarised in Table 10:1.

Table 10.1: Concepts of hospitality from *Hospitality: A Social Lens*

Perspective	Concepts of hospitality	Author
Anthropology	Moral obligations defining social and cultural expectations about behaviour as host and guest – intra-tribal hospitality and reciprocity	Cole
Architecture	Hotel space designed to create an ambience of hospitality experiences – symbolism and the rhetoric of hospitality adapts to address developments in consumer expectations	Wharton
Classics	Historical insight into religious and cultural obligations for hosts and guest in Greek, Roman and early Christian settings	O'Gorman
Culture	Ethical hospitality – differences between powerful hosts and vulnerable guests – the widespread fear of global strangers	Sherringham and Daruwalla
Cultural geography	Use of bars, restaurants, clubs and boutique hotels in the regeneration of city centre spaces – role of hospitality experiences in establishing and reinforcing lifestyle experiences.	Bell
Gastronomy	Eating and drinking as focus of gastronomy – reflection on the acts of hosting and the manners of being guests	Santich
History	Multicultural evolution of the 'hospitality industry' in the various colonial hotels and pubs of Melbourne in the nineteenth century	O'Mahony
Human resource management	Commercial control through looking good and sounding right – hospitality experiences require selection and development of service staff who sound and look the 'part' as defined by the brand and the market it is supposedly servicing	Nixon and Wahurst
Socio-linguistics	Demonstrating how fast food restaurants manufacture, control and process customers in a set of predicable processes shaping customer tastes and expectations supporting Ritzer's theory	Robinson and Lynch
Sociology	Commercial home of the micro-business being operated as a guest house or hotel – represent a forum for both private and commercial acts of hospitality	Di Domenico and Lynch
Sociology	Component parts of the of the theory of McDonaldization are an anathema to spontaneous hospitable behaviour	Ritzer

From Table 10:1 the diversity contained in the book is clearly illustrated. It is an in-depth and social science oriented view of hospitality. It is directed at increasing knowledge and understanding of the phenomenon of hospitality without the need to be overtly relevant towards immediate industry concerns. Lashley *et al.* (2007, p. 187) also propose a bold research agenda to deepen the study of hospitality, in particular stating: 'the study of hospitality would benefit from turning its gaze outwards to the ways in which hospitality interacts with society'. One of their broad recommendations for hospitality research is:

> *Investigate the content and facets of the socially constructed connection between host and guest towards the satisfaction of psychological and physiological needs, transforming a 'stranger into a friend', recognising that the host, guest and hospitality space are co-creators in the process of production, consumption and communication. Recognition also needs to be made of the potentiality of a dichotomy of host/guest reference points that may not share a common moral universe, albeit negotiated between the two extremes of hospitality and hostility.*

> *(Lashley et al., 2007, p. 188)*

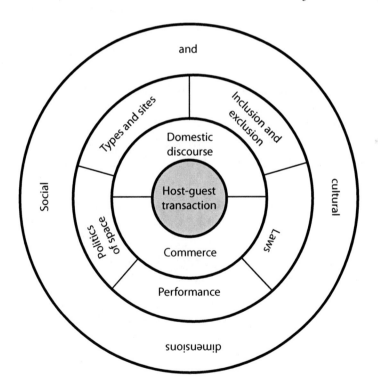

Figure 10.1: The Hospitality Conceptual Lens.
Source: Lashley *et al.*, 2007, p. 175

They also propose investigation into historical conceptualisations, features and characteristics of hospitality. In the words of the editors, the chapters provide 'a rich cornucopia of ways of viewing, understanding, and knowing hospitality, across multiple disciplines, interpretations, times, forms, purposes, sites, and social and cultural contexts' (Lashley *et al.*, 2007, p. 173). In their analysis of the chapters, Lashley *et al.* (2007) present 'the hospitality conceptual lens', shown in Figure 10.1, as an emergent conceptual framework for future research into the phenomenon of hospitality.

This Hospitality Conceptual Lens contains nine robust themes with the host/guest transaction seen as the central focus of the hospitality phenomenon. The content of these themes are presented in summary form in Table 10.2.

Table 10.2: Dominant themes of the hospitality conceptual framework. Source: Lashley *et al.* 2007, p. 174f

Host/guest transaction	The extent to which a host takes responsibility for the care and management of a guest and a guest accepts or rejects the authority of the host
Inclusion/ exclusion	Symbolism of the host welcoming of an 'other' (guest) across thresholds signifying inclusion, the converse is the exclusion of leaving unwelcome 'others' on the outside
Social and cultural dimensions	Hospitality causes the host and guest to construct a temporary common moral universe, involving a process of production, consumption, and communication that defines the host/guest transaction
Laws	Socially and culturally defined obligations, standards, principles, norms and rules associated with hospitality, defining duties and the behaviours of both host and guest
Performance	Host/guest transaction can be depicted as actors performing their respective roles, on a stage that is deliberately constructed to convey symbolism and meaning; thus highlighting authenticity
Domestic discourse	Reflects the domestic roots of hospitality and symbolic connotations of practices, language and gendered roles relative to host/guest transaction within other types and sites
Politics of space	Concept of boundaries and meanings of a social, spatial and cultural nature that denote inclusions/exclusions, and defines the level of intimacy/distance within the host/guest transaction once across the thresholds
Types and sites	Differentiates between and acknowledges the multi-manifestation of forms and locations for experiencing hospitality and host/guest transaction
Commerce	Refers to particular types and sites of commercial hospitality where the host/guest transaction explicitly contains economic dimensions alongside those of the social

This conceptual framework has been presented as a means that can be 'employed to examine social situations where hospitality is involved in order to understand aspects of the society in which the hospitality act occurs' and correspondingly it offers a modern base for future hospitality research.

On the whole, the book seems to be an attempt to apply critical ideas from a management perspective, focusing on what guests do in the host's premises. Within this context the Hospitality Social Lens seems to be a retro-fit of the book which has evolved a posteriori from the chapters. In addition the book tends to present hospitality from the perspective of the hosts rather than guest; a possible legacy of hospitality management where the literature has tended towards a view from a provider's perspective.

Further examination of the nine themes presented by Lashley *et al.* (2007) suggests that the host/guest relationship is not just limited by the extent to which a host takes responsibility for the care and management of a guest and a guest accepts or rejects the authority of the host but is actually significantly influenced by the other eight themes. Therefore, the data can be structured around the eight modified themes of the Hospitality Social Lens focused on the host/guest transaction. The other eight themes are all in effect qualifiers of the host/guest transaction, which cannot be understood, unless contextualised by the other eight themes.

Initial reconsideration of the data

The data from the various chapters of this book can be structured and presented in as a set of aspects of hospitality within the focused themes of the Hospitality Social Lens. Initially this was done but it was not without problems:

Types and sites

Inevitably the types and sites of hospitality in Classical Antiquity separate into three clear subdivisions: domestic, civic and commercial. This highlights and acknowledges the three principal contexts where the host/guest transaction takes place and reinforces the threefold typology.

Laws

Those that govern the hospitality transaction in Classical Antiquity pertain to the socially and culturally defined or established obligations, standards, principles, norms and rules defining duties and the behaviours of both host and guest. Furthermore, what becomes clear is that there are two main groups of laws: divine and human. At one level it could be argued that divine law does not actually exist, as it is a human construct. However, during the analysis, it was seen that divine law governed a great deal of the hospitality transaction so this particular subdivision helps to illustrate the profound complexity to the host/guest transaction.

Inclusion/exclusion

Aspects of inclusion and/or exclusion that exist within hospitality transactions in Classical Antiquity can also be subdivided and grouped into three subdivisions: domestic, civic and commercial. Here there seems to exist an underlying tension in the literature. At first, in early Classical Antiquity, all strangers/guests were treated equally; however, as society became more urbanised, guests began to be differentiated according to needs and status whilst certain expectations of both the host and the guest need to be met. It is also rich in symbolism where the host, regardless of context, welcomes the guest across their threshold and placing them under their protection. As the urban societies began to develop certain groups in society, often the poor or under-privileged were excluded from hospitality transactions.

Transactional expectations

The theme of transactional expectations was labelled 'Commerce' by Lashley *et al.* (2007) in the original classification of the themes of the Hospitality Lens. It referred to particular types and sites of commercial hospitality where the host/guest transaction explicitly contains economic dimensions; however, the original economic classification did not allow for other benefits to the host or the guest. However, frequently the benefits or expectations that the host and/or the guest expected from the hospitality relationship far exceeded economic benefit. Therefore, this category is now renamed transactional expectations as this is a considerable more encompassing delimiter and now includes subdivisions of: spiritual benefit, reciprocity and commerce.

Politics of space

Aspects of the hospitality transaction categorised as 'politics of space' are focused on the concept of boundaries and meanings of a social, spatial and cultural nature and also helps to define the level of intimacy or distance within the host/guest relationship, including the emphasis placed on boundaries and thresholds. The aspects of politics of space have been subdivided into those that emphasises the threshold itself and those that are categorised as behavioural after the guest has crossed the host threshold. This reinforces that the guest and host need to enter the same space in order for the hospitality transaction to take place.

Social and cultural dimensions

The social and cultural dimensions illustrate the richness and complexity of the hospitality transaction. Lashley *et al.* (2007) observe that the act of giving or receiving hospitality causes the host and guest to construct a temporary common moral universe. Within this temporary moral universe the host and the guest define their behaviour through the sharing of hospitality. This is borne out by the research; however, the research also clearly indicates that social and cultural dimensions both influence and delimit the expectations shared by the guest and host. These expectations come from both the attitude in which they approach the hospitality transaction and any underlying religious connotations that may also influence their philosophy of hospitality. Another social and cultural factor was the importance of hospitality networks as a means of communication between individuals and, as societies progressed to become more urbanised, between states. Thus the social and cultural dimensions have been subdivided into: communication system; attitude and religious connotations.

Domestic discourse

Domestic discourse reflects the domestic roots of hospitality and symbolic connotations of practices, language and gendered roles relative to host/ guest transaction. Normally these tend to transcend the actual context of the hospitality relationship. In order to increase the clarity in the aspects under consideration the theme would have to be subdivided into: domestic roots; symbolic connotations and gendered roles.

Performance

The host and the guest can be depicted as two actors performing their respective roles on a stage that has been is deliberately constructed to convey symbolism and meaning; thus highlighting authenticity. However, this research indicated that often these elements of performance highlight deeply-held expectations of the guest or the host and are central to the hospitality relationship. This is further reinforced with subdivision for the needs of the guest and particular rituals that take place within the hospitality transaction.

Developing clarity

Considering the aspects of hospitality from Classical Antiquity within the eight separate themes allowed for comparisons to be made between the themes of the Social Lens. The richness and depth of understanding of hospitality in Classical Antiquity is remarkable in itself. However, certain cognate aspects of hospitality are repeated across the themes and the subdivisions that had evolved. To reduce this repetition and make the presentation more clear, the eight themes of lens can be brought together into three groups where the aspects of hospitality are clearly related or analogous in nature.

These three groupings are:

◊ Location and context of the hospitality relationship ;

◊ Expectational norms in the hospitality relationship;

◊ Symbolism in the hospitality relationship.

The analogous nature of these three groups is based on the textual comparison between the aspects of hospitality. This is not to highlight some form of semantic similarity between them, but rather to reflect, identify and reinforce their character and function.

Location and context of the hospitality relationship

This brings together 'types and sites', 'laws' and 'inclusion/exclusion'. These govern the transaction and impose obstacles and barriers on the hospitable relationship imposed frequently by the host on the guest. Another modification that took place at this stage was the discussion based on the laws of hospitality. The distinction between human and divine, which evolved during the analysis, became increasingly artificial as divine laws were presumed on the gods by humanity and then imposed on humanity by mankind. The philosophical abstraction was therefore changed to reflect how the various laws were imposed across the domestic, civic and commercial spheres of the hospitality relationship.

Expectational norms in the hospitality relationship

These are governed by 'transactional expectations', 'politics of space' and 'social and cultural dimensions' with the sub-themes of spiritual benefits, reciprocity, commerce, behaviour, thresholds, communication system, attitude and religious connotations. Often these expectations may not be realistic on the part of either guest or the host. However, it is the management of these expectations that result in either disappointment or satisfaction within the hospitality process.

Symbolism in the hospitality relationship

This brings together 'domestic discourse' with 'performance' together with the sub-themes of domestic roots; symbolic connotations; gendered roles; needs and rituals influence aspects of symbolism within the hospitality relationship.

The identification of the three cognate groupings of hospitality, based on the themes of the Hospitality Social Lens, provided a way of organising and tabulating the aspects of hospitality in Classical Antiquity.

Location and context in the hospitality relationship

The details of the results are presented in Table 10.3 In this table, redacted from the data, it is clear that the separation of the contexts of hospitality into domestic, civic and commercial hospitality continues to exist. Although the origins of hospitality are located in the home, the developments of civil and commercial hospitality have brought features uniquely associated with them. Domestic, civic and commercial hospitality may superficially be seen to have similar characteristics. However, detailed examination shows that they clearly exist differently within each of the three contexts. In other words although hospitality in the three contexts always requires the adoption of hospitable behaviours, the nature of the context of the hospitality event means that the nature of the hospitality offered is inherently different.

The needs of the host and the guest have always varied. In consequence, hospitality has always had to be able to respond to a range of needs. The exploration of Classical Antiquity shows that the basis for a diverse range of types of places for the provision of hospitality in order to meet the needs of the full spectrum of society already existed. Although initially centred on the home, higher levels of hospitality and service were established over time, as a direct consequence of the ability of the higher classes to afford to travel to new lands and to demand environments there that were commensurate with their wealth and status. Hospitality has never been homogeneous and its provision has been increasingly codified. As societies became more sophisticated, the codification of hospitality provided reference points for how to treat a range of guests/strangers, according to a variety of criteria. The increased separations of the contexts of domestic, civic and commercial hospitality are also reinforced. Additionally as civic and business hospitality develops, hospitality professionals emerge, with particular individuals being recognised as having formal and defined responsibilities for hospitality. Other features identified, which increasingly become more formal as the societies develop, include legal governance, more sophisticated approaches to codification, and the establishment of contractual relationships.

Table 10.3: Aspects that govern the location and context in the hospitality relationship

Types and Sites

Domestic

- As societies develop they go through different stages in the provision of hospitality
- Hospitality practices evolved from domestic hospitality
- Home refers to the entire household not just family members
- Reputation for being hospitable led to growth in stature and status of household

- All guests to be treated hospitably and hospitality must be genuinely and freely offered
- Hospitality becomes legally defined
- Established by individuals or through mediation
- Hereditary hospitality established by exchange of tokens
- Sacred in nature where hospitality ties became more important than blood ties
- Personal duty of the head of the household for hospitality should not be delegated to slaves

Civic

- Diplomatic relations established and strengthened by mutual ties of hospitality between states
- Exchange of hospitality ambassadors lead to deepening of relationships
- Civic receptions and freedom of the city important part of diplomatic process
- Hospitality used to foster strategic alliances between states
- Citizen rights recognised in foreign states where formal hospitality relationships exist
- Mutual bonds of hospitality between the churches created a hospitality network
- Charitable hospitality for the sick, poor and pilgrims gives rise to organised, community-based hospitality networks

Commercial

- Commercial hospitality is a distinct and separate sector
- Large-scale provision for food, beverage and accommodation
- Needed to support and attract travellers and necessary for business and traders
- Recognised as a valuable source of income
- Hospitality management professionals established reputations through professional practice and writings
- Stratified and diversified commercial hospitality industry exists and hospitality establishments become clustered within cities
- Provision of commercial hospitality affected by demand
- Monastic hospitality became aligned to commercial hospitality

Inclusion /Exclusion

Domestic

- Hospitality in the home was offered to the stranger
- Hospitality offered to all guests on an equal basis and then tailored to meet the needs of the guest
- Higher classes had extensive networks of peer-to-peer domestic hospitality
- Hospitality builds interdependent social networks with whom hospitality is freely shared
- Hospitality in the home offered to the stranger and is a personal duty of the head of the household
- All are welcome, but some are more welcome than others

Civic

- The state provides a higher level of hospitality to its own citizens
- Civic hospitality is stratified and guests are offered hospitality depending on their rank, status and purpose of visit
- Hospitality alliances formed for strategic reasons
- Monastic hospitality provision based on ontological orientation
- Hospitality transforms relationships; when practised by the state can cause social change

Commercial

- Commercial hospitality exists for those who do not have a network of private hospitality or receive hospitality by the state
- Stratified levels of provision offered different levels of service
- Commercial hospitality must be paid for and more money bought better provision
- Establishments gained reputations through the quality of their staff and standard of service and clientele
- Commercial hospitality provision subject to fluctuations in demand

---

Laws

Domestic

- Domestic hospitality placed under the spiritual protection of the gods
- Hospitality must not be abused; condemnation and punishment for violation of transcendent laws of hospitality brought divine punishments on individuals or the state
- Behavioural expectations in duty of hospitality to the stranger with particular emphasis placed on hospitality to the needy
- Strangers when receiving hospitality should be controlled and contained but not molested
- Domestic hospitality was formed by formal contract and declaration
- Emphasis given to the importance of transcendental hospitality
- Guest has a duty not to disturb the realm of the host

Civic

- Civic relationships are placed under the spiritual protection of the gods
- Violation of any hospitality ethical code was considered a crime
- Hospitality alliances demanded mutual recognition of each other's deities
- Hospitality was a method of judging the worth of a person both by individuals and society as a whole
- Free hospitality was limited to three days
- Hereditary hospitality to three subsequent generations and verified by exchange of tokens

Commercial

- Commercial industry and those employed within it increasingly subject to legal control

Expectational norms in the hospitality relationship

The details of the results are presented in Table 10.4. From the data it was clear that hospitality has been a primary feature in the development of the societies that have been considered. It is an essential part of human existence, especially as it deals with basic human needs (food, drink, shelter and security). In addition, the concept of hospitality as being based on meeting the basic needs that guests have at the time, rather than the type of people that they are, was also established.

Hospitality was initially concerned with the protection of others in order to be protected from others. Additionally, within Classical Antiquity, and reinforced by all religious teaching and practice, it is considered that the offer of hospitality is an inherently good thing to do. Alongside this it is also well established that failure to provide hospitality is viewed as both an impiety and a temporal crime. However, what is equally established is the concept of reciprocity: for any act of hospitality there is always the expectation (explicit or implied) of a benefit that will arise from its provision. Initially, this is simply to be protected from the stranger, but it also can include monetary, spiritual reward, prestige, or benefit exchange. Moreover, the concept of reciprocity within the hospitality event does not just apply to the provider of the hospitality; it also applies to the receiver of the hospitality. There are expectations on the guests, again explicit or implied, either in material terms or in requirements to observe specific behaviours, or both.

Expectational norms also reinforce the notion that in addition to the broad distinctions between the contexts of domestic, civic and commercial hospitality, the geographic location of the context, the cultural (including religious) influences, and the level of development of the society at the time, all affect the contexts differently. Again the nature of the hospitality offered becomes more inherently different depending both on the context of the hospitality event and the wider influences upon it.

Table 10.4: Aspects that govern the expectational norms in the hospitality relationship

Transactional expectations

Spiritual benefits

- Spiritual rewards included long life, happiness, and good fortune for individuals and for the state
- Ultimate benefit was eternal recognition on the earth, entry into the afterlife and eternal recognition in the heavens
- Hospitality offered particularly to the weakest led to eschatological rewards

Reciprocity

- Hospitality was given to the stranger in order to be protected from them
- Hosts received metaphysical benefits and guests physical benefits
- Domestic hospitality relationships would guarantee food, beverage and accommodation and representation in law courts, citizen rights, access to games and sporting events
- Tangible benefits to host include exchange of gifts and military support
- Prestige and honour gained through hospitality is central to the self-interest of the host
- Civil/state hospitality included mutual recognition of gods and military support in conflicts and war
- Guest receiving hospitality of the community must work for the good of the community
- Breaches in the codes of hospitality reciprocity could lead to war

Commerce

- Commercial hospitality as source of revenue for the state and individuals
- Fine commercial hospitality establishments enhanced the standing of the city
- Hospitality professionals commanded high reputations within society
- Religious hospitality is only free for a limited period time, then guests must work for the good of the community

Politics of space

Behaviour

- Guests bring blessing to the home of the host
- Receive all who ask
- Whilst in the place of hospitality the host cannot harm the guest in any way
- Guests must not harm the host or their property
- Guest made aware they are on the territory of the host demonstrating the moral superiority of the host
- When connected by bonds of hospitality the host must receive guest
- Once established, bonds of hospitality can only be dissolved by formal declaration
- Hospitality must be tailored to the needs of the stranger/guest
- Abuse of hospitality is condemned
- Important for guest not to overstay the welcome and put an undue burden on the host

Thresholds

- Hospitality should be offered as if in the home
- Crossing thresholds guaranteed hospitality and provided physical protection, sanctuary and security
- Crossing the threshold of hospitality begins the process by means of which an outsider's status is changed from stranger to guest
- Potential for social change through protection of the vulnerable and those without status, provide aid to those in need and welcoming those who are alienated

Social and cultural dimensions

Communication system

- Information gathering using hospitality networks with guests seen as means of news exchange
- Alliances born out of hospitality also subverted for espionage and political gain
- Patronage shown through hospitality in particular the giving of meals in restaurants
- Hospitality networks allowed for exchange of strategic information
- Theologically mandated hospitality was a central factor in the spreading of the particular message of the religious groups
- Hospitable gestures can have a darker character of espionage
- Hospitality as a means of social control and manipulation
- Hospitality allows individuals to connect with a community and also interconnection of communities

Attitude

- Cultural value on which society is founded as well as a societal need
- Guests seen as a gift from the gods and hosts always to be prepared to offer hospitality
- Provision of hospitality is giving due honour to the gods who watch over the process
- Respect for the guest and non-inquisitorial towards the guest before hospitality is provided
- Hospitality when properly given should lead to lasting friendship
- Hosts should portray an openness to guests
- Mutual courtesy and consideration should be shown at all times
- The needs of the guest should be put before the needs of the host
- Hospitality contained the concepts of: duty; loyalty; and reciprocity.
- Hospitality is to be offered even in adversity and absolutely welcoming

Religious connotations

- Hospitality is rich in religious symbolism
- Mankind is god's guest in the universe
- Hospitality was means of paying homage to the gods
- Guest should be welcomed as gift from the gods
- The guest is sacred and seen as a gift from the gods
- The host and the guest were under the protection of the gods
- Spiritual redemption often through provision of hospitality
- Common recognition of deities between hospitably aligned states
- Hospitality is a moral practice and self-sacrifice was central to a hospitable attitude
- Hospitable motivation included human need and eschatological rewards
- Hospitality was moral virtue that included clothing the poor, feeding the hungry, protecting the vulnerable

Symbolism in the hospitality relationship

The details of the results are presented in Table 10.5. From the texts, and also demonstrated in this table, hospitality has been central to the development of all societies since the beginning of human history. It is the catalyst that has facilitated human activities, including those that enhance civilisation. It is also identified as being the central feature of human endeavour and celebration, through until the end of time. Relationships between individuals, households and friends were developed through mutual hospitality between the original partners, and then subsequently given to their descendants, and their wider circle of friends. This also establishes the concept of continuing shared benefits between the individuals and households, which is also reflected within the practices of the civic and commercial contexts. In this sense, hospitality becomes a means of networking and strategic alliances.

The vocational nature of hospitality was established through the original concept of hospitality as homage to a superior being, or pursuit of a higher ideal. This provides a basis for the view that hospitality management should be recognised as a true profession because of its strong vocational origins. However, there is also a whole range of stereotypical roles associated with hospitality both in terms of gender and status. These roles appear and are accepted as normal, mostly reflecting the practices of the home and the household at the time. Inevitably, through the adoption of the customs and practices of hospitality from the home context into the civic and commercial contexts, these stereotypical roles have continued to be adopted and expected, mainly because, at the time, neither the existence of them nor the rationale for them was questioned. There are also similarities within the nature of rituals associated with hospitality. Again, the origins of the home are evident in civic and commercial contexts of hospitality; although they do become more prescribed and documented the further the hospitality practice is separated from the origins of the home and the household.

Table 10.5: Aspects that govern the expectational norms in the hospitality relationship

Domestic discourse

Domestic roots

- Hospitality always linked to roots in the home
- Hospitality practices emerged from those of the home
- Hospitality operates within culturally established norms and protocols often taken from domestic practices

- Hospitality is an extended system of friendship and allows the guest to find a home
- Monastic hospitality has its roots in the home but hosts and guests are kept separate

Symbolic connotations

- Home is symbolic of the hospitality transaction also providing sanctuary and security
- Commercial hospitality establishments often converted homes
- Transition from stranger to guest to friend
- Relief of homelessness
- Religious hospitality presented accommodation as the guest's home in God's house

Gendered roles

- Men tend to be seen as master of the household and the host, with women taking the role of cooking and serving
- Woman played an important role in hospitality relationships, fulfils the role of head of the household when the role holder absent
- Where servants and slaves existed within the household they fulfilled hospitable tasks
- Hospitality roles were differentiated by gender and stereotypical roles of, for example, male chef and female barmaids started to emerge but true hospitality transcends gender

Performance

Needs

- Welcoming with emphasis on those in need
- Provision of food, drink and accommodation
- Depending on need could also include clothing, alms and medical care

Rituals

- Specified welcoming gestures, acceptance into the activities of the household, provision of entertainment
- Religions reinforced the characteristics of welcoming strangers and devoted and congenial reception
- Ritualistic symbolism surrounding the meal and food as an art form in every-day life
- Bounteous hospitality was a display of social status an hospitality became quasi-theatrical and spectacular in its staging and production
- Hospitality goes though a ritualised process and that in turn transforms the stranger into a guest who is under the protection of host
- Guests become friends for the duration of the hospitality transaction, maybe longer
- Appropriate ontological orientated when providing hospitality

10.2 Dynamic model of hospitality

Undeniably the modified Hospitality Social Lens is a useful means for classifying data. However, the process of doing so should not overly reduce the aspects of understanding of hospitality in Classical Antiquity; rather it must allow the richness and depth of the data to be exposed, thus giving a true depiction of hospitality in Classical Antiquity. Although the modified Social Lens proves to be a useful framework for organising data it is not a dynamic model. The new model presented in this chapter is a development of the Hospitality Social Lens in light of the outcome of exploration of Classical Antiquity represented in this book and its use in organising and presenting data.

For the purposes of this new model the thresholds of hospitality are illustrated by the eight revised themes of the Hospitality Social Lens: 'type and sites'; 'inclusion/exclusion'; 'laws'; 'transactional expectations'; 'politics of space'; 'social and cultural dimensions'; 'domestic discourse'; and 'performance'. These thresholds are normally imposed on the guest by the host and differ greatly depending on the type of hospitality that is being offered even within the typology of domestic, civic and commercial hospitality.

Hospitality never seemed to be offered unconditionally, and at the very least the host always expects some benefit from their hospitable actions, either physical or metaphysical benefits. To illustrate this, Figure 10.2 splits the guest from the host, leaving the host at the centre, whilst the guest is shown in the outer circle. The middle circle shows the eight thresholds of hospitality from revised themes of the Hospitality Social Lens grouped together in the three influencing categories of hospitality relationship: location and context; expectational norms; and symbolism. These three influencing categories evolved a priori from the research. By placing these influencing categories between the guest and the host, the model is then able to further illustrate the thresholds that the guest has to cross and therefore shows them as the barriers put in place by the host.

Figure 10.2 shows the guest/host relationship incorporating the modified Hospitality Social Lens and would serve to illustrate a generic hospitality relationship. However, as has been discussed there is really no such thing as a generic hospitality relationship not least because it exists within three distinct contexts of domestic, civic and commercial. This means that the new model would have to be adaptable to illustrate different hospitality relationships within these different contexts. However, as was discussed in Chapter 2 (page 35), care must be taken to avoid any possibility of creating a Teleological Fallacy. Therefore, the examples illustrated here are taken from Classical Antiquity and the temptation to draw parallels to modern or any other times has been resisted.

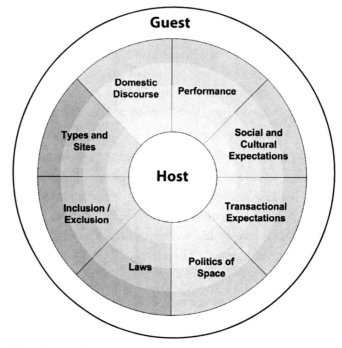

Figure 10.2: Generic hospitality relationship

Domestic hospitality

In the domestic sphere, there are plenty of texts that record the process of the host welcoming the guest into their home. Throughout the writings of Homer particular emphasis is placed on domestic hospitality, highlighting that this must not be abused. Violation of these transcendent laws of hospitality results in condemnation and punishment, and brought divine punishments on the individuals. From these earliest times, the research has consistently demonstrated that if the host or the household had a reputation for being hospitable this would directly lead to a growth both in the stature and the status of household and the host. However, hospitality offered at home has always brought expectations that the guest expects to be fulfilled: food; a comfortable place to sit; charming company; and entertainment. These expectations are fulfilled by Abraham and the other Judaeo-Christian characters, Solon, Socrates, and subsequently by the citizens of Rome. Hospitality was often held to be sacred in nature, particularly where bonds of hospitality became more important than blood ties. Towards the end of Classical Antiquity, and certainly within the flourishing Christian communities, domestic hospitality had taken on the mantel of a theological virtue. Throughout the whole period under investigation it was clear that hospitality was a personal duty of the head of the household that should not be delegated to slaves or servants.

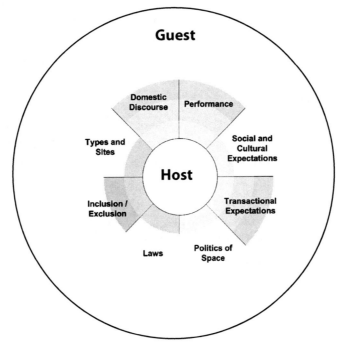

Figure 10.3: Domestic hospitality relationship

Within the domestic hospitality relationship there is a great deal of importance placed on symbolism. Performance is dependent upon both the host and the guest knowing what norms of behaviour they are expected to conform to. This is coupled with domestic discourse, as everyone is aware of the roles they are meant to play, transcendental or physical. However, transactional expectations are great as reciprocity is probably expected on both sides, be these a cooperative working relationship, better promotion prospects or interpersonal loyalty.

Finally, the factors that govern the location and context are possibly the least influential thresholds. However, the exception to that would be 'Inclusion/Exclusion'. Hopefully the host and the guest feel a mutual embrace within the hospitality relationship. Moreover, depending on the context there are those others who were not invited so, metaphorically speaking, are left outside looking in.

Civic hospitality

As societies develop they go through different stages in the provision of hospitality. However, on the whole the research has shown that the vast majority of hospitality practices and customs have evolved from domestic hospitality. The second example of how the model can show different hospitality relationships is taken from the civic sphere. Civic hospitality both originated and abounded within Classical Antiquity. It was seen a necessity for the state with the civic and religious measure of virtue. Figure 10.4 represents the guest/host relationship at a state visit, arguably one of the most stratified hospitality occasions.

Within this hospitality relationship the entire guest–host relationship is delimited by thresholds, some of which are deliberately designed to impose distance between the host and their guests. The symbolism around a state visit is designed to show the power and the influence of the host and often the importance of the principal guest; the performance threshold highlights this. Hospitality at this level becomes quasi-theatrical, spectacular in its staging and production. The guest of honour takes on the persona of a friend for the duration of the hospitality transaction, maybe longer. All the other guests are relegated to the audience, which can include participation, sometimes by

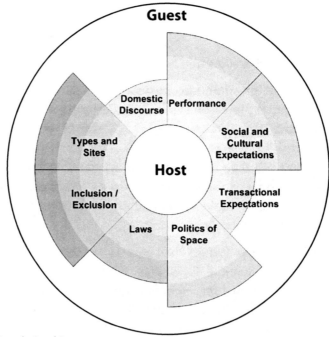

Figure 10.4: Civic hospitality relationship

joining in the meals. However, often involvement is solely or largely just as observers, merely validating the actions of the host. Domestic discourse is significantly diminished when servants of the host take all the gendered roles and gender itself becomes aspecific. However, certain limited elements remain: for example the host's home becomes symbolic of the country. Within civic hospitality the location and context in which the hospitality is provided is particularly important.

Diplomatic relations have always been established and strengthened by mutual ties of hospitality between states. Of course, civic hospitality is intensely stratified and guests are offered hospitality depending on their rank, status and purpose of visit. It is not unusual for alliances that are formed for strategic reasons to be cemented with formal hospitality. These hospitality relationships when used in a particularly strategic manner can actually transform the interpersonal relationship between the guest and the host and even can be catalysts for social change.

Finally, the expectational norms of the state occasion play a significant part in the civic hospitality relationship. There is still a great deal of prestige and honour to be gained through state hospitality, and its provision is often central to the self-interest of both the host and the guest. State occasions normally contain significant public occasions including: welcome ceremonies, state banquets; return dinners where the guest becomes the host of their host; mutual gift giving and departure ceremonies. However, at the individual level, even civic hospitality is still tailored by the host to the needs, or more often the personal interests, of the guest.

Commercial hospitality

Unequivocally the commercial hospitality sector is one of the world's oldest industries. A commercial hospitality relationship is depicted in Figure 10.5; this represents a typical hotel as described by Xenophon or found in Pompeii.

Hostels and inns in Mesopotamia date back to at least 2000 BC and they were controlled by the laws of the time. Two thousand years later, towns like Pompeii had a flourishing diversified and stratified commercial hospitality industry. There was a wide range of facilities on offer providing a diverse range of services, from the large central hotels located in the middle of a town and other complementary facilities to smaller countryside establishments along the main roads between the towns.

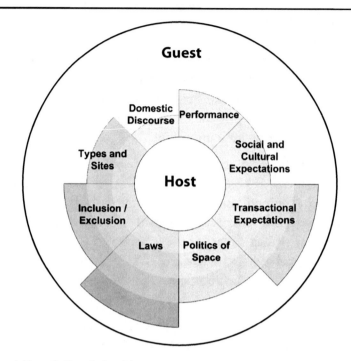

Figure 10.5: Commercial hospitality relationship

Within the performance segment there are limited gendered roles; roles are differentiated by gender and stereotypical roles. For example, male chefs and female barmaids started to emerge but commercial hospitality provision tends to transcend gender. The commercial sector tends to exhibit the characteristics of welcoming strangers and devoted and congenial reception. However, these would tend to be disingenuous pseudo-theatrical performances rather than a genuinely hospitable ontological orientation. The aspects that govern the expectational norms in the hospitality relationship are often the most significant the host places on his guest within the commercial hospitality relationship. Commercial hospitality has always been seen as a source of revenue both for the state and for individuals. The reciprocity that is expected by the host for the hospitality that the guest is given is monetary. Often the guest will not pay if the hospitality that is received is not perceived to be of an acceptable standard. As such, in commercial hospitality, hospitality does involve the satisfaction or manipulation of the guests' perceptions. Manipulation or subterfuge is nothing unusual within the guest/host relationship. In Classical Antiquity information gathering used hospitality networks, with guests seen as means of news exchange. However, these networks born out of hospitality were also subverted for espionage and strategic gain. Outstanding establishments within the commercial hospitality sphere have always been considered enhancement to the standing of the city and provided a source of revenue. Similarly, hospitality professionals commanded high reputations within society frequently established through professional practice and writings in Classical Antiquity. However, crossing thresholds of commercial hospitality guaranteed and provided physical protection, sanctuary and security.

In examining the location and context of the commercial hospitality relationship it became evident that in Classical Antiquity, the commercial hospitality sector was already distinct and separate from domestic and civic hospitality. There was already a large-scale provision of food, beverage and accommodation and the sector supported and attracted travellers and was necessary and integral for business and served the needs of merchants. Stratified and diversified commercial hospitality industry existed and hospitality establishments become clustered within cities. In other words, the supply of commercial hospitality was already subject to the demand of market forces focused on urban centres to which the merchants were attracted. Commercial hospitality existed for those who did not have an extensive network of private hospitality or were either insufficiently privileged to receive the hospitality of the state or in such an impoverished personal situation that they required it. The commercial provision was not homogeneous, and stratified levels of provision offered different levels of service. Indeed, commercial hospitality had always to be paid for and more money bought a better provision and quality of service. Establishments quickly gained reputations through the quality of their staff and standard of service provided, and equally through the character and behaviour of their clientele. Finally, one constant and unremitting aspect of the commercial industry and those employed within it was the increasing legal control they were subject to.

10.3 Further development of the dynamic model of hospitality

The Generic Model of Hospitality given in Figure 10.2 and its three contextual derivations (Figures 10.3, 10.4 and 10.5) can be further developed to allows for comparison and contrasting of the themes of the Social Lens and to draw conclusions on three specific determinants, all of which define the host/guest relationship:

◊ Types of hospitality behaviour;

◊ Nature of the hospitality relationship, and

◊ The level of intimacy.

To illustrate this visually Figure 10.6 has been constructed.

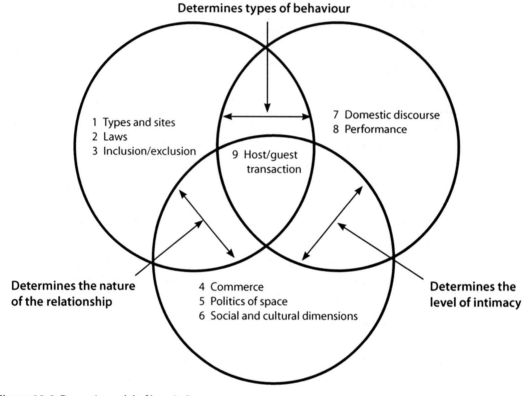

Figure 10.6: Dynamic model of hospitality

◊ **The Nature of the Behaviour** is determined by the linkages that exist between types and sites, laws and inclusion/exclusion and domestic discourse and performance.

◊ **The nature of the relationship** is determined by the linkages between types and sites, laws and inclusion/exclusion and commerce, politics of space and social and cultural dimensions

◊ **The level of intimacy** is determined by the linkages between commerce, politics of space and social and cultural dimensions and domestic discourse and performance.

10.4 The key outcomes

The identification of the key outcomes presented here takes account of the Five Dimensions of Hospitality identified in Chapter 6 (section 6.2), the content of the subsequent chapters, and the analysis of the aspects of hospitality identified when applying the Social Lens, as discussed in Section 10.1 above.

Initial overview

As its main focus, this book was aimed at exploring the extent to which origins of hospitality were founded in ancient and classical history. Overall, it is clear that hospitality has its origins early in human history and has been evolving since that time.

Hospitality has been a central feature in the development of all the societies that have been considered. These are societies with urban foci and centralised political control. In these societies, hospitality is the catalyst that has facilitated human activities, including those that enhance civilisation. It is also an essential part of human existence, especially as it deals with basic human needs (food, drink, shelter and security). Also, the vocational nature of hospitality is established through the original concept of hospitality as homage to a superior being, or pursuit of a higher ideal. This provides a basis for the view that hospitality management should be recognised as a true profession because of its strong vocational origins. It also impels a view that hospitality is about mutual expectations and the management of those, as much as it is about the management of activities or resources.

It seems in the societies considered within this book that it is inherent in human nature to offer hospitality, and that the societies and all the contemporaneous religious teachings support and reinforce this trait. Throughout Classical Antiquity the structures and organisation within societies are inexorably linked with religion. Consequently domestic, civil and commercial hospitality are always under the influence of religious doctrine as much as civil codes. The extensive discussions on hospitality and impiety highlighted a classic chicken and egg position: if faith and belief are human constructs and if these govern everyday life, then does this reinforce the view that hospitality is inherently a basic human trait?

The importance of context

The provision of hospitality clearly takes place within three specific and different contexts: domestic, civil and commercial. Reviewing the content of this book only serves to reinforce this continued separation. The needs of hosts and guests have always varied; hospitality, therefore, has always had to be able to respond to a range of differing needs and contexts. Hospitality has never been homogeneous and its provision has been increasingly codified. Additionally, the nature of the hospitality offered becomes more inherently different depending both on the context of the hospitality event and the wider influences upon it.

In addition to context, the nature of the hospitality event is affected by its geographic location, the cultural (including religious) customs of the society, and the specific time in history. The modern literature has in many cases ignored these differing influences on the hospitality event and there is evidence of supporting or criticising hospitality customs based on largely spurious notions of what hospitality could or should be. The potential for the Teleological Fallacy (as discussed in Chapter 3, page 53) is evident and especially in the philosophical literature (as discussed in Chapter 2). At best, this literature helps with the understanding of human interaction; at worst the discussions and the interpretations of hospitality events are based not only on spurious notions of what hospitality is but also on attempts to relate different contexts, as well as making comparisons that link, for instance, separate societies, customs, locations and times in history. Such reductionist thought holds a general view from pre-assumed premises, rather than building a general view from premises pertinent in diverse contexts.

Although civic hospitality is different to the hospitality of the home, it is closely related to the hospitality of the home, with societies often acting as in effect as large households. However, commercial hospitality is something else entirely. An extreme view questions whether commercial hospitality is in fact hospitality at all. Although commercial hospitality requires welcoming and caring behaviour for it to be conducted, does this actually mean that it is offered as true hospitality? Is it not simply a service provided in a hospitable way? The other perspective to consider here is that the commercial hospitality is not offered in isolation. It is only offered when the customer is offering to pay for it and only continues for as long as the customer has the means to pay. One more complex question to explore is: who is actually the host in the commercial hospitality relationship? It could be argued that the customer is the host who, being away from their own household, is simply seeking to re-create their own household somewhere else.

Hospitality is a two-way process

What can often be overlooked, or simply ignored, is the fact that hospitality is a process linking the host and the guest. The guest is linked to the host by the very act of the host providing food, drink and often accommodation to the guest; the level of service provided being initially dependent on the needs of the guest at the time and the capability of the host. However, as time progresses rank, ontological or otherwise, and status do tend to be determining factors of the hospitality on offer.

What is equally established is the concept of reciprocity: for any act of hospitality there is always the expectation (explicit or implied) of a benefit that will arise from its provision. Initially this may be simply to be protected from the stranger but also can include monetary, spiritual reward, prestige or benefit exchange. Moreover, the concept of reciprocity within the hospitality event does not just apply to the provider of the hospitality; it also applies equally to the receiver. There are always expectations on the guests, again explicit or implied, either in material terms or in requirements to observe specific behaviours, or both. The host does not need to be fully altruistic in their endeavour as reciprocity, temporal or metaphysical, is an important part of the hospitality transaction.

The two-way process and the concept of reciprocity reinforce that hospitality is not friendship; it is not even a commercial friendship. Once friendship is established then the relationship changes. The stranger becomes a friend and the potential ultimate goal of hospitality has been achieved. However, this is only the potential goal as, depending on the context, that goal may never be achieved, and in many cases it may never have been the intention of the hospitality process to reach that goal: as for example in commercial hospitality. Friends have a relationship that ideally is based on the purest of motivations this is often demonstrated with some or all of the following characteristics: the tendency to desire what is best for the other; sympathy; empathy, and mutual understanding. These are not characteristics that readily appear in the hospitality relationship. The hospitality relationship is one of stresses and barriers: thresholds that a guest has to cross before they are welcomed. This tension in the guest/host relationship has been reflected constantly throughout the literature and exists in domestic, civic and commercial hospitality.

Difference in perspectives

One criticism of the hospitality literature is that the vast majority of it tends to be written from the host or providers' perspective, with very little from the consumers' or guests' perspectives. However, The Dynamic Model of Hospitality presented in this chapter can be inverted, enabling the hospitality transaction to be viewed from the guests' or consumers' perspectives. This reinforces both the two-way process and the concept of reciprocity. The potential inverting of the guest and host, within the same dynamic model, makes the model adaptable to visually represent the hospitality transaction in the different contexts.

Overall summary

By way of an overall summary the original identification of the Five Dimensions of Hospitality first given in Chapter 6 is presented here in a modified form. This is shown in Table 10.6 and identifies the five dimensions and provides a summary of the aspect of hospitality that underpin it.

Table 10.6: The five dimensions of hospitality

Dimension	Summary of aspects of hospitality
Honourable tradition	Within the ancient and classical worlds, often reinforced by religious teaching and practice, hospitality was considered as an inherently good thing to provide. The vocational nature of hospitality was established. The concept of reciprocity – monetary, spiritual, or exchange – was already understood, as was the concept of failure in providing hospitality being viewed as both an impiety and a temporal crime.
Fundamental to human existence	Hospitality is a primary feature in the development of societies, especially as it deals with basic human needs (food, drink, shelter and security).
Stratified	As the societies become more sophisticated, the codification of hospitality provided reference points for how to treat a range of guests/strangers, according to a variety of criteria. Typologies of hospitality also became apparent: private, civic, and business/commercial. Hospitality professionals emerged as civic and business hospitality developed.
Diversified	Hospitality had always to be able to respond to a broad range of needs and this provided the basis for a diverse range of types of hospitality and establishments.
Central to human endeavour	Since the beginning of human history, hospitality was the mechanism that has been central to the development of societies, at both the individual and collective levels. It was the catalyst used to facilitate human activities, especially those that were aimed at enhancing civilisation.

10.5 The ultimate conclusion

Throughout the work undertaken to develop the text for this book, one aspect of the phenomenon of hospitality that has been a constant throughout is reflected in the etymology: the terms of 'guest' and 'stranger' were originally synonyms (see Chapter 1, page 12). Is it really here that the clue to the nature of hospitality has been there all along? If hospitality is primarily about defence (protection from the stranger) and if the relationship between a host and a guest needs to be established to achieve harmony of reciprocity (mutual benefit) then are not the acts of hospitality simply the mechanisms by which this happens? Or, in other words, hospitality represents the thresholds over which both the host and the guest have to cross in order to inhabit the same space. Being hospitable is then the description of the set of behaviours and expectations that can take place between the host and the guest. Hospitality is the term for the two arriving into the same universe, which allows these behaviours to happen, their expectations to be met and the two-way process to obtain. This also then means that the provision of hospitality as a service is inherently about the management of these behaviours and expectations. And what is wrong with that?

Appendices

A   Glossary of names and terms

Abraham In the Bible and Qur'ān Jews, Christians and Muslims regard him as the founding patriarch of the Israelites and of the Nabataean people. Famous for his hospitality to three strangers at an oasis among the 'Oaks of Mamre'.

Aeneas Leader of the Trojans, according to Virgil, Romulus and Remus were both descendants of Aeneas through their mother, and thus he was responsible for founding the Roman people.

Apicius Apicius was the proverbial cognomen for several connoisseurs of food. The most famous (and probably the second), Marcus Gavius Apicius, lived in the early Empire (c.30 BC); he kept an academy, in the manner of a philosopher. A third Apicius, or a group of Apicii, lived in the late fourth or early fifth century and redacted the surviving Roman cookbook bearing his name.

Aristocles Believed to be the real name for Plato.

Aristotle (384–322 BC) Ancient Greek philosopher, who wrote books on many subjects, including physics, poetry, zoology, logic, rhetoric, government, and biology; student of Plato at the Academy.

Classical Antiquity The broad term for the period of cultural history centred on the Mediterranean Sea, which begins with the earliest-recorded Greek poetry of Homer (c.770 BC), and coincides with the traditional date of the founding of Rome in 753 BC. The end is disputed and includes the end of the Western Roman Empire in AD 476 and AD 529 with the closure of Plato's Academy in Athens.

Cicero Marcus Tullius Cicero (106–43 bc) Orator and statesman of Ancient Rome, and is generally considered the greatest Latin orator and prose stylist.

Cyclops The notorious one-eyed monster that was famous for killing then devouring his guests.

Dido Queen of Carthage (in modern-day Tunisia) She is best known from the account given by the Roman poet Virgil, the Aeneid, however she is also mentioned by Ovid.

Dionysius of Halicarnassus (c.60–7 BC) was a Greek historian and teacher of rhetoric, who flourished during the reign of Caesar Augustus.

Elissa Greek name for Dido (see Dido)

Euripides (c.480–406 BC) was considered to be one of the great tragedians of classical Athens. Ancient scholars thought that Euripides had written 92 plays; 18 of them have survived complete.

Herodotus Herodotus of Halicarnassus (484–c.425 bc) Historian famous for writing The Histories, a collection of stories on different places and peoples he learned about through his travels. Often claimed to be the first travel writer.

Homer Legendary early Greek poet traditionally credited with the composition of the Iliad and the Odyssey, commonly assumed to have lived in the eighth Century BC.

Jupiter In Roman mythology, Jupiter held the same role as Zeus in the Greek pantheon, as the patron deity of the Roman state, the god of laws, social order and, in particular, hospitality.

Livy	Titus Livius (59 BC– AD 17) wrote a history of Rome, Ab urbe condita libri, from its founding (traditionally dated to 753 BC) through to the reign of Augustus.
Menelaus	King of Sparta married to Helen. When Paris, a Trojan prince, came to Sparta and left with Helen it caused the Trojan War. After the Greek victory, Helen returned to Sparta with Menelaus.
Nestor	An Argonaut, who in the Odyssey, receives Telemachus in a most hospitable manner and entertains him lavishly as a guest.
Odysseus	Hero of Homer's Odyssey, most famous for the ten years it took him to return home from the Trojan War. Odysseus was the king of Ithaca, husband of Penelope and father of Telemachus.
Ovid	Publius Ovidius Naso (43 BC–AD 17), a Roman poet who wrote on topics of love, abandoned women, and mythological transformations.
Petronius	(c. AD 27–66) A Roman writer who was a noted satirist. Amongst scholars there remains confusion over his real name, being identified as C. Petronius Arbiter, but the manuscript text of the Satyricon, used in this volume calls him Titus Petronius.
Plato	(c.427–c.347 BC) Ancient Greek philosopher, who wrote on many philosophical issues, dealing especially in politics, ethics, metaphysics and epistemology. He was a student of Socrates, writer of philosophical dialogues, and founder of the Academy in Athens.
Plautus	Titus Maccius Plautus (254–184 bc) A comic playwright in the time of the Roman Republic. He wrote approximately 130 plays, of which 21 survive.
Plutarch	Mestrius Plutarchus (c. AD 46–127), Greek historian, biographer, and essayist. He was a priest of the Delphic temple and a magistrate; he represented his home on various foreign missions.
Roman Empire	The Roman Empire followed the Roman Republic. Several dates are traditionally offered for the transition from Republic to Empire: Julius Caesar's appointment as dictator (44 BC), Battle of Actium (31 BC), and the Senate's declaration of Octavian as Augustus (27 bc). At its territorial peak, the Empire was approximately 6 million sq km of land. The end of the Roman Empire is traditionally, if not strictly accurately, placed at AD 476.
Roman Republic	The phase of the ancient Roman civilization characterised by a republican form of government, began with the overthrow of the monarchy c.509 bc and lasted over 450 years until its subversion, through a series of civil wars, into the Roman Empire.
Sarah	Wife of Abraham.
Socrates	(c.470–399 BC) Greek philosopher who is widely credited for laying the foundation for Western philosophy; principal source of information on him comes from Plato's dialogues.
Telemachus	Son of Odysseus and Penelope. After his father had been gone for nearly 20 years, young Telemachus is advised to travel in search of news of his father depending on hospitality throughout his voyage.
Thucydides	(c.455–c.400 BC) Ancient Greek historian and the author of the History of the Peloponnesian War, which recounts the war between Sparta and Athens in the 5th century bc. This work is widely regarded a classic, and represents the first work of its kind.
Ulysses	Odysseus in Roman mythology (see Odysseus).
Virgil	Publius Vergilius Maro (70–19 BC), Latin poet, the author of the Aeneid, an epic poem of twelve books that became the Roman Empire's national epic.
Xenophon	(427–355 BC) Ancient Greek soldier, mercenary and an admirer of Socrates. He is known for his writings on the history of his own times, the sayings of Socrates, and the life of Greece.
Zeus	In Greek mythology he is the king of the gods, the ruler of Mount Olympus, and god of the sky and thunder, amongst his other roles was watching over the law of hospitality. (In Roman mythology his equivalent is Jupiter.)

B   Frequently used Latin and Greek Terms

Term	Translation	Meaning
Caupona	Restaurant	Commercial hospitality establishment that served food and drink, offered sit-down meals; this term was often used to describe public eating-houses and sometimes included a few rooms.
Clientela	Client city	When a town wanted to establish a formal hospitality relationship with Rome, it entered into *clientela* to some distinguished Roman, who then acted as patron of the client-town; next stage *municipia*.
Hospes	Guest	A person connected with a Roman by ties of hospitality was deemed even more sacred, and to have greater claims upon the host, than that of a person connected by blood or affinity.
Hospes publicus	Public guest	The custom of granting the honour of the title *hospes publicus* to a distinguished foreigner by a decree of the senate; similar to modern concept of freedom of the city.
Hospitium	Hotel/hostel	Larger commercial hospitality establishments that offered rooms for rent, and often food and drink to overnight guests; often specifically built for business purposes.
Hospitium privatum	Private hospitality	Various obligations came with the connection of hospitality with a foreigner imposed upon a Roman, amongst those obligations included: reception of a guest when travelling; duties of protection; and, in case of need, to represent him as his patron in the courts of justice.
Ius hospitii	Law of hospitality	Those joined in a relationship of private hospitality was established by mutual presents, or by the mediation of a third person, Jupiter was thought to watch over the *ius hospitii*.
Katagogion κατὰ γογιον	Inn/hostel	Purpose-built for the provision of commercial hospitality in the Greek city-states.
Lumpanar	Brothel	Provided a full range of services of a personal nature, sometimes even including food, beverage and accommodation.
Municipia	Town	Name given to a town that had an established formal hospitality relationship with the City of Rome; stage after the relationship of *clientela*.
Oikos Οἶκος	home, household	This includes not only the resident 'family' in biological sense of the term, but also all those who live in the house as well as those who depended upon the household and contribute to its wealth and survival. This may include slaves; illegitimate children; normally the offspring of the master and female slaves; resident in-laws; and 'adopted' persons who serve as retainers or 'squires'.
Philoxenos Φιλόξενος	Love of strangers	Greek law/custom of offering protection and hospitality to strangers; its antithesis is still in common English usage today of 'xenophobia'.
Popina	Restaurant	Alternative name for a restaurant; seen under *caupona*.

Proxenos πρόξενος	Guest-friend	Literally the 'guest-friend' of a city-state; looking after the interests of a foreign state in his own country
Stabula	Coaching inn	Buildings with open courtyard surrounded by a kitchen, a latrine, and bedrooms with stables at the rear. Often found just outside the city, close to the city gates; offered food, drink and accommodation.
Taberna	Bar	Sold a variety of simple foods and drink. They usually contained a simple L-shaped marble counter, about six to eight feet long
Tessera hospitalis	Hospitality token	When bond of hospitality was formed, the two friends used to divide between themselves a token by which, afterwards, they themselves or their descendants might recognise one another.
Xenia Ξένία	Guest/stranger	In Greek it had the interchangeable meaning of guest or stranger, thus the first of many hospitality paradoxes is seen. Also has the sense of 'hospitable reception'.
xenodaites ξενοδαίτης	Guest-eater	Literally 'one that devours guests', a concept epitomised by the Cyclops; one of the two most serious breaches of the hospitality code, the other being killing guests.
xenokonos ξενοκτόνος	Guest-killer	Literally 'slaying of guests and strangers', one of the two most serious breaches of the hospitality code; the other being eating guests.
Xenos ξένος	Guest/stranger	See Xenia

C   Methodological issues

Much of the research carried out for the preparation of this text had to depend upon on textual data, as there are very few other practical ways of accessing Classical Antiquity. The notes in this appedix provide an insight into some of the methodological considerations taken into account when the original doctoral research, which supports the content of this book, was being undertaken. The appendix considers phenomenological hermeneutics, explores issues to do with the translations of texts and give a brief outline of the underpinning philosophy.

Phenomenological hermeneutics

The exploration of literature pervades the entire book, with the focus of the original research that underpins the content of the book based on textual analysis. This research was being carried out within the interpretivist paradigm as it is seeking to observe the general trends and perceptions of a social phenomenon. As the research is concerned with seeking an understanding of different perceptions of hospitality contained in the texts of Classical Antiquity combined with the selection of the interpretivist paradigm, the application of hermeneutics was used.

Hermeneutic phenomenology attempts to be descriptive, to show how things look, to let things speak for themselves and, in the context of the hermeneutic project, it is interpretive. While there may be, at first glance, an implicit contradiction between description and interpretation, Van Manen (1990, p. 180) feels that this may be resolved, 'if one acknowledges that the (phenomenological) "facts" of lived experience are always already meaningfully (hermeneutically) experienced. Moreover, even the 'facts' of lived experience need to be captured in language (the human science text) and this is inevitably an interpretive process.' Denzin (1989, p. 53) also notes the hermeneutic nature of interpretive research when he argues that:

> Interpretive research enters the hermeneutic circle by placing the researcher and subject in the center [sic] of the research process. The subject who tells a self or personal experience story is, of course, at the center of the life that is told about. The researcher who reads and interprets a self-story is at the center of his or her interpretation of that story. Two interpretive structures thus interface one another.

The Greek word hermēneia, meaning interpretation or understanding, encapsulated a wide range of interpretation and clarification, which covered speech, translation, and commentary. Hermeneutics has now become the theory of textual interpretation. Originally concerned with interpreting sacred texts; it has developed over time into a scientific methodology (Bohman, 1999). According to Alvesson and Sköldberg (2004, p. 53) 'hermeneutics has its roots in the Renaissance in two parallel and partly interacting currents of thought, the Protestant analysis of the Bible and the humanist study of the ancient classics.' This was the first time that Biblical texts were to be critically evaluated; previously they were held as the divinely inspired word of God and were considered beyond critical interpretation.

Edmund Husserl is generally considered to be the founder of phenomenology. He considered it to be a foundational science underlying all of the sciences and sought to clarify, through the use of critical reflection and description, the foundation and constitution of knowledge in consciousness. Husserl (1931) claimed that the phenomena that form our conscious experience manifest essences or structures. To be specific, he viewed experience as consisting of both concrete particulars and the categories of meaning to which they belong. To illustrate this Hein and Austin (2001, p. 4) use the following example of apples:

> Although we may have experiences of a variety of apples, which vary in color, size, and texture, these are all instances of 'appleness', which is also experientially real. The meaning 'appleness' therefore remains the same despite variations in how it is manifested concretely. In other words, the structure of 'appleness' provides us with concrete instances of apples.

This is a development from Aristotelian metaphysics where Aristotle argued for the independent existence of the social world as distinct from the physical world. Similarly, when investigating hospitality over a period, there can be a variety of instances of hospitality – all of these are experientially real; it is the overriding concept of hospitality that is being investigated. Husserl (1931) saw the task of phenomenology as describing these metaphysical structures, including their constituent parts and their interrelationships.

Due to the complexity of the research, the hermeneutic circle (Alvesson and Sköldberg, 2004) developed into a hermeneutic helix. This helical, rather than the conventional circular, process is illustrated in Figure C.1 Derived hermeneutical helix. It allowed for a dynamic and engaging methodology through revisiting the presuppositions and the texts themselves. It also became more critical as it permitted development though simultaneously, focusing and increasing clarity in the distillation of the essence of hospitality that was emerging from the text.

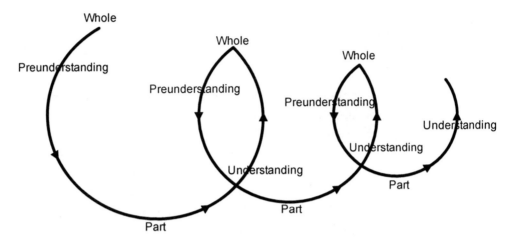

Figure C.1: Derived hermeneutical helix

This research, in line with the traditional hermeneutic circle, began with examining the textual corpus as a whole, through exploring own presuppositions and pre-understandings of the texts. This was done, first, by developing a personal reflectivity. This reflexive writing process is repeated at the two subsequent points where the helix returns to the pre-understanding and presuppositions stage, in order to reflect further on personal bias towards the texts. Second, a review of the Judaeo-Christian theological and biblical studies literature was conducted to lay down background details before the inductive textual analysis was undertaken.

In keeping with the traditional hermeneutic circle, after the pre-understandings and the textual corpus as a whole were reflected upon, the texts themselves were considered individually. The pericopes (small extracts of text from a larger work) that referred to hospitality or hospitality issues, which had been previously identified, formed the basis for the initial inductive analysis. This inductive engagement could have been the end point of the hermeneutical process, and conventionally would have been. However, the presentation of the results initially tended towards being descriptive and thus not overtly analytical. The results did not seem clear and the essence of hospitality still seemed to transcend the description of hospitality that was presented.

What was clear was a need to revisit the personal presuppositions and pre-understandings of the texts. In order to do this, a literature review of contemporary authors in classics and hospitality was conducted. The ideas that emanate from the analysis of these authors become the pre-understandings for the second twist of the helix, when the individual pericopes are reviewed for a second time. What became evident from the texts is that they were about delivery of hospitality whereas philosophical literature added a dimension of experience of hospitality.

The final stage of the helix saw the need to integrate the ideas and research into the area of hospitality studies. Auspiciously this was contemporaneous with the publication of *Hospitality – A Social Lens* (Lashley *et al*, 2007). Thus, the structure of the lens was to form the pre-understanding for the third and final twist of helix; a reflective analysis using the lens. As a consequence of the application of the hermeneutical helix a new hospitality model is presented in three different contexts and from two perspectives (Chapter 10). The new model offered is a natural progression of the Hospitality Social Lens in light of the discoveries made through this research.

Translation of texts

Since all writing is the product of a particular time and culture, the views expressed in it and the language in which they are expressed reflect a particular cultural conditioning. A literal translation lets aspects, such as the poetic structure, and whether the same word is being used in several passages, be seen. It is useful if working with a detailed commentary that is discussing the original language or the literary form. Using this type of translation, it is possible to misunderstand the meaning of the text, whereas dynamic translation attempts to transfer the same meaning and impact to a modern reader just as the original would have to its readers. It departs from a literal translation for a number of reasons: idiom; words which have several meanings, the choice of which is based on a combination of context and grammar; words that have no direct equivalent in English that are best rendered by a phrase, or the choice of different wording; and lastly differences in grammatical and stylistic conventions.

English translations show differing levels of constancy in translation and this is demonstrated in detail using the example of the text of Romans 12:13.

The Greek text for Romans 12:13 is as follows:

'ταῖς χρείαις τῶν ἁγίων κοινωνοῦτες τὴν ψιλοξενίαν διώκοντες'.

A morphological analysis of the texts is shown in Table C.1.

Table C.1: Morphological analysis of Romans 12:13

Word	Base	Morphology	Translation
ταῖς	ὅ	definite article: dative plural feminine	The
Χρείαις	Χρεία	noun: dative plural feminine	Need: to / for needs
Τῶν	ὅ	definite article: genitive plural masculine	Of the
ἁγίων	ἅγιος	adjective: genitive plural masculine	holy, saint: of saints
κοινωνοῦτες	Κοινωέω	verb: present active participle, nominative plural masculine	contribute (and related synonyms)
Τήν	ὅ	definite article: accusative singular feminine	The
ψιλοξενίαν	Ψιλοξενία	noun: accusative singular feminine	love of strangers: hospitality
Διώκοντες	Διώκω	verb: present active participle, nominative plural masculine	pursue (and related synonyms)

This has been rendered in Latin in the vulgate as: 'Necessitatibus sanctorum communicantes hospitalitatem sectantes'. Whilst a literal translation of the text would be: 'to the necessities of the saints contributing; the hospitality pursuing'. More than 100 translations of the New Testament are in existence. The translations of Romans 12:13 given below, taken from some of the most popular translations, start with the most formal and end with the most dynamic.

Within Table C.2 it can be seen that the translations vary in length from nine words to 32 words, that the verse splits into two parts 'ταῖς χρείαις τῶν ἁγίων κοινωνοῦτες' and 'τὴν ψιλοξενίαν διώκοντες'.

The central word for this study 'ψιλοξενίαν' is translated in general, as hospitality, with some notable exceptions. The New Revised Standard version encourages the extension of hospitality 'to strangers', this emphasises the more literal translation of 'ψιλοξενίαν' –'love of strangers' – but is rather exclusive as true hospitality should be open to all, friend and stranger alike. The more dynamic translations offer various interpretations of the meaning of hospitality: 'ready to take people into your houses'; 'open your homes to strangers'; 'bring strangers in need into your homes'; 'be glad to take care of strangers in your house'; 'give meals and a place to stay to those who need it'; and finally the most 'dynamic' translation 'and get into the habit of inviting guests home for dinner or, if they need lodging, for the night'.

Table C.2: Translations of Romans 12:13

King James Version	Distributing to the necessity of saints; given to hospitality
New King James Version	Distributing to the needs of the saints, given to hospitality
Wycliffe Version	Giving good to the needs of saints, keeping hospitality
Rheimes New Testament	Communicating to the necessities of the saints. Pursuing hospitality.
Darby Translation	Distributing to the necessities of the saints; given to hospitality
Revised Standard Bible	Contribute to the needs of the saints, practice hospitality
New Revised Standard Version	Contribute to the needs of the saints; extend hospitality to strangers
New International Version	Share with God's people who are in need. Practice hospitality
New American Standard Bible	Contributing to the needs of the saints, practising hospitality.
New American Bible	Contribute to the needs of the holy ones, exercise hospitality.
The Bible in Basic English	Giving to the needs of the saints, ready to take people into your houses.
English Standard Version	Contribute to the needs of the saints and seek to show hospitality.
God's Word Translation	Share what you have with God's people who are in need. Be hospitable.
Jerusalem Bible	If any of the saints are in need you must share with them; and you should make hospitality your special care.
New Jerusalem Bible	Share with any of God's holy people who are in need; look for opportunities to be hospitable.
Good News Translation	Share your belongings with your needy fellow Christians, and open your homes to strangers.
New Century Version	Share with God's people who need help. Bring strangers in need into your homes.
World Wide English Version	Give to God's people who need it. Be glad to take care of strangers in your house.
New Life Version	Share what you have with Christian brothers who are in need. Give meals and a place to stay to those who need it.
New Living Translation	When God's children are in need, be the one to help them out. And get into the habit of inviting guests home for dinner or, if they need lodging, for the night.

This example shows that translation is a multi-dimensional approximation – there are many differences between the languages: sentence structure; the tenses and moods; and the implied logic contained in the words. Without doubt, there are bad translations; that is to say, translations that make unnecessary changes to the meaning of the text. However, there can be no such a thing as a best translation. There has always been some debate on how ancient and classical texts can be 'properly' translated. Oppenheim (1977), a philologist and Assyriologist, did much to make Mesopotamian texts as understandable in the modern world, as those of Greece and Rome. In the introduction to *Ancient Mesopotamia: Portrait of a Dead Civilization,* he wrote:

> *translated texts tend to speak more of the translator than of their original message. It is not too difficult to render texts written in a dead language as literally as possible and to suggest to the outsider, through the use of quaint and stilted locutions, the alleged awkwardness and archaism of a remote period… A step nearer to the realization of the legitimate desire to make the texts "speak for themselves"… with a critical discussion of the literary, stylistic, and emotional setting of each translated piece.*
>
> *(Oppenheim, 1977, p. 10)*

The standard and accessible versions of these texts, in English translation, are by Matthews and Benjamin; in their introduction to the texts, they state:

> *In preparing [our translation] we tried to meet Oppenheim's challenge. Our readings are not literal or visual, text-oriented, translations, but responsible, reader-oriented, paraphrases. The English vocabulary and idiom emphasises the relationship between the ancient Near Eastern parallel and the Bible. It imitates commonly used patterns of speech today. It avoids awkwardness and archaism'*
>
> *(Matthews et al., 1991b, p. xii)*

The definition of an acceptable translation is what the person who is reading the translation will accept, thus it will change with each text, and even with the same text if it is translated at a different time or for a different purpose. This is why different translations of the Bible are needed for different times and people; the audience has changed, and the needs of the audience have changed. For example, a translation of the Bible used for prayerful meditation would not be the same as one used for textual analysis; similarly, a poetic translation of Homer's works would not be very useful in a critical analysis of hospitality encounters in the ancient world.

Underpinning philosophy

Gorgias, a fifth century Sophist, is remembered for his provocative aphorisms the most notable is his treatise *On What is Not*:

Firstly ... nothing exists;

secondly ... even if anything exists, it is incomprehensible by man;

thirdly .., even if anything is comprehensible, it is guaranteed to be inexpressible and incommunicable to one's neighbour.

(*Gorgias 500 BC, quoted in Aristotle, De Melisso Xenophane Gorgia 980a:*
19–20)

Gorgias' treatise could be seen as just a rhetorical parody of philological and rhetorical philosophical doctrines; however it may also be an epistemology and a genuine philosophy of rhetoric. That said, Gorgias could also be a nihilist, attacking the doctrines of the Pre-Socratic ontological approach. Nevertheless it is a succinct summary of the problems of research and dissemination.

St Anselm, the 11th century philosopher and Archbishop of Canterbury, wrote, 'I do not seek to understand so that I may believe, but I believe so that I may understand' (Anselm, *Proslogion* 154–5). St Anselm asserts that nothing is achieved or ascertained by merely speculating from the sidelines; a certain level of committed involvement is necessary. The theory of the independent existence of the social world was established by Aristotle (*c.*350 BC) when he argued that something exists apart from the concrete thing:

If, on the one hand, there is nothing apart from individual beings, and the individuals are infinite in number, how is it possible to get knowledge of the infinite individuals? For all things that we know, we know in so far as they have some unity and identity, and in so far as some attribute belongs to them universally. But if this is necessary, and there must be something apart from the individuals, it will be necessary that something exists apart from the concrete thing.

(*Aristotle, Metaphysics 999a: 25–8*)

In 1781 Immanuel Kant published his *Critique of Pure Reason* ([1781] 1998). This caused a Copernican revolution in philosophy. Kant argued that there are ways of knowing about the world other than through direct observation, and that people use these all the time; this proposition provided the platform for the launch of many of the ideas associated with qualitative research methodology. Kant's view proposes considering not how our representations may necessarily conform to objects as such, but rather how objects may necessarily conform to our representations. From a pre-Copernican view, objects are considered just by themselves, totally apart from any intrinsic cognitive relation to our representations; it is mysterious how they could ever be determined a priori. Kant theorised that things could be considered just as phenomena (objects of experience) rather than noumena (things in themselves specified negatively as unknown beyond our experience). Therefore, if human faculties of representation are used to study these phenomena, a priori conceptualisations can be envisaged. Kant ([1781] 1998) also showed how flawless logic can prove the existence of God; at the same time he showed how flawless logic proves that there is no God at all; illustrating that opposing philosophies can be equally logical and at the same time contradictory and incomplete, a salient warning to any emergent researcher defending their philosophical stance.

D   Augmented Bibliography

Classical sources

References to ancient Greek, Latin, Biblical, and Patristic texts employ the standard English-language citation system: the author's name; followed by the conventional Latin name for the work, spelled out in full rather than abbreviated; and followed by Arabic numerals that guide the reader to chapter, paragraph, and line. For discussions of authors and their texts, please see *The Oxford Classical Dictionary*, edited by S. Hornblower and A. Spawforth (2003).

All biblical translations are the author's own and the two versions of the bible used are:

◊ The *Biblia Hebraica Stuttgartensia* (Elliger and Rudolph, 1990) is generally considered to be the definitive edition of the Hebrew Bible. Widely regarded as a reliable edition of the Hebrew and Aramaic scriptures and is the most widely used original-language edition among scholars; it is based on the Leningrad Codex a nearly exact copy of the Masoretic Text (*c.* ninth century AD) the oldest complete Hebrew/Aramaic Bible still preserved.

◊ The *Nestle-Aland Novum Testamentum Graece* is the critical scholarly work redacted from over 5400 complete or fragmented Greek manuscripts. The most recent edition (Aland *et al.*, 2007) shows a nearly exhaustive list of variants but includes only the most significant witnesses for each variant. The Greek text has paragraph and section breaks, cross references in the margins and includes synoptic parallels.

In the following list of ancient works cited in this book, the Loeb Classical Library, the ongoing series, begun early in this century, encompasses both Greek and Latin authors and provides the Greek or Latin text on the left-hand page, with a good English translation facing it. For texts not available in the Loeb series, a standard critical edition of the text has been cited. In the case of the Patristic writers the 220 volumes of Jacque Paul Migne's comprehensive compilation of the Patristic works (*PL*) has been cited.

Acta Proconsularia Cypriani	*Translations and Reprints from the Original Sources of European History*, trans. Dana Carleton Munro and Edith Bramhall, volume 4.1 University of Pennsylvania, Pennsylvania, 1900.
Apocrypha	*The Apocryphal New Testament, being all The Gospels, Epistles and other pieces now extant attributed in the first four centuries to Jesus Christ, His Apostles, and their companions and not included in The New Testament*, William Hone, London 1821.
Anselm, St, *Proslogion*	*Proslogion. with, A reply on behalf of the fool by Gaunilo; and, The author's reply to Gaunilo translated, with an introduction and philosophical commentary, by M. J. Charlesworth*, Clarendon Press, Oxford (1965).
Aristotle, *Athenian Constitution*	*The Athenian Constitution translated with introduction and notes by P.J. Rhodes*, Penguin Books, Harmondsworth 1984.
Aristotle, *Metaphysics*	*Metaphysics, Oeconomica, and Magna Moralia*, Loeb Classical Library, volume 17, Heinemann 1968.
Athenaeus, *Deipnosophistae*	*The Learned Banqueters*, Loeb Classical Library, volume 372–5, Heinemann, 2007/08.
Bede, *Historica* I	*Baedae Opera Historica*, Loeb Classical Library, volume 248, Heinemann, 1930.
Chrysostom, St	*J. Patrologiae Graecae: S.P.N. Joannis Chrysostomi, Archiepiscopi Constantinopolitani opera omnia quæ exstant*, J.P. Migne, Lutetiæ Parisiorum, 1862–3, volumes XLVII–LXIV.
Cicero, *De Officiis*	*De Officiis*, Loeb Classical Library, volume 30. Heinemann, 1913.
Cicero, *Pro Deiotaro*	*Pro T. Annio Milone, In L. Calpurnium Pisonem, Pro M. Aemilio Scauro, Pro M. Fonteio, Pro C. Rabirio Postumo, Pro M. Marcello, Pro Q. Ligario, Pro rege Deiotaro*, Loeb Classical Library, volume 252. Heinemann, 1931.
Clement of Alexandria, *The Stromata*	*The Stromata*, Loeb Classical Library, volume 92, Heinemann, 1919.
Corpus Inscriptionum Latinarum	17 volumes, edited by Theodor Mominsen *et al.* Berlin, 1863.
Council of Carthage	*Dionysii Exigui, Viventioli, Trojani, Pontiani, S. Cæsarii Arelatensis episcopi, Fulgentii Ferrandi et rustici quorum prior Carthaginensis, posterior Romanæ ecclesiæ diaconus, necnon Justi, Facundi, Urgellensis et Hermianensis episcoporum, opera omnia.* J.P. Migne, volume LXVII, Lutetiæ Parisiorum, 1865.
Didache,	*Didache ton dwdeka avpostolon: The teaching of the twelve apostles – recently discovered and published by Philotheos Bryennios, Metropolitan of Nicomedia*, edited with a translation by Roswell D. Hitchcock and Francis Brown, J.C. Nimmo, London, 1885.

Justinian, *Codex Iustinianus*	*Digesta Instiniani. The Digest of Justinian*, Latin text edited by Theodor Mommsen, English translation by Alan Watson, Philadelphia, 1985.
Epictetus, *Arrian*	*The Discourses as Reported by Arrian*, Loeb Classical Library, volumes 131 and 218, Heinemann 1925 and 1928.
Euripides, *Cyclops*	*Electra, Orestes, Iphigeneia in Taurica, Andromache, Cyclops*, Loeb Classical Library, volume 10, Heinemann, 1913.
Euripides, *Hecuba*	*Iphigeneia at Aulis, Rhesus, Hecuba, The daughters of Troy, Helen*, Loeb Classical Library, volume 9, Heinemann, 1912.
Euripides, *Medea*	*Alcestis and Medea*, Loeb Classical Library, volume 10, Heinemann, 1994.
Gratian, *Distinctio*	*Decretum Gratiani, emendatum et variis electionibus simul et notationibus illustratum, Gregorii XIII pont. max. jussu editum post Justi Henningii Boehmeri curas.* J.P. Migne. Parisiis: apud Garnier fratres, 1891.
Herodotus, *Historia*	*Historia*, Loeb Classical Library, volumes 117–120, Heinemann, 1920–25.
Homer, *The Odyssey*	*The Odyssey*, Loeb Classical Library, volumes 104–5, Heinemann, 1919.
Homer, *Demeter*	*Hesiod, the Homeric hymns and Homerica*, Loeb Classical Library, volume 57, Heinemann, 1914.
Horace, *Satires*	*Horace: Satires, Epistles and Ars Poetica*, translated by H. Rushton, Fairclough, Cambridge, MA, 1926.
Isidore, *PL LXXXIII.786*	*Sancti Isidori, Hispalensis episcopi, Opera omnia, Romæ anno Domini MDCCXCVII excusa recensente Faustino Arevalo, qui Isidoriana præmisit ; variorum præfationes, notas, collationes, qua antea editas, qua tunc primum edendas, collegit; accurante et denuo recognoscente.* J.P. Migne. Lutetiæ Parisiorum 1850.
Juvenal, *Satires*	*Satires by Juvenal and Persius*, Loeb Classical Library, new volume, Heinemann, 2004.
Lactantius, *Epitome Divinarum Institutionum*	*Epitome Divinarum Institutionum*, edited by Eberhard Heck and Antonie Wlosok, Teubner, Stuttgart, 1994. *The Divine Institutes, Books I-VII* , translated by Sister Mary Francis McDonald, Catholic University of America Press, Washington, 1964.
Livy, *Ab Urbe Condita*	*Ab Urbe Condita*, Loeb Classical Library, assorted volumes, Heinemann, 1916–49.
Martyrdom of Polycarp	*S. Clementis Romani, S. Ignatii, S. Polycarpi, Patrum apostolicorum, quae supersunt: accedunt S. Ignatii et S. Polycarpi martyria ad fidem codicum recesuit, adnotationibus variorum et suis illustravit, indicibus instruxit Gulielmus Jacobson*, Oxonii e typographeo Academico, 1840.

Origen, *Contra Celsus* *Contra Celsum*, translated with an introduction and notes by Henry Chadwick, Cambridge University Press, Cambridge, 1953.

Ovid, *Metamorphoses* *Metamorphoses*, Loeb Classical Library, volumes 42–43, Heinemann, 1916.

Pausanias, *Achaia* *Description of Greece*, Loeb Classical Library, volume 93, Heinemann, 1918.

Petronius, *Satyricon* *Satyricon*, Loeb Classical Library, volume 15, Heinemann, 1913.

Philostratus, *Vita Apollonii* *The Life of Apollonius of Tyana, the Epistles of Apollonis and the Treatise of Eusebius*, Loeb Classical Library, volumes 16–17, Heinemann, 1912.

Eunapius, *Vitae Sophistarum* *The Lives of the Sophists*, Loeb Classical Library, volume 134, Heinemann, 1922.

Pindar, *Odes* *Olympian Odes, Pythian Odes*, Loeb Classical Library, volume 56, Harvard University Press, 1997.

Plato, *De Legibus* *Laws*, Loeb Classical Library, volumes 187–92, Heinemann, 1926.
Plato, *Timaeus and Critias* *Timaeus and Critias*, Loeb Classical Library, volume 234, Heinemann, 1929.

Plautus, *Poenulus et Cistellaria* *Poenulus et Cistellaria* in *The Little Carthaginian, Pseudolus, The Rope*, Loeb Classical Library, volume 163, Heinemann, 1921.

Pliny (the Elder), *Naturalis Historia* *Natural History*, Loeb Classical Library, 10 volumes, Heinemann, 1938–62.

Plutarch, *Quaestiones Convivales* *Morals and Table Talk*, 16 volumes. Loeb Classical Library, Heinemann, 1927–69.

Plutarch, *Vitae Parallelae* *Plutarch's Lives*, Loeb Classical Library, 11 volumes, Cambridge,MA. 1949–59.

Polybius, *Historia* *Historia* or *The Histories*. Loeb Classical Library Volumes: 128; 137-138; 159-161. London: Heinemann, 1922-1927.

Pseudo-Acro, *Pseudoacronis Scholia* *Pseudoacronis Scholia in HoratiumVvetustiora*, edited by Otto Keller, 2 volumes, Leipzig, 1902–04.

Seneca (the Elder), *Controversiae* *Controversiae. Suasoriae*, Loeb Classical Library, volumes 463–4, Heinemann, 1974.

Seneca (the Younger), De *Vita Benta et Consolatione ad Helviam* *De Consolatione ad Marciam. De Vita Beata. De Otio. De Tranquillitate Animi. De Brevitate Vitae. De Consolatione ad Polybium. De Consolatione ad Helviam*, Loeb Classical Library, volumes 132, Heinemann, 1932.

Tacitus, *Annales* *Annales*, Loeb Classical Library, volumes 132–7, Heinemann, 1932.

Tertullian, *De Praescriptione haereticorum* *Quinti Septimii florentis Tertulliani de praescriptione haereticorum ad martyras, Ad scapulam*, edited with introductions and notes by T. Herbert Bindley, Clarendon Press, Oxford, 1893.

Codex Theodosius	Codex Theodosianus cum perpetuis commentariis Iacobi Gothofredi. Praemittuntur chronologia accuratior, cum chronico historico, et prolegomena: subjiciuntur notitia dignitatum, prosopographia, topographia, index rerum, et glossarium nomicum. Lugduni, 1665.
Thucydides, *Peloponnesian War*	*History of the Peloponnesian War*, Loeb Classical Library, volumes 108–10, Heinemann, 1919.
Virgil, *Aeneid*	*Eclogues, Georgics et Aeneid*. Loeb Classical Library Volumes: 63-64. Harvard University Press, 1999-2000
Xenophon, *Anabasis*	*Anabasis and Hellenica*, Loeb Classical Library, volume 88–90, Heinemann, 1919–22,
Xenophon, *Ways and Means*	*Scripta Minora*, Loeb Classical Library, volume 183, Heinemann, 1925.

Modern sources

al-Mulk, N. (1994). *Siyāsatnāmah*. Tehran: Shirkat-i Intisharat-i Ilm va Farangi.

al-Muqaddasī, M.A. (1877). *Kītāb absan al-taqāsīm fī ma'rifat al-aqālīm*. Brill: Lugduni Batavorum.

al-Narshakhī, M. (1954). *The History of Bukhara by Muhammad Narshakhī; translated from a Persian abridgement of the Arabic original by Narshakhī*. Cambridge, MA: Mediaeval Academy of America.

al-Tabarī. (1989). *Ta'rīkh al-rusul wa al-mulūk*. Albany: State University of New York Press.

Aland, B., Aland, K., Karavidopoulos, J., Martini, C.M. and Metzger, B.M. (eds). (2007). *Nestle-Aland Novum Testamentum Graece*. Stuttgart: Deutsche Bibelgesellschaft.

Alvesson, M. and Sköldberg, K. (2004). *Reflexive Methodology: New Vistas for Qualitative Research*. London: Sage Publications.

André, J. (1981). *L'Alimentation et la Cuisine à Rome*. Paris: Les Belles Lettres.

Baker, P. (2005). Bush Winds Up Asia Trip With a Taste of Mongolia. *Washington Post*, 22 November, p. 25.

Bakker, E. J. (1997). *Poetry in Speech: Orality and Homeric Discourse*. Ithaca, NY: Cornell University Press.

Balsdon, J.P.V.D. (1969). *Roman Women: Their History and Habits*. Westport, CT: Greenwood Press.

Barber, M. (1994). *The New Knighthood: A History of the Order of the Temple*. Cambridge: Cambridge University Press.

Bardi, J.A. (2007). *Hotel Front Office Management*. Hoboken, NJ: John Wiley & Sons.

Basnyat, B. and Murdoch, D.R. (2003). High Altitude Illness. *The Lancet*, 361, 1967-1974.

Ben Jelloun, T. (1999). *French Hospitality: Racism and North African Immigrants*. New York: Columbia University Press.

Benedict XVI (2005). Missa Pro Eligendo Romano Pontifice. Retrieved 25/09/08, from http://www.vatican.va/gpII/documents/homily-pro-eligendo-pontifice_20050418_en.html

Benveniste, E. (1969). *Indo-European Languages and Society*. Coral Gables: University of Miami Press.

Flavio Biondo of Forlí, *Historiarum ab Inclinatione Romanorum Imperii Decades* (*Decades of History from the Deterioration of the Roman Empire*

Bickford, I. (2002). 'Host' semantic histories taken from the project sponsored by the Stanford Humanities Laboratory and the Seaver Institute, Crowds is a collaborative research project which focuses on the rise and fall of the crowd – particularly the revolutionary crowd – in the Western socio-political imagination between 1789 and the present. Retrieved 19/12/03, from http://shl.stanford.edu/Crowds/hist/host.htm

Böckmann, A. (1988). Xeniteia-Philoxenia als Hilfe zur Interpretation von Regula Benedicti 53 im Zusammenhang mit Kapitel 58 und 66. *Regulae Benedicti Studia*, 14/15, 131-144.

Bohman, J. (1999). Hermeneutics. In R. Audi (ed.), *The Cambridge Dictionary of Philosophy* (pp. 89-91). Cambridge: Cambridge University Press.

Bolchazy, L.J. (1993). *Hospitality in Early Rome. Livy's Concept of its Humanizing Force*. Chicago: Ares.

Borias, J. (1974). Hospitalité Augustinienne et Bénédictine. *Revue de Histoire de Spiritualité* 50, 3-16.

Browning, R. (1975). *The Emperor Julian*. London: Weidenfeld and Nicolson.

Burton, J. (1998). Women's Commensality in the Ancient Greek World. *Greece and Rome*, 45(2), 143-165.

Campbell, C.W. (1903). Journeys in Mongolia. *Geographical Journal*, 22(5), 485-512.

Caputo, J.D. (2002). *Deconstruction In A Nutshell: A Conversation with Jacques Derrida*. New York: Fordham University Press.

Carepino, J. (1940). *Daily Life in Ancient Rome*. New Haven, CT: Yale University Press.

Cavindish, G. (1962). *Thomas Wolsey, Late Cardinal, his Life and Death. Editor Roger Lockyer*. London: Folio Society.

Chaumartin, H. (1946). *Le mal des ardents et le feu Saint-Antoine*. Vienne la Romaine: Les Presses de l'Imprimerie Ternet-Martin.

Conrad, L.I. (1995). The Arab-Islamic medical tradition. In L.I. Conrad, M. Neve, V. Nutton, R. Porter and A. Wear (eds), *The Western Medical Tradition: 800 BC to AD 1800* (pp. 93-138). New York: Cambridge University Press.

Constable, O.R. (2001). Funduq, Fondaco, and Khān in the Wake of Christian Commerce and Crusade. In A.E. Laiou and R.P. Mottahedeh (eds), *The Crusades from the Perspective of Byzantium and the Muslim World*. Washington: Dumbarton Oaks.

Cornford, F.M. (1903). *The Cambridge Classical Course: An Essay in Anticipation of Further Reform*. Cambridge: W.H. Heffer & Sons.

Crum, K. (1976). *The Interpreter's Dictionary of the Bible: an Illustrated Encyclopaedia*. Nashville, TN: Abingdon Press.

D'Avino, M. (1967). *The Women of Pompeii*. Naples: Loffredo.

De Vaux, R. (1961). *Ancient Israel*. London: Darton, Longman & Todd.

Denzin, N.K. (1989). *Interpretive Interactionism*. Newbury Park, CA: Sage.

Derrida, J. (1981). *Dissemination*. Chicago: University of Chicago Press.

Derrida, J. (1994). *Specters of Marx: The State of the Debt, the Work of Mourning, and the New International*. New York: Routledge.

Derrida, J. (1997a). *Of Grammatology: Corrected edition*. Baltimore, MD: Johns Hopkins Press.

Derrida, J. (1997b). The Villanova Roundtable: A Conversation with Jacques Derrida. In J. D. Caputo (ed.), *Deconstruction in a Nutshell: A Conversation with Jacques Derrida*. New York: Fordham University Press.

Derrida, J. (1998a). Hospitality, Justice and Responsibility: A Dialogue with Jacques Derrida. In R. Kearney and M. Dooley (eds), *Questioning Ethics: Contemporary Debates in Philosophy*. London: Roudedge.

Derrida, J. (1998b). *Monolinguism of the Other or the Prosthesis of Origin*. Stanford, CA: Stanford University Press.

Derrida, J. (1999a). *Adieu to Emmanuel Lévinas*. Stanford, CA: Stanford University Press.

Derrida, J. (1999b). Responsabilité et hospitalité. In M. Seffahi (ed.), *Manifeste pour l'hospitalité*. Paris: Paroles l'Aube.

Derrida, J. (1999c). *Sur Parole: Instantanés philosophiques*. Paris: Editions de l'aube.

Derrida, J. (2000a). Hostipitality. *Angelaki: Journal of the Theoretical Humanities*, 5(3), 3-18.

Derrida, J. (2000b). *Of Hospitality*. Stanford, CA: Stanford University Press.

Derrida, J. (2002). *Acts of Religion*. New York: Routledge.

Dimock, J. F. (ed.). (1876). *Giraldi Cambrensis Opera*. London: Longman, Green, Longman, and Roberts.

Dols, M.W. (1987). The origins of the Islamic Hospital: Myth and reality. *Bulletin of Historical Medicine*, 61, 367-390.

Driver, G. R. and Miles, J.C. (1952). *Code of Hammurabi in English and Akkadian*. Oxford: Clarendon Press.

Duval, M. (ed.). (1984). *Œuvres Complètes de Antoine Louis Leon De Saint Just 1767-1794*. Paris: Gérard Lebovici.

Elliger, K. and Rudolph, W. (eds). (1990). *Biblia Hebraica Stuttgartensia* Stuttgart: Deutsche Bibelgesellschaft.

Ellis, S.J.R. (2004). The Distribution of Bars at Pompeii: Archaeological, spatial and viewshed analyses. *Journal of Roman Archaeology*, 17, 371-384.

Etymologiarum, seu Originum Libri XX (*Twenty Books of Etymologies*, or *Origins*,

Evans-Pritchard, E.E. (1965). *Theories of Primitive Religion*. Oxford: Clarendon Press.

Evans, A.J. (1921). *The Palace of Minos: A comparative account of the successive stages of the early Cretan civilization as illustrated by the discoveries at Knossos*. London: Macmillan.

Fagles, R. (1990). *Iliad*. London: Viking.

Field, D.H. (1994). Hospitality. In D.J. Atkinson and D.H. Field (eds), *New Dictionary of Christian Ethics and Pastoral Theology*. London: Inter-Varsity Press.

Finley, M.I. (1983). *Ancient Slavery and Modern Ideology*. Oxford: Clarendon Press.

Firth, C.M. and Quibell, J.E. (1936). *Excavations at Saggard: The Step Pyramid Service des Antiquités de l'Égypte*. Cairo: Le Caire.

Fowler, J.T. (ed.). (1964). *Rites of Durham: Being a description or brief declaration of all the ancient monuments, rites, & customs belonging or being within the monastical church of Durham before the suppression written 1593*. London: published for the Society by Andrews & Bernard Quaritch.

Frazer, J.G. (1911). *Taboo and the Perils of the Soul, The Golden Bough: A study in magic and religion* (Vol. 3). London: Macmillan.

Frazer, J.G. (1923). *Folk-lore in the Old Testament: studies in comparative religion, legend and law*. London: Macmillan.

Fry, T. (1981). *RB 1980: The Rule of St. Benedict, In Latin and English with Notes*. Collegeville<<??state>>: Liturgical Press.

Gabel, L.C. (ed.). (1960). *Memoirs of a Renaissance Pope: The commentaries of Pius II*. London: Allen & Unwin.

Gardner, J.F. (1991). *Women in Roman Law and Society*. Bloomington: Indiana University Press.

Garnsey, P. (2002). *Food and Society in Classical Antiquity*. Cambridge: Cambridge University Press.

Gelb, I.J. (1956). *The Assyrian Dictionary of the Oriental Institute of the University of Chicago*. Chicago: Oriental Institute.

Gibson, R.K. (1999). Aeneas as hospes in Vergil, *Aeneid* 1 and 4. *Classical Quarterly, New Series*, 49, 184-202.

Graziosi, B. (2005). *Homer: The resonance of epic*. London: Duckworth.

Hall, C.M. (2004). Reflexivity and tourism research: Situating myself and/with others. In L. Goodson. and J. Phillimore (eds), *Qualitative Research in Tourism: Ontologies, Epistemologies and Methodologies*. London: Routledge.

Hamarneh, S. (1974). Ecology and the therapeutics in medieval Arabic medicine. *Sudhoffs Archive*, 5, 166-185.

Hamāsa. (1970). *Kitāb al-wahshīyāt: wa-huwa al-Hamāsa al-sughrā li-Abī Tammām Habīb ibn Aws al-Tā'ī; 'allaqa 'alayhi wa-haqqaqahn 'Abd al-'Azīz al-Maymanī al-Rājkūtī; wa-zāda fī hawāshīhi Mahmūd Muhammad Shākir*. al-Qāhirah Dar al-Ma'ārif bi-Misr.

Heal, F. (1990). *Hospitality in Early Modern England*. Oxford: Clarendon Press.

Hein, S.F., and Austin, W.J. (2001). Empirical and Hermeneutic Approaches to Phenomenological Research in Psychology: A Comparison. *Psychological Methods*, 6(1), 3-17.

Heissig, W. (1980). *The Religions of Mongolia*. London: Routledge and Kegan Paul.

Herzfeld, M. (1987). As in Your Own House: Hospitality, Ethnography and the Stereotype of Mediterranean Society. In D.D. Gilmore (ed.), *Honor and Shame and the Unity of the Mediterraean* (pp. 75-89). Washington, DC: American Anthropological Association.

Herzfeld, M. (1991). *A Place in History: Social and Monumental Time in a Cretan Town*. Princeton, NJ: Princeton University Press.

Hobbs, T.R. (1993). Man, Woman and Hospitality: 2 Kings 4.8-36. *Biblical Theology Bulletin*, 23(1), 91-100.

Hobbs, T.R. (2001). Hospitality in the First Testament and the 'Teleological Fallacy.'. *Journal for the Study of the Old Testament*, 26, 3-30.

Holzherr, G. (1982). *Die Behediktsregel: Eine Anleitung Zu Christlichem Leben*. Verlag: Benziger.

Horn, W. and Born, E. (1979). *The Plan of St Gall: A study of the architecture & economy of, and life in a paradigmatic Carolingian monastery*. Berkeley: University of California Press.

Hornblower, S. and Spawforth, A. (2003). *The Oxford Classical Dictionary*. Oxford: Oxford University Press.

Hume, E.E. (1940). *Medical work of the Knights Hospitallers of Saint John of Jerusalem*. Baltimore, MD: Johns Hopkins Press.

Humphrey, C. (1974). Inside a Mongolian Tent. *New Society*, 30, 273-275.

Husserl, E. (1931). *Ideas Toward a Pure Phenomenology and Phenomenological Psychology*. New York: Humanities Press.

ibn Abd al-Hakam, A. (1922). *Kitāb Futūh Misr wa-ahb ārihā*. New Haven, CT: Yale University Press.

ibn Anas, M. (1999). *al-Muwatta' lil-Imām Mālik ibn Anas*. al-Qāhirah: Dār al-Hadīth.

Imamuddin, S.M. (1978). Maristan in Medieval Spain. *Islamic Studies*, 17, 45-55.

Jacobsen, T. (1970). *Toward the image of Tammuz and other essays on Mesopotamian history and culture*. Cambridge, MA: Harvard University Press.

Janzen, W. (1994). *Old Testament Ethics: A Paradigmatic Approach*. Louisville, KY: John Knox Press.

Janzen, W.V.N. (2002). Biblical Theology of Hospitality. *Vision, A Journal for Church and Theology*, 3(1), 4-15.

Jones, T.B. and Snyder, J. W. (1961). *Sumerian Economic Texts from the Third Ur Dynasty. A catalogue and discussion of documents from various collections*. Minneapolis: University of Minnesota Press.

Kant, I. (ed.). ([1780] 1998). *Kritik der Reinen Vernunft. Critique of Pure Reason*. Cambridge: Cambridge University Press.

Kardong, T.G. (1984). *Together Unto Life Everlasting, An Introduction to the Rule of Benedict*. Richardton, ND: Assumption Abbey Press.

Kardong, T.G. (1996). *Benedict's Rule: A Translation and Commentary*. Collegeville MN: Liturgical Press.

Kerr, J. (2002). The Open Door: Hospitality and Honour in Twelfth/Early Thirteenth-Century England. *History, The Journal of the Historical Association*, 87, 322-335.

King, C. (1995). What is hospitality? *International Journal of Hospitality Management*, 14(3/4), 219-234.

King, E.J. (1931). *The Knights Hospitallers in the Holy Land*. London: Methuen.

Kleberg, T. (1957). *Hôtels, Restaurants et Cabarets dans L'antiquité romaine: Études Historiques et Philologiques*. Uppsala: Almqvist & Wiksell.

Koenig, J. (1992). Hospitality. In D. Noel (ed.), *The Anchor Bible Dictionary* (vol. 3, pp. 299-301). New York: Freeman Doubleday.

Kurzová, H. (1981). *Der Relativsatz in den Indoeuropäischen Sprachen*. Prague: Academia.

Lashley, C., Lynch, P. and Morrison, A. (2007). *Hospitality: A Social Lens*. Oxford: Elsevier.

Latham, R. (1958) The Travels of Marco Polo, London: Penguin Classics

Lattin, G.W. (1989). *The Lodging and Food Service Industy*. East Lansing, MI: Educational Institute of the American Hotel & Motel Association.

Leclereq, J. (1968). *The Spirituality of the Middle Ages*. London: Burns and Oates.

Lenoir, A. (1856). *Architecture Monastique*. Paris: Imprimerie Nationale.

Levy, H.L. (1963). The Odyssean Suitors and the Host-Guest Relationship. *Transactions and Proceedings of the American Philological Association*, 94, 145-153.

Liddell, H.G., Scott, R., Jones, H.S., McKenzie, R., Thompson, A.A. and Glare, P.G.W. (1996). *Greek-English Lexicon: Revised Supplement*. Oxford: Clarendon Press.

Liebeschuetz, J.H.W.G. (2001). *Decline and Fall of the Roman City*. Oxford: Oxford University Press.

Lindsay, J. (1960). *The Writing on the Wall*. London: Frederick Muller.

Long, T.G. (1997). *Hebrews*. Louisville, KY: John Knox Press.

Lord, A.B. (1960). *The Singer of Tales*. Cambridge, MA: Harvard University Press.

Malina, B.J. (1985). in *Harper's Bible Dictionary*. Paul J. Achtemeier (e.d) London: Harper & Row.

Mallory, J.P. and Adams, D.Q. (2006). *The Oxford Introduction to Proto-Indo-European and The Proto-Indo-European World*. Oxford: Oxford University Press.

Mango, C. (1986). A Late Roman Inn in Eastern Turkey. *Oxford Journal of Archaeology*, 5, 223-231.

Matthews, V.H. (1991a). Hospitality and Hostility in Judges 4. *Biblical Theology Bulletin*, 21, 13-21.

Matthews, V.H. (1991b). *Old Testament Parallels: Laws and Stories from the Ancient Near East*. New York: Paulist Press.

Matthews, V.H. (1992). Hospitality and Hostility in Genesis 19 and Judges 19. *Biblical Theology Bulletin*, 22(1), 3-11.

Medlik, S. and Ingram, G. (2000). *The Business of Hotels*. Oxford: Butterworth Heinemann.

Miller, T.S. (1978). The Knights of Saint John and the Hospitals of the Latin West. *Speculum*, 53(4), 709-733.

Ministry of Road Transport and Tourism (2005). *The Yearbook of Mongolian Tourism Statistics, 2005 Edition*. Ulaanbaatar: Ministry of Road Transport and Tourism.

Mollat, M. (1978). *Les pauvres au Moyen âge: étude sociale*. Paris: Hachette.

Mommsen, T.E. (1942). Petrarch's Conception of the 'Dark Ages.'. *Speculum*, 17(2), 226-242.

Morrison, A. (2001). Entrepreneurs transcend time: a biographic analysis. *Management Decision*, 39(9), 784-790.

Mostaert, A. (1956). Matériaux ethnographiques relatifs aux Mongols ordos. *Central Asiatic Journal*, 2(4), 241-294.

Mostaert, A. (1962). À propos d'une prière feu. Indiana University. *Uralic and Altaic Series*, 13, 191-223.

Muhlmann, W.E. (1932). Hospitality. In E.R.A. Seligman (ed.), *Encyclopaedia of the Social Sciences*. New York: Macmillan.

Mynors, R.A.B., Thomson, R.M. and Winterbottom, M. (1998). *Gesta Regum Anglorum. The History of the English Kings by William of Malmesbury (1090 - 1143)*. Oxford: Clarendon Press.

Nutton, V. (1995). Medicine in Medieval Western Europe. In L.I. Conrad, M. Neve, V. Nutton, R. Porter and A. Wear (eds), *The Western Medical Tradition: 800 BC to AD 1800* (pp. 139-198). New York: Cambridge University Press.

O'Gorman, K.D. (2007). Discovering commercial hospitality in ancient Rome. *Hospitality Review*, 9(2), 44-52.

O'Gorman, K.D., Baxter, I. and Scott, B. (2007). Exploring Pompeii: Discovering hospitality through research synergy. *Tourism and Hospitality Research*, 7(2), 89-99.

O'Connor, D. (2005). Towards a new interpretation of 'hospitality'. *International Journal of Contemporary Hospitality Management*, 17(3), 267-271.

Oden, A.G. (2001). *And You Welcomed Me: A Sourcebook on Hospitality in Early Christianity*. Nashville, TN: Abingdon Press.

Ong, W.J. (1987). *Oralidad y escritura: Tecnologías de la Palabra*. Mexico City: Fonda de la cultura Económica.

Oppenheim, A.L. (1967). *Letters from Mesopotamia: Official, business, and private letters on clay tablets from two millennia*. Chicago: University of Chicago Press.

Oppenheim, A.L. (1977). *Ancient Mesopotamia: Portrait of a Dead Civilization*. Chicago: University of Chicago Press.

Parry, M. (1936). On Typical Scenes in Homer. *Classical Philology*, 31, 357-360.

Patlagean, E. (1981). *Structure social, famille, chrétienté a Byzance, IVe – XIe siècle*. London: Variorum Reprints.

Pedrick, V. (1988). The Hospitality of Noble Women in the *Odyssey*. *Helios*, 15(2), 85-101.

Petersen, A. (1994). The Archaeology of the Syrian and Iraqi Hajj Routes. *World Archaeology*, 26, 47-56.

Petrarchae, F. (1554). *Francisci Petrarchae Opera quae extant omnia. Adiecimus eiusdem Authoris, quæ Hetrusco sermone scripsit carmina*. Basileæ: Henrichus Petri.

Pike, R. (1965). *Love in Ancient Rome*. London: F. Mueller.

Pitt-Rivers, J. (1971). *People of the Sierra*. Chicago: University of Chicago Press.

Pitt-Rivers, J. (1977). *The fate of Shechem, or, The politics of sex: essays in the anthropology of the Mediterranean*. Cambridge: Cambridge University Press.

Pohl, D.C. (1999). *Making Room: Recovering Hospitality as a Christian Tradition*. Grand Rapids, MI: Eerdmans.

Pope John Paul II (1994). *Crossing the Threshold of Hope*. London: Alfred A Knopf.

Porter, R. (1997). *The Greatest Benefit to Mankind: A Medical History of Humanity from Antiquity to the Present*. London: Fontana Press.

Porter, R. (2003). *Blood and Guts: A Short History of Medicine*. London: Penguin Press.

Poter, W. (1858). *A History of the Knights of Malta or The Order of the Hospital of Saint John of Jerusalem*. London: Longman, Brown, Green, Longmans, & Roberts.

Pritchard, J.B. (1955). *The Ancient Near East in pictures relating to the Old Testament*. Princeton, NJ: Princeton University Press.

Reece, S. (1993). *The Stranger's welcome: oral theory and the aesthetics of the Homeric hospitality scene*. Michigan: University of Michigan Press.

Regnault, L. (1990). *La Vie Quotidienne de Pères du Désert en Egypte au IVe Siècle*. Paris: Hachette.

Renfrew, C. (1990). *Archaeology and Language: The Puzzle of Indo-European Origins*. Cambridge: Cambridge University Press.

Retief, F.P. and Cilliers, L. (2005). The Evolution of Hospitals from Antiquity to Renaissance. *Acta Theologica Supplementum*, 7, 213-233.

Richard, Y. (1990). Land of a thousand and one courtesies - Iran - The Art of Hospitality'. *UNESCO Courier,* 30 February.

Richardson, M.E.J. (2000). *Hammurabi's Laws: Text, translation and glossary.* Sheffield: Sheffield Academic Press.

Riddle, D.W. (1938). Early Christian Hospitality: A Factor in the Gospel Transmission. *Journal of Biblical Literature,* (2), 141-154.

Rinchen, B. (2005). Hospitality And Customs Of Mongolia. In G. Purevsambuu (ed.), *Mongolian Cultural Heritage.* Ulaanbaatar: Montsame.

Rinchen Yöngsiyebü, B. (1984). White, Black, and Yellow Shamans among the Mongols. *Journal of the Anglo-Mongolian Society,* 9(1-2), 19-24.

Ringe, D. (2006). *A History of English: From Proto-Indo-European to Proto-Germanic.* Oxford: Oxford University Press.

Robertson, J.C. (ed.). (1875). *Materials for the History of Thomas Becket: Archbishop of Canterbury canonized by Pope Alexander III., A. D. 1173.* London: Longman.

Robertson Smith, W. (1927). *Lectures on the Religion of the Semites: Fundamental Institutions.* London: A. & C. Black.

Rosello, M. (2001). *Postcolonial Hospitality: The Immigrant as Guest.* Stanford, CA: Stanford University Press.

Rosello, M. (2002). European Hospitality without a home: Gypsy communities and illegal immigration in Van Cauwelaert's Un Aller simple. *Studies in 20th Century Literature,* 26(1), 172-193.

Rutes, W. and Penner, R. (1985). *Hotel Planning and Design.* New York: Watson-Guptill.

Sánchez Caro, J.M. (1989). *Biblia y palabra de dios.* Navarra: Verbo Divino.

Sause, B.A. (1962). *The principles of monasticism. Original title Praecipua ordinis monastici elementa. by Maurus Wolter, 1825 - 1900.* St Louis, MO: Herder.

Schérer, R. (1993). *Zeus Hospitalier: Eloge de l'hospitalité.* Paris: Armand Colin.

Shokoohy, M. (1983). The Sasanian Caravanserai of Dayr-i gachin, South of Ray, Iran. *Bulletin of the School of Oriental and African Studies, University of London,* 46(3), 445-461.

Silberbauer, G. (1993). Ethics in Small-Scale Societies. In P. Singer (ed.), *A Companion to Ethics.* Oxford: Blackwell.

Smith, D.H. (1986). Hospitality. In J. Macquarrie and J. Childress (eds), *New Dictionary of Christian Ethics.* London: SCM Press.

Smith, J.M.H. (2005). *Europe after Rome: a new cultural history 500-1000.* Oxford: Oxford University Press.

Strong, R. (2003). *Feast: A Grand History of Eating.* London: Random House.

Tanner, N.P. (ed.). (1990). *Decrees of the Ecumenical Councils* London: Sheed & Ward.

Telfer, E. (1996). *Food for Thought: Philosophy and Food.* London: Routledge.

Telfer, E. (2000). The Philosophy of hospitableness. In C. Lashley and A. Morrison (eds), *In Search of Hospitality – Theoretical Perspectives and Debates.* Oxford: Butterworth Heinemann.

Thomas, C.G. and Conant, C. (2005). *The Trojan War.* London: Greenwood Press.

Tierney, B. (1959). *Medieval poor law: a sketch of canonical theory and its application in England.* Berkeley: University of California Press.

Trevijano Etcheverría, R. (1997). *Estudios Sobre el Evangelio de Tomás.* Madrid: Editorial Ciudad Nueva.

Trevijano Etcheverría, R. (1998). *Patrología.* Madrid: Biblioteca de Autores Cristianos.

UNESCO. (1996). *World Heritage List Extract: Pompei and Ercolano, Italy*. Paris: UNESCO World Heritage Centre.

Van Cauwelaert, D. (1994). *Un Aller Simple*. Paris: Librairie Générale Française.

Van Manen, M. (1990). *Researching Lived Experience*. Ontario: State University of New York Press.<<A to confirm that it wasn't New York as well/primary pub place>>

Vermes, G. (1997). *The Complete Dead Sea Scrolls in English*. London: Penguin.

Vogüé, A. (1977). *La Règle de saint Benoît, VII, Commentaire Doctrinal et Spiritual*. Paris: Les editions du Cerf.

Wahnich, S. (1997a). L'hospitalité et la Révolution française. In D. Fassin, A. Morice and C. Quirninal (eds), *Les lois de l'inhospitalité: Les politiques de l'immigration à l'épreuve des sans-papiers*. Paris: La Découverte.

Wahnich, S. (1997b). *L'impossible Citoyen: L'étranger dans le discours de la révolution française*. Paris: Albin Michel.

Ward-Perkins, J.B. (2005). *The Fall of Rome: and the end of civilization*. Oxford: Oxford University Press.

Watkins, C. (2000). *Indo-European and the Indo-Europeans in The American Heritage Dictionary of the English Language*, 4th edn, Boston, MA : Houghton Mifflin.

Webber, A. (1989). The Hero Tells His Name: Formula and Variation in the Phaeacian Episode of the *Odyssey*. *Transactions of the American Philological Association*, 119, 1-13.

William of Rubruck (1990). *The mission of William of Rubruck: His journey to the court of the Great Khan Möngke 1253-1255*. London: Hakluyt Society.

Wiltshire, S.F. (1989). *Public and private in Vergil's Aeneid*. Amherst, MA: University of Massachusetts Press.

Wolter, M. (1880). *Praecipua Ordinis Monastici Elementa*. Brugis: Desclée.

Wood, R.C. (1994). Some Theroetical Perspectives on Hospitality. In A.V. Seaton, C.L. Jenkins, R.C. Wood, P.U.C. Dieke, M.M. Bennett, L.R. Maclellan and R. Smith (eds), *Tourism the State of the Art* (pp. 737-742). Chichester: Wiley.

Wood, R.C. (1999). Traditional and alternative research philosophies. In B. Brotherton (ed.), *The Handbook of Contemporary Hospitality Management Research*. Chichester: John Wiley.

Wright, T. (ed.). (1848). *Early travels in Palestine: Comprising the narratives of Arculf, Willibald, Bernard, Sæwulf, Sigurd, Benjamin of Tudela, Sir John Maundeville, De la Brocquière, and Maundrell*. London: H.G. Bohn.

Yavuz, A.T. (1997). The Concepts That Shape Anatolian Seljuq Caravanserais. *Muqarnas*, 14, 80-95.

Yoyotte, J. (1960). *Les pèlerinages dans l'Égypte ancienne. Les pèlerinages en Sources Orientales*. Paris: Seuil.

Yu, L. and Goulden, M. (2006). A comparative analysis of international tourists' satisfaction in Mongolia. *Tourism Management*, 27, 1331-1342.

Zumthor, P. (1983). *Introduction à la poésie orale*. Paris: Seuil.

Index

Strategy for Tourism

by John Tribe, Professor and Head of Tourism, Surrey University, UK

Strategy for Tourism is an internationally focused text which explains strategic management, analysis and implementation specifically in the tourism industry. It covers strategic management in a variety of tourism contexts, such as organizations, destinations, governments, NGOs and IGOs, as well as for special purposes (e.g. ad hoc events, sustainability, inclusion, pro-poor). Using global case studies, it provides a complete overview of all the factors required when establishing a strategic plan.

ISBN: 978-1-906884-07-9

Hard copy: £29.99: €32.99:$48 E-Book: £22.59 E-Chapter: £2.50: March 2010

Tourism Research: a 20:20 vision

Edited by Professor Douglas Pearce is Professor Tourism Management, Victoria Management School, New Zealand and Professor Richard Butler, Professor in the Department of Hospitality and Tourism Management of University of Strathclyde

Tourism research continues to expand at a rapid rate and this explosion in output has meant it is more and more difficult to keep pace with what is being produced, as well as the quality of what is produced. *Tourism Research: a 20:20 vision* examines how research agendas have evolved and might develop in coming years, considers conceptual and methodological advances, discusses obstacles that have been encountered and suggests ways forward.

ISBN: 978-1-906884-10-9

Hard copy: £49.99: €49.99:$60 E-Book: £39.99 E-Chapter: £2.50: March 2010

Tourism and Political Change

Edited by Wantanee Suntikul, Assistant Professor in Tourism Planning and Development at the Institute for Tourism Studies in Macao, China and Richard Butler, Professor in the Department of Hospitality and Tourism Management of University of Strathclyde

Tourism is a vital tool for political and economic change – the use of tourism to initiate political discussions, increased pressure for fair trade, and tourist boycotts all reflect the huge impact the tourism industry has on political change. With international contributions from an esteemed list of experienced individuals, *Tourism and Political Change* addresses these issues of great current relevance and importance focussing on events and their impacts.

ISBN: 978-1-906884-11-6

Hard copy: £34.99: €34.99:$40 E-Book: £25 E-Chapter: £3.99 : April 2010

Global Geotourism Perspectives

Edited by David Newsome, Associate Professor, Environmental Science and Ecotourism, Murdoch University, Australia and Ross Dowling, Foundation Professor of Tourism, Edith Cowan University, Australia

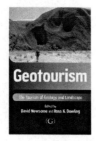

The field of geotourism is a rapidly emerging one. It expands and develops a new area of natural area tourism. This edited collection is divided into four sections to cover the globe, encompassing Australasia, Europe and Scandinavia, USA, and Asia. With chapters authored by international experts in the field from industry and academia, it examines specific sites to discuss best practice, issues of sustainability, planning, sensitive development and active management.

ISBN: 978-1-906884-09-3

Hard copy: £29.99: €29.99:$40 E-Book: £22.50 E-Chapter: £2.99 : April 2010

Tourism and Crime: Key Themes

Edited by David Botterill, freelance academic and higher education consultant and Professor Emeritus in the Welsh Centre for Tourism Research, University of Wales Institute Cardiff, and Trevor Jones, Reader in Criminology and Criminal Justice at the School of Social Sciences, University of Cardiff

The tourist as victim or offender? With contributions from international experts *Tourism and Crime: Key Themes* is the first text to addresses the tourism-crime nexus, including issues such as drugs tourism, sex tourism and alcohol-related crime and disorder among holidaymakers, the 'naming and shaming' of specific 'danger travel spots', the governance of safety in 'stateless' spaces, cooperation between justice authorities in different jurisdictions, and much more.

ISBN: 978-1-906884-14-7

Hard copy: £34.99: €34.99:$40 E-Book: £25 E-Chapter: £3.99 : May 2010

For more details on these and other Goodfellow Publisher products, and to order inspection copies, visit the website at <u>www.goodfellowpublishers.com</u> or email us at customerservice@goodfellowpublishers.com.

Also available from all good book retailers.

WWW.GOODFELLOWPUBLISHERS.COM

Lightning Source UK Ltd.
Milton Keynes UK
08 May 2010

153924UK00001B/8/P